TAPESTRY

THRESHOLDS
IN READING

TAPESTRY

❖

The **Tapestry** program of language
materials is based on the concepts
presented in *The Tapestry of
Language Learning: The Individual
in the Communicative Classroom* by
Robin C. Scarcella &
Rebecca L. Oxford.

❖

Each title in this program focuses on:

❖

Individual learner strategies and
instruction

❖

The relatedness of skills

❖

Ongoing self-assessment

❖

Authentic material as input

❖

Theme-based learning linked to task-
based instruction

❖

Attention to all aspects of
communicative competence

THRESHOLDS IN READING

Martha Grace Low

Heinle & Heinle Publishers
An International Thomson
Publishing Company
Boston, Massachusetts, 02116, USA

The publication of *Thresholds In Reading* was directed by the members of the Heinle & Heinle Global Innovations Publishing Team:

Elizabeth Holthaus, Global Innovations Team Leader
David C. Lee, Editorial Director
John F. McHugh, Market Development Director
Lisa McLaughlin, Production Services Coordinator

Also participating in the publication of this program were:

Publisher: Stanley J. Galek
Assistant Editor: Kenneth Mattsson
Manufacturing Coordinator: Mary Beth Hennebury
Full Service Project Manager/Compositor: PC&F, Inc.
Interior Design: Maureen Lauran
Cover Design: Maureen Lauran

Manufactured in the United States of America

ISBN: 0-8384-5336-8

Heinle & Heinle Publishers is an International Thomson Publishing Company.

10 9 8 7 6 5 4 3 2 1

For my parents,
who taught me to read

PHOTO CREDITS

TEXT CREDITS

WELCOME TO TAPESTRY

*E*nter the world of Tapestry! Language learning can be seen as an ever-developing tapestry woven with many threads and colors. The elements of the tapestry are related to different language skills like listening and speaking, reading and writing; the characteristics of the teachers; the desires, needs, and backgrounds of the students; and the general second language development process. When all these elements are working together harmoniously, the result is a colorful, continuously growing tapestry of language competence of which the student and the teacher can be proud.

This volume is part of the Tapestry program for students of English as a second language (ESL) at levels from beginning to "bridge" (which follows the advanced level and prepares students to enter regular postsecondary programs along with native English speakers). Tapestry levels include:

Beginning
Low Intermediate
High Intermediate
Low Advanced
High Advanced
Bridge

Because the Tapestry Program provides a unified theoretical and pedagogical foundation for all its components, you can optimally use all the Tapestry student books in a coordinated fashion as an entire curriculum of materials. (They will be published from 1993 to 1996 with further editions likely thereafter.) Alternatively, you can decide to use just certain Tapestry volumes, depending on your specific needs.

Tapestry is primarily designed for ESL students at postsecondary institutions in North America. Some want to learn ESL for academic or career advancement, others for social and personal reasons. Tapestry builds directly on all these motivations. Tapestry stimulates learners to do their best. It enables learners to use English naturally and to develop fluency as well as accuracy.

Tapestry Principles

The following principles underlie the instruction provided in all of the components of the Tapestry program.

EMPOWERING LEARNERS

Language learners in Tapestry classrooms are active and increasingly responsible for developing their English language skills and related cultural abilities. This self direction leads to better, more rapid learning. Some cultures virtually train their students to be passive in the classroom, but Tapestry weans them from passivity by providing exceptionally high interest materials, colorful and motivating activities, personalized self-reflection tasks, peer tutoring and other forms of cooperative learning, and powerful learning strategies to boost self direction in learning.

The empowerment of learners creates refreshing new roles for teachers, too. The teacher serves as facilitator, co-communicator, diagnostician, guide, and helper. Teachers are set free to be more creative at the same time their students become more autonomous learners.

HELPING STUDENTS IMPROVE THEIR LEARNING STRATEGIES

Learning strategies are the behaviors or steps an individual uses to enhance his or her learning. Examples are taking notes, practicing, finding a conversation partner, analyzing words, using background knowledge, and controlling anxiety. Hundreds of such strategies have been identified. Successful language learners use language learning strategies that are most effective for them given their particular learning style, and they put them together smoothly to fit the needs of a given language task. On the other hand, the learning strategies of less successful learners are a desperate grab-bag of ill-matched techniques.

All learners need to know a wide range of learning strategies. All learners need systematic practice in choosing and applying strategies that are relevant for various learning needs. Tapestry is one of the only ESL programs that overtly weaves a comprehensive set of learning strategies into language activities in all its volumes. These learning strategies are arranged in eight broad categories throughout the Tapestry books:

Forming concepts
Personalizing
Remembering new material
Managing your learning
Understanding and using emotions
Overcoming limitations
Testing Hypotheses
Learning with Others

The most useful strategies are sometimes repeated and flagged with a note, "It Works! Learning Strategy . . ." to remind students to use a learning strategy they have already encountered. This recycling reinforces the value of learning strategies and provides greater practice.

RECOGNIZING AND HANDLING LEARNING STYLES EFFECTIVELY

Learners have different learning styles (for instance, visual, auditory, hands-on; reflective, impulsive; analytic, global; extroverted, introverted; closure-oriented, open). Particularly in an ESL setting, where students come from vastly different cultural backgrounds, learning styles differences abound and can cause "style conflicts."

Unlike most language instruction materials, Tapestry provides exciting activities specifically tailored to the needs of students with a large range of learning styles. You can use any Tapestry volume with the confidence that the activities and materials are intentionally geared for many different styles. Insights from the latest educational and psychological research undergird this style-nourishing variety.

OFFERING AUTHENTIC, MEANINGFUL COMMUNICATION

Students need to encounter language that provides authentic, meaningful communication. They must be involved in real-life communication tasks that cause them to *want* and *need* to read, write, speak, and listen to English. Moreover, the tasks—to be most effective—must be arranged around themes relevant to learners.

Themes like family relationships, survival in the educational system, personal health, friendships in a new country, political changes, and protection of the environment are all valuable to ESL learners. Tapestry focuses on topics like these. In every Tapestry volume, you will see specific content drawn from very broad areas such as home life, science and technology, business, humanities, social sciences, global issues, and multiculturalism. All the themes are real and important, and they are fashioned into language tasks that students enjoy.

At the advanced level, Tapestry also includes special books each focused on a single broad theme. For instance, there are two books on business English, two on English for science and technology, and two on academic communication and study skills.

UNDERSTANDING AND VALUING DIFFERENT CULTURES

Many ESL books and programs focus completely on the "new" culture, that is, the culture which the students are entering. The implicit message is that ESL students should just learn about this target culture, and there is no need to understand their own culture better or to find out about the cultures of their international classmates. To some ESL students, this makes them feel their own culture is not valued in the new country.

Tapestry is designed to provide a clear and understandable entry into North American culture. Nevertheless, the Tapestry Program values *all* the cultures found in the ESL classroom. Tapestry students have constant opportunities to become "culturally fluent" in North American culture while they are learning English, but they also have the chance to think about the cultures of their classmates and even understand their home culture from different perspectives.

INTEGRATING THE LANGUAGE SKILLS

Communication in a language is not restricted to one skill or another. ESL students are typically expected to learn (to a greater or lesser degree) all four language skills: reading, writing, speaking, and listening. They are also expected to develop strong grammatical competence, as well as becoming socioculturally sensitive and knowing what to do when they encounter a "language barrier."

Research shows that multi-skill learning is more effective than isolated-skill learning, because related activities in several skills provide reinforcement and refresh the learner's memory. Therefore, Tapestry integrates all the skills. A given Tapestry volume might highlight one skill, such as reading, but all other skills are also included to support and strengthen overall language development.

However, many intensive ESL programs are divided into classes labeled according to one skill (Reading Comprehension Class) or at most two skills (Listening/Speaking Class or Oral Communication Class). The volumes in the Tapestry Program can easily be used to fit this traditional format, because each volume clearly identifies its highlighted or central skill(s).

Grammar is interwoven into all Tapestry volumes. However, there is also a separate reference book for students, *The Tapestry Grammar,* and a Grammar Strand composed of grammar "work-out" books at each of the levels in the Tapestry Program.

Other Features of the Tapestry Program

PILOT SITES

It is not enough to provide volumes full of appealing tasks and beautiful pictures. Users deserve to know that the materials have been pilot-tested. In many ESL series, pilot testing takes place at only a few sites or even just in the classroom of the author. In contrast, Heinle & Heinle Publishers have developed a network of Tapestry Pilot Test Sites throughout North America. At this time, there are approximately 40 such sites, although the number grows weekly. These sites try out the materials and provide suggestions for revisions. They are all actively engaged in making Tapestry the best program possible.

AN OVERALL GUIDEBOOK

To offer coherence to the entire Tapestry Program and especially to offer support for teachers who want to understand the principles and practice of Tapestry, we have written a book entitled, *The Tapestry of Language Learning. The Individual in the Communicative Classroom* (Scarcella and Oxford, published in 1992 by Heinle & Heinle).

A Last Word

We are pleased to welcome you to Tapestry! We use the Tapestry principles every day, and we hope these principles—and all the books in the Tapestry Program— provide you the same strength, confidence, and joy that they give us. We look forward to comments from both teachers and students who use any part of the Tapestry Program.

Rebecca L. Oxford
University of Alabama
Tuscaloosa, Alabama

Robin C. Scarcella
University of California at Irvine
Irvine, California

PREFACE

To the Student

A *threshold* is the bottom part of a door frame, the part you step over when you enter a room. We also use the word to describe the beginning of a new experience. This book is entitled *Thresholds* because it may be your first encounter with unsimplified reading in English and with the higher-level academic activities that you will need to do if you enter an English-language college or university.

The focus of the book is reading and vocabulary. The readings are unsimplified and are taken from a variety of sources: books, encyclopedias, newspapers, magazines, and personal journals. The keywords that you will study include some of the most common academic vocabulary in English; these are words that you will encounter again and again in your future reading and that you will want to use in your writing. Whether or not you are planning to use English for higher-level academic study, they are words that every well-educated speaker of English knows and uses, and they will serve you well.

Although you may find the level of some of the readings challenging, don't be discouraged. One purpose of the book is to show you ways, or *strategies,* of approaching unsimplified reading so that you can understand its main ideas. These strategies are keys that can unlock material that you might have thought was unavailable to you.

Finally, each chapter in this book explores several ways of looking at a controversial topic. One of the most important purposes of education is to show students all sides of an issue so they will become well informed. The purpose of these readings is not to lead you in particular directions, but to enable you to reach well-informed opinions.

To the Teacher

Thresholds is a high-intermediate reading text that features unsimplified passages and common academic vocabulary. It serves students training to study at English-language colleges or universities, those studying English out of personal interest, and those who want more English in order to further their career opportunities.

The book was written primarily to meet the needs of a reading course, but it is equally usable in a course that includes a writing component. The Instructor's Manual gives guidelines for use in both kinds of courses.

Particular skills and tasks are explained in detail when they are introduced. After that, they are recycled in later chapters. If you skip chapters or activities, you may wish to know where these introductory explanations are given.

Chapter 2: The Columbus Controversy
    Vocabulary in context
    Making vocabulary cards
    Keyword study and exercises
    Making a chart
    Taking notes from reading

Chapter 3: The First North Americans
    Anticipating information in a reading passage
    Developing good habits during reading
    Paraphrasing
    Distinguishing between topic and main idea

Chapter 4: Alternative Education
    Projects
    Summarizing
    Jigsaw reading
    Taking notes using graphic formats
    Identifying the topic sentence

Chapter 6: Lies and Truth
    Paraphrasing (in more detail than in Chapter 3)
    Identifying issues and taking positions
    Anticipating test questions
    Recognizing the structure of a reading passage

Chapter 8: Bigfoot and Company
    Analyzing an author's position on a controversy
    Arguing both sides of an issue

CHAPTER FEATURES

Chapter 1 is a preliminary unit in which students perform diagnostic tasks, take a reading inventory, and set goals according to their individual academic, career, and personal interests.

Chapters 2 through 8 each centers around a series of readings related to a central topic. Within the chapter, each new passage enlarges upon the previous perspective and provides schema activation for the next, so that by the end, students can synthesize information from several readings in their discussion and writing activities. In addition, certain themes link the content across units: for example, the influence of cultural values on topics such as education, history, and the treatment of endangered species.

Chapters 5 and 7 are consolidation chapters that serve to solidify skills previously presented.

Each chapter opens with schema-activation activities for both vocabulary and content. Reading skill-builders are directly tied to the content of each topic and therefore contribute to comprehension of the whole. Comprehension and skills are developed through interactive activities and through writing assignments that range from personal response and narration to expository and persuasive writing. Reading passages are used as the basis for training in writing from outside sources: e.g., summarizing, paraphrasing, and synthesizing, though not to the extent of writing a full-fledged research paper. You, the teacher, will decide to what extent writing will be emphasized.

Each reading passage is the focus of the following activities:

Identifying the circled reference words
Comprehension questions
Scanning exercises
True-false questions (using paraphrases from the reading)
Identifying the main idea, or taking notes
Vocabulary-in-context exercises
Keyword exercises

If you follow this sequence of activities slavishly, your students will quickly become bored with the repeated format. Pick and choose from what's available in the book in order to vary the way class time is spent. Interspersed in each chapter you'll also find a variety of activities calling for discussion, freewriting, essay writing, cultural surveys, and longer projects. Design your class to stimulate student interest.

SUPPLEMENTARY WORK

If your program has a reading laboratory, use it to supplement the text. At the high-intermediate level, students are ready to begin speed-reading exercises such as those provided in the computer program Speed Reader II and in SRA's Mark II reading kit. If your course integrates reading and writing, you may wish to teach your students the rudiments of word processing in a computer laboratory. A computer lab with a large overhead screen connected to a computer enables you to demonstrate the process of generating first drafts of essays, then going back to reorganize, develop, and edit them.

ANCILLARY MATERIALS

This book is accompanied by a tape; the selections that it includes are indicated in the text.

The Instructor's Manual includes answers to the exercises, tests with answer keys, and suggestions for facilitating activities. It gives guidelines for picking and choosing if you can't use all of the text in one term, models for adapting the book to semester- or quarter-length terms, and suggestions for integrating a writing component. The manual also includes lists of optional longer readings related to each topic and guidelines for writing sentences with selected keywords.

Acknowledgements

Thanks to Rebecca Oxford, Robin Scarcella, and Dave Lee for conceiving of and carrying out the whole Tapestry project. I am very grateful to Dave, my editor, for his quiet, wise leadership; to Ken Mattsson, assistant editor, for his unflagging helpfulness and good cheer; and to Amy Jamison, who coordinated the developmental reviews and synthesized them into a meaningful summary. My colleagues Jeanne Andersen and Jill Bishop piloted the manuscript with me and gave me encouragement, constructive suggestions, and marvelous ideas for improvements. A special thanks goes out to the students at the American English Institute who helped us refine the text; their responses told me better than anything else what was working and what needed rethinking.

During the course of writing this manuscript I developed a special place in my heart for the Diamond Peak Wilderness, where I spent many happy hours not even thinking about the task at hand, and from where I always came back refreshed. But I reserve my deepest gratitude for my husband, Tracy Daugherty, who made everything possible.

Thanks also to the following reviewers:

Diane Starke, El Paso Community College
Edith Williams, Northern Virginia Community College
Laura Le Dréan, University of Houston Downtown Campus
Pamela Friedman, Alameda, CA
Patricia Johnson, The American University
Betty Payne, Montgomery College
Ayse Stromsdorfer, St. Louis University

And thanks to more-distant "colleagues" who field-tested parts of the manuscript:

Wynell C. Biles, Texas A&M University
Mala R. Farmer-Bailey, Texas A&M University
Michelle Remaud, Northeastern University
Priscilla Taylor, California State University, Los Angeles

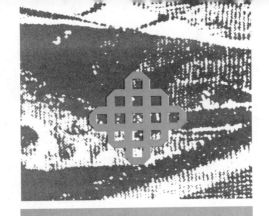

CONTENTS

Appendix   *245*

Getting Started

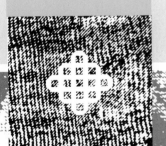

Your teacher will use the following activity to get an idea of your ability in several English skills: listening, reading, speaking, writing, and grammar. Please don't read the story yet. This is what you're going to do:

1. You'll listen as your teacher reads the story aloud. You may ask for a second reading if you wish.
2. You'll read the story silently as many times as you like for about 10 minutes. When you finish, you may ask anything you wish about the events in the story or the vocabulary.
3. Without looking at the story, you'll have about 15 minutes to do a fill-in-the-blank exercise (called a *cloze* exercise).
4. You may study the story again for a few minutes. Then you'll put it aside and you'll work with a partner. Each of you will take turns telling the story to each other. This will give you practice in speaking and will also prepare you for the next step.
5. You may study the story again for a few minutes. Then you'll put it aside and try to write it. You'll have about 15 minutes for this. If you're good at working from memory, feel free to copy any sentences that you can remember; but what's important is that you retell the meaning of the story, not the exact wording.

STORY: THE KING'S DECISION

Many years ago there lived a king who was widely known for his wisdom. It was said that he was the wisest man who had ever lived.

One day two women came before him. One of them was carrying a living baby, but the other's baby was dead. The first woman said, "Great king, this woman and I live in the same house. Our babies were born only three days apart. Then one night, she rolled over on her baby in her sleep, and it died. So she exchanged her dead baby for my live one while I was sleeping. When I woke up in the morning, I thought my baby had died! Then I noticed through my tears that it was not my son, but hers."

"Great king, this woman is lying," protested the second woman. "It was her son that died, and now she wants mine. Do not let her take away my only child!"

The king was silent for a moment. Then he spoke. "Each woman claims that the living baby is hers," he said. "Who can decide such a matter when no one else was there to see what really happened?" He turned to one of his guards. "Bring me a sword," he commanded. The sword was brought. "Now," he ordered the guard, "divide the living baby into two parts, and give each woman half."

The guard raised his sword over the screaming baby. "No!" cried the first woman. "Don't do it! Give the baby to her, but don't kill him!"

The other woman said, "No, go ahead and divide him. It's a fair decision."

The guard looked at the king for his orders. The king smiled. "Give the living baby to the first woman," he said. "She is his real mother. She loves her son so much that she would rather give him up than see him harmed."

Cloze Exercise

Instructions: Write only one word in each blank.

Many years ago there lived a _____ who was widely known

for his _____. It was said that he was _____

wisest man who had ever lived.

_____ day two women came before him. _____

of them was carrying a living _____, but the other's baby was

dead. _____ first woman said, "Great king, this _____

and I live in the same _____. Our babies were born only three

_____ apart. Then one night, she rolled _____

on her baby in her sleep, _____ it died. So she exchanged her

_____ baby for my live one while _____ was

sleeping. When I woke up _____ the morning, I thought my

baby _____ died! Then I noticed through my _____

that it was not my son, _____ hers."

"Great king, this woman is _____," protested the second

woman. "It was _____ son that died, and now she _____

mine. Do not let her take _____ my only child!"

The king was _____ for a moment. Then he spoke.

"_____ woman claims that the living baby _____

hers," he said. "Who can decide _____ a matter when no one else

_____ there to see what really happened?" _____

turned to one of his guards. "_____ me a sword," he commanded.

The _____ was brought. "Now," he ordered the _____,

"divide the living baby into two _____, and give each woman half."

The _____ raised his sword over the screaming _____.

"No!" cried the first woman. "Don't _____ it! Give the baby to

her, _____ don't kill him!"

The other woman _____, "No, go ahead and divide him.

_____ a fair decision."

The guard looked _____ the king for his orders. The

_____ smiled. "Give the living baby to _____

first woman," he said. "She is _____ real mother. She loves her son

_____ much that she would rather give _____

up than see him harmed."

Instructions: Complete the chart and answer the questions below.

GOOD	VERY GOOD		BAD	VERY BAD
		Are these good or bad reading habits?		
_____	_____	**a.** When you read silently, read every word.		
_____	_____	**b.** Every time you find a word that you don't know, stop and look it up in your dictionary.	_____	_____
_____	_____	**c.** Begin at the beginning and read straight through without stopping.		
_____	_____	**d.** Use your dictionary only at the end of each section.	_____	_____
_____	_____	**e.** Don't use a dictionary.	_____	_____
		f. As you read, try to mentally translate the passage into your native language.		
		g. If you find something that you don't understand, stop and think about it. Don't go on to the next part until you understand it.	_____	_____
_____	_____	**h.** Say the words in your head as you read them.	_____	_____
_____	_____	**i.** Look over the passage briefly from start to finish before you actually read it.	_____	_____
		j. If possible, mark important ideas and words (or unknown words) as you read.		
_____	_____	**k.** Read a little bit more quickly than is comfortable for you.	_____	_____
_____	_____	**l.** Guess what the unknown words mean.	_____	_____
		m. Try to understand the organization of the passage and the relationships between the ideas.	_____	_____

1. How well do you read in your native language?_____

In English? _____

2. Do you enjoy reading in your native language? _____

In English?_____

3. What do you find hardest about reading in English? (vocabulary, grammar, speed, concentration, interest, etc.)

_____

4. What do you like to read for pleasure?

_____

5. What reading skills would you like to improve in this course?

_____

How much vocabulary do you need?

First of all, how many English words do you think you know now? Think about your reading/listening vocabulary, which is much larger than your writing/speaking vocabulary.

How much vocabulary you need depends on what you want to use English for. If you want to study in a college or university where English is the language of instruction, you'll need a broad vocabulary that includes both everyday and academic words. Most native-speaking undergraduate students have a reading vocabulary of around 20,000 words. Then every year of their studies, they add another one to two thousand words.

Remember this: reading is a process. Vocabulary is a very important part of the process of reading comprehension, probably the most important part. However, if you interrupt your reading to use your dictionary in the middle of a sentence or a paragraph, you may improve your vocabulary a little, but you won't improve your reading at all. Wait to use your dictionary until you come to a good stopping place. Then carefully decide which new words to look up. If you try to look up all of them, you'll still be working when all your friends have closed their books and gone out to enjoy their free time. Worse yet, you'll become discouraged and you may come to hate reading in English. Life is short! Look up only the words that you absolutely need in order to understand the idea of the material. If there are other words that would be useful for you to know, your teacher or this book will point them out to you.

What's the best way to learn new vocabulary?

It's important to understand that you won't remember much new vocabulary unless you find a systematic way of recording it and studying it. There are a number of ways of doing this, including keeping a vocabulary notebook, writing meanings in the margins of a text, or using small vocabulary cards. Different ways work well for different people. You may want to try several in order to find the one that fits your learning style. Or you may have a special way of your own that works for you. If so, tell your teacher and your classmates about it.

How fast should you read?

College students who are native speakers of English generally read at the following speeds:

Very careful study reading	200 words per minute
Normal study reading	300 words per minute
Skimming	450 words per minute
Scanning	600 words per minute

Note two things:

1. The rate of reading depends on what kind of reading you're doing, and that depends on your purpose. "Normal study reading" is the rate used when you're reading a homework assignment in your textbook for the first time. "Very careful study reading" is the rate used when you're reading something very difficult or important or when you're studying for a major examination. Skimming and scanning will be discussed below.
2. These rates are high! If your school has materials to measure your reading speed, your teacher will show you how to use them so that you can find out how fast you can read. If you're planning to attend (or are already attending) a college or university in an English-speaking country, you'll want to build your speed as closely as possible to the rates given above. The amount of reading you'll have to do is very great, and if you are a slow reader, you may fall behind in your work and have trouble catching up.

Skimming and scanning are different from study reading in that they're much faster. When you do them, you don't read everything on the page. They are described below.

What is skimming, and what good is it?

Do you know what skim milk is? In milk production, skimming is the process of taking the cream off the top of the milk. In reading, skimming is similar: you're looking at the top, the surface, but not reading deeply to catch all the information. You just want to know the topic and the main points.

When you skim, do this:

1. Read the title.
2. Read any subheadings.
3. Look at any pictures, charts, graphs, etc. that are included.
4. Read all of the first paragraph.
5. Look for the main points of the following paragraphs. They're usually in the first sentence; if not there, try the last sentence; if not there, look inside the paragraph.
6. Read all of the last paragraph. It will probably contain a summary or some other type of important conclusion.

Here's what skimming looks like: Turn back to page 2 to "The King's Decision." If you were to skim it, here's what you would read:

Skimming: "The King's Decision"

Many years ago there lived a king who was widely known for his wisdom. It was said that he was the wisest man who had ever lived.

One day two women came before him. One of them was carrying a living baby, but the other's baby was dead. . . . . she exchanged her dead baby for my live one . . . . it was not my son, but hers."

"Great king, this woman is lying," . . . .
. . . .
    The king was silent for a moment. . . . .
. . . .
. . . . "Bring me a sword," . . . .
. . . . "divide the living baby into two parts, and give each woman half."
    The guard raised his sword . . . . "No!" . . . .
"Give the baby to her . . . ."
    The other woman said, "No, go ahead and divide him. . . . ."
    The guard looked at the king for his orders. The king smiled. "Give the
living baby to the first woman," he said. "She is his real mother. She loves her
son so much that she would rather give him up than see him harmed."

Notice that if you read only these parts, you would understand the general idea of
the story.

Why skim? It's one of the most useful pre-reading skills that you can use.
Before reading any homework assignment or important material, follow the six
steps listed above. Skimming identifies the topic for you and "programs" your
brain to know what kind of information it will be receiving. Then when you read,
you'll be able to read faster, to understand the material better, and to remember it
longer. You'll practice skimming throughout this textbook, and you should make a
point of doing it in your outside reading.

What's scanning, and what good is it?

Scanning is looking for specific information in a reading passage. It does not
include reading every word, nor even reading for the main idea. Notice that it's the
fastest kind of reading on the reading speed table given above. For instance, you
might be in the library looking for good materials to use in a research paper. You
pick up a book with a title that looks useful. You scan the table of contents to see
if your subject is there. You find a chapter title that looks promising. You turn to
that chapter and run your eyes quickly down the pages, looking for key words that
are related to your topic. That's scanning. If you find what you're looking for, then
you might sit down to do some careful study reading. But study reading is different
from scanning.

Scanning is a very important reading skill because it saves you time and it
directs you to useful information. The secrets to good scanning are:

1. Knowing which "key words" to look for. If you can't find the one you're
   looking for, try another that means the same thing.
2. Not wasting time reading whole sentences. Just look for the key words or
   phrases.

Scanning is a skill that you'll practice in this book, but don't stop here. Use it
in your outside reading. It'll save you time and make you a stronger reader.

Build your reading comprehension.

There are many ways to strengthen your reading comprehension. This book
will give you practice in identifying the main ideas of reading passages, taking
notes from your reading, paraphrasing information in your own words,
summarizing passages into a single sentence or a short paragraph, using
information from readings in papers of your own, and anticipating test questions.

Outside reading is important.

The materials in this book are designed to interest you, to build your reading skills, and to increase your vocabulary. But a textbook alone isn't enough to make you a strong reader. You should supplement it with outside reading that fits your own interests and needs. It's especially important that you read some longer materials than this book contains. If your school has a reading laboratory, you might find some materials there that interest you. If it doesn't, go to the library and look for books or magazines that are interesting and that don't seem too difficult.

How difficult is "too difficult"? The decision is really yours, but in general, if there's a great deal of new vocabulary and if the grammar of the sentences is very hard for you to follow, you should look for something simpler. That's because very difficult material makes such slow reading that you can't remember what the first part of the sentence was by the time you finish the last part. Or you can't remember what was said in the sentence before, or back at the beginning of the paragraph. If you can read through a paragraph and keep the general ideas in your head from start to finish, that's probably a good level for you, even though there may be new vocabulary and some difficult sentences.

SETTING YOUR OWN GOALS

Your reasons for being in this class might be different from everyone else's. Your strengths and weaknesses in reading and vocabulary are different. So are your interests. That's why it's important for you to set some goals of your own for this course. Consider the following questions.

1. What are you going to use English for after you finish this program?
   What reading and vocabulary abilities will you need in order to do that?
   What kind of materials will you be reading then?
2. In past language courses, what were you good at?
   What ways of studying worked well for you? (For example, studying with a partner, studying rules, just reading a lot, asking a teacher to help you, writing notes, writing in your textbook, talking about what you were learning, etc.)
   Are you good at memorizing vocabulary?
   How do you learn it best?

You'll find it helpful to set short-term objectives for yourself with every chapter in this book. That's because your first objectives may not be very realistic, and you may want to change them. Don't set objectives that you can't possibly achieve, because you'll become discouraged. Take into consideration your interests, your needs, and your abilities.

You should also choose a longer goal for the term, which you can re-evaluate periodically. Take a moment to think about this now, and write it down. Keep it in your notebook or binder. Review it from time to time, and change it as you need or want to.

FREEWRITING: THINKING ABOUT GOALS

Here are some things you'll want to consider in setting goals:

1. How much material you want to read outside of class, and what kind
2. What kind of material you want to learn to read (personal interest, major field, etc.)
3. How fast you want to read by the end of this course
4. What level of comprehension you'd like to reach (for example, 65% comprehension of unsimplified reading passages)
5. How many vocabulary words you want to learn each week
6. How much to learn about them: part of speech? pronunciation? example-sentences? how to use them in your writing?
7. What score you'd like to make on the TOEFL or another examination
8. What you especially want to improve in this course

The Columbus Controversy

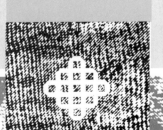

PLANNING YOUR LEARNING

Your teacher will show you the overall goal statement that you wrote at the end of Chapter 1. Review what you wrote and think about how you can work to meet your goal as you study this new chapter.

- How many words do you want to learn? (minimum 39, the number of "keywords" in the chapter)
- What grade would you like to make on the vocabulary section of the exam at the end of the chapter?
- What grade would you like to make on the reading comprehension section of the exam?
- What are you going to read outside of class?

PREVIEWING THE CHAPTER

- Think about the title of this chapter. What is a controversy? What's controversial about Christopher Columbus?
- Look in the Table of Contents at the titles of the four readings in this chapter. Look through the chapter at the map and the pictures. What are some things that you expect to learn about?
- Which reading do you think you'll be most interested in?

FREEWRITING: WHO WAS CHRISTOPHER COLUMBUS?

- What do you know about Christopher Columbus? Take a few minutes to write everything that you have ever learned. This is *freewriting:* Concentrate on content and on expressing yourself so that people can understand you; don't spend much time worrying about vocabulary or grammar. Try to write as much as you can in the time you have.
- After you finish writing, form a group with two or three classmates and tell each other what you wrote. Did your partners have any information that was different from yours?

LEARNING STRATEGY

Managing Your Learning: Sharing information with partners is a good way to get some idea of what to expect from a reading.

PREPARING TO READ: CONTENT

Working in small groups, try to answer as many of the following questions as you can. The answers provide basic information that will help you to understand the readings about Columbus in this chapter.

1. What did Columbus want to do that had never been done before?
2. How many ships did he take on his first voyage, and what were their names?
3. What were the names of the king and queen of Spain at that time?
4. What problems did he and his men have on their first voyage?
5. What did they find when they reached land?
6. How many voyages did Columbus make to America?
7. Tell two results of Columbus's voyages.

When he started out he didn't know where he was going, when he got there he didn't know where he was, and when he got back he didn't know where he had been.
—*Author unknown*

PREPARING TO READ: VOCABULARY

The following "vocabulary preview" will make your reading easier when you encounter these words and concepts. Work with a partner; you can use your dictionary if you like. Don't worry if you can't guess some of the words.

1. A trip that you make on a ship is called a v_____.

2. Columbus s_____ed from Spain to America in 1492.

3. The men who traveled with Columbus and who worked on his ships were called his c_____.

4. Columbus's title was "The A_____ of the Ocean Sea."

5. Columbus was looking for the I_____s.

6. He wasn't trying to d_____ America, which he didn't even know existed.

7. After he traveled to America, Europeans began to call America "The _____ World," and Europe "The _____ World."

8. The dominant religion in Europe in Columbus's time was C_____.

9. The country that Columbus departed from was S_____. Its people were called S_____s, and their language was sometimes called S_____.

10. Two groups of Indians that Columbus met in America were the G_____ and the A_____.

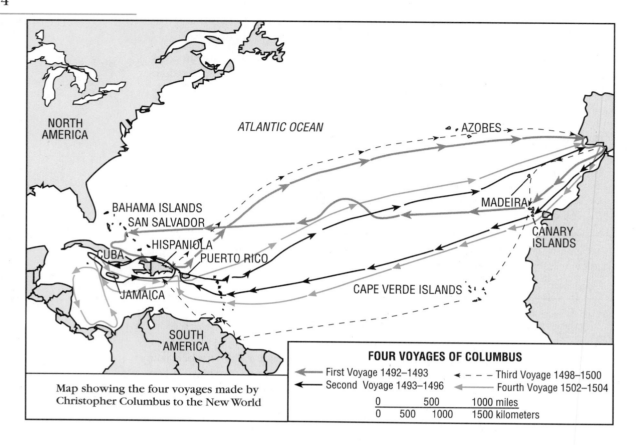

Map showing the four voyages made by
Christopher Columbus to the New World

FOUR VOYAGES OF COLUMBUS

First Voyage 1492–1493   Third Voyage 1498–1500
Second Voyage 1493–1496   Fourth Voyage 1502–1504

0		500	1000 miles
0	500	1000	1500 kilometers

Reading a Map

1. Which voyage took the longest time?
2. Which voyage was made in the shortest time?
3. Which voyage took Columbus the farthest south?
4. What was the length of time between Columbus's first departure from Spain and his last arrival back in Spain?
5. How far is it from the Canary Islands to San Salvador?
6. Look at the places where Columbus landed. How many of these countries can you identify by their modern names?

Columbus's first voyage to the Americas is memorable partly because no European had ever sailed so far west into the Atlantic Ocean before, at least not from southern Europe. (It seems that Vikings from Iceland had landed on the North American coast, but they had crossed the Atlantic much farther north.) Consequently there were no accurate maps of where they were going, and no one was sure if they would really find land or how long the voyage might take.

They had enough food and water for about four weeks; if they hadn't found land by then, they would die. It's easy to understand why Columbus's crew were nervous as the Canary Islands disappeared behind them. As the voyage lengthened into days and then weeks, they grew more and more worried and frightened. The following passages are simplifications of an English translation of Columbus's daily journal.

NOTE: This reading is also on the tape.

Reading process: Very quickly skim the passage by reading the first sentence of every entry. Then read more carefully. Mark all the vocabulary items that you don't know, but don't stop to use your dictionary yet.

COLUMBUS'S FIRST VOYAGE

1   *Monday, 3 September, 1492.* Gutierrez has already acquired all of the wood and water necessary for the voyage, (which) I estimate will last twenty-one days. However, to be on the safe side, in case of contrary winds or currents, I ordered Gutierrez to prepare for a voyage of twenty-eight days. I anticipate[1] no problem in replenishing our supplies when we reach the Indies.

2   *Wednesday, 5 September, 1492.* All is ready for the voyage. Tonight I shall order a special service of thanksgiving; at sunrise I will lift anchors to begin the journey westward.

3   *Thursday, 6 September, 1492.* Shortly before noon I sailed and set my course for the west. I sailed all day and night with very little wind.

4   *Sunday, 9 September, 1492.* This day we completely lost sight of land. Many men sighed and wept for fear they would not see it again for a long time. I comforted them with great promises of lands and riches. I decided to count fewer miles than we actually made. I did this so the sailors might not think themselves as far from Spain as they really were. For myself I kept a confidential,[2] accurate[3] reckoning. Tonight I made ninety miles.

5   *Saturday, 15 September, 1492.* I sailed west day and night for eighty-one miles. Early this morning I saw a marvelous meteorite fall into the sea twelve or fifteen miles away. Some people took this to be a bad omen, but I calmed them by telling them of the numerous[4] times that I have seen (such events.) I have to confess that this is the closest a falling star has ever come to my ship.

6   *Sunday, 23 September, 1492.* The crew is grumbling about the wind. The changing wind, along with the flat sea, has led the men to believe we will never get home. I told them being near land keeps the sea smooth. Later, when waves arose without wind, they were astonished. I saw (this) as a sign from God. Soon the wind arose and the sea grew rougher. The crew was relieved. The men tried to catch fish but could not get any to bite at the hooks. Eventually they harpooned several.

7   *Monday, 24 September, 1492.* I am having serious trouble with the crew, despite the signs of land that we have.

8   All day long and all night long those who get together never stop complaining. They fear they will not return home. They have said that it is insanity[5] and suicidal[6] to risk their lives. They say I am willing to risk my life to become a great Lord and that I have deceived[7] them to further my ambition.[8] I am told by a few trusted men (and these are few in number!) that if I persist in going onward, that the best course of action will be to throw me into the sea some night. They will say I fell overboard while taking the position of the North Star.

9   *Tuesday, 25 September, 1492.* At sunset Pinzon called to me that he saw land and claimed the reward. I fell to my knees to give thanks to Our Lord. The *Niña*'s crew all climbed the mast and rigging, and claimed that it was land. I myself was sure it was land about seventy-five miles to the southwest.

10   *Wednesday, 26 September, 1492.* After sunrise I realized[9] that what we all thought was land was nothing more than squall clouds, (which) often resemble land. I returned to my original course of west in the afternoon, once I was positive I had not seen land. Day and night I sailed ninety-three miles, but recorded seventy-two. The sea was like a river and the air sweet and balmy.

11   *Wednesday, 10 October, 1492.* Between day and night I made one hundred seventy-seven miles. I told the crew one hundred thirty-two miles, but they could stand it no longer. They grumbled and complained of the long voyage. I told them that, for better or worse, they had to complete the voyage. I cheered them on, telling them of the honors and rewards they would receive. I told them it was useless[10] to complain. I had started to find the Indies and would continue until I (had.)

Threads

A hero is a person who knows how to hang on one minute longer.

Norwegian proverb

After You Read

Identify the circled reference words: Write the meanings of these words in the margin beside the reading.

COMPREHENSION QUESTIONS

1. Find the names of two men in the passage. _____

_____

How did you find them? _____

What was the job of the first man? _____

2. Look at the entry for 9 September. In your own words, explain what Columbus did on this day. _____

_____

Do you think he should have done it? _____

3. Name three dangers that Columbus faced.

   a. _____

   b. _____

   c. _____

4. On what day were Columbus and his men greatly disappointed?

   _____

   What disappointed them? _____

5. Find two entries that show Columbus's belief in God. What were the dates?

   _____

   _____

6. Look at the entry for 25 September. What do you think "the reward" was for?

   _____

7. Find a date when it was windy. _____

   Find a date when there was no wind. _____

8. How did Columbus encourage the men? _____

   _____

9. Columbus's ships finally reached land on 12 October 1492. How long had

   their voyage lasted? _____

10. In your opinion, what are three adjectives that describe Columbus's
    personality? Write the date of the entry that made you think of each one.

    Adjectives   *Date*

    a. _____   _____

    b. _____   _____

    c. _____   _____

LEARNING STRATEGY

**Personalizing: You can get a better understanding of another
person's actions if you try to identify yourself with his or her
point of view.**

FREEWRITING: VALUES AND POINTS OF VIEW

Columbus's *point of view* was the way he felt about what he was doing. In order to understand his point of view, imagine that you are Columbus. Why do you want to make this voyage? If you succeed, what will you gain? Write an entry about this for your secret journal.

Now imagine that you are just an ordinary sailor on one of Columbus's ships. Why did you agree to make this voyage? What will you gain if Columbus succeeds? If he fails, you fear that you will never see land again. Write a letter home that you plan to put into a bottle, cork up, and throw into the sea.

Columbus's point of view came partly from his *values*—the ideas and actions that were important to him. One common human value is the desire to stay alive. Why was Columbus willing to make such a dangerous trip when everyone else on the ships was telling him that they feared they would all die?

LEARNING STRATEGY

Managing Your Learning: Look up only the most important words in the dictionary.

Vocabulary

VOCABULARY STUDY: CHOOSING THE MOST IMPORTANT NEW WORDS

Look at the entry for 3 September. When you were reading, you marked all the vocabulary items that you didn't know; now tell them to your teacher, who will write them on the blackboard. Look at them together. Which ones keep you from understanding the general idea of the entry for that date? Those are the only ones you should worry about for the sake of comprehension.

Look at the whole passage in this way. Choose not more than ten of such words and write them here. You're going to look them up in a moment.

1. _____   6. _____

2. _____   7. _____

3. _____   8. _____

4. _____   9. _____

5. _____   10. _____

Now work with a partner and compare your lists. Discuss differences; you can change your list if you think your partner's is better.

LEARNING STRATEGY

Forming Concepts: Use the context to help you understand new vocabulary.

VOCABULARY IN CONTEXT

Some of the unknown words can be understood in a general way because of other information that is provided in the same passage. This surrounding information is called the *context* of the words. In the entry for 3 September, for instance, the word *supplies* may be new to you, but the first sentence contains two examples of supplies. What are they?

In the entry for 5 September, the context helps you to understand the meaning of *journey*. What is another word in the entry that means the same thing?

In the entry for 15 September, the word *meteorite* is probably new to you. It is not a common or very important word in English, but in the last sentence Columbus gives you a *synonym*—a phrase that means the same thing. What is it?

You can't always guess the meaning of new words by looking at their context, but often you can learn enough about the word that you can understand the passage in a general way. Usually this general kind of understanding is enough. If it's not—if you really can't guess the meaning of the word and you know that it's central to an understanding of the passage—then look it up when you come to a good stopping place, such as the end of a section or a chapter.

LEARNING STRATEGY

Remembering New Material: Recording new words on cards that you can rearrange makes it easier to remember them.

USING VOCABULARY CARDS

You can buy blank cards ranging in size from very small (like business cards) to much larger, depending on how much information you want to write. But you should choose a size that you can handle easily.

Here is some information you may want to write on each card:

- the word on one side and its definition (preferably in English) on the other
- its pronunciation
- its part of speech
- a sample sentence or phrase containing the word

But you may find that recording *all* this information for every word slows you down and discourages you. Find a balance that's helpful but manageable.

Think about how much information you want to record; then go out and buy a stack of cards. Record the ten words that you wrote above. Then add cards for the following words—not because they are necessary in order to understand the general idea of the passage, but because they are useful.

These words will be called **keywords** in this book. A list of all the keywords in this chapter is on page 38.

KEYWORDS

NOTE: Following each keyword in the list below is the number of the paragraph (¶) in the reading where the keyword appears.

1. anticipate* ¶1
2. confidential ¶4
3. accurate ¶4
4. numerous* ¶5
5. insanity ¶8

6. suicidal ¶8
7. deceive* ¶8
8. ambition ¶8
9. resemble* ¶10
10. useless ¶11

---

* Part of your vocabulary study will include making sentences of your own with the keywords marked with an asterisk (*). Study the sentences they appear in, and then imitate the sentence structure when you write your own sentences.

KEYWORD EXERCISE

In this exercise, the keywords are printed in italics.

1. What's the most *accurate* way to count the population of a city?

   EXAMPLE: Columbus kept an *accurate* record of his distance in a secret journal.

2. What are the two most important elements of meaning in the word *confidential?*

   information   secret   to explain   completely   to imagine

   EXAMPLE: Columbus never showed his *confidential* journal to the crew.

3. *Matching:*

   _____ 1. *useless*

   _____ 2. *anticipate*

   _____ 3. *numerous*

   _____ 4. *insanity*

   _____ 5. *suicidal*

   _____ 6. *deceive*

   _____ 7. *resemble*

   _____ 8. *ambition*

   a. antonym (= opposite): few

   b. acting in a very dangerous way

   c. synonym: look like

   d. not helpful

   e. madness or foolishness

   f. desire to be rich, powerful, successful

   g. prepare for something before it happens

   h. antonym: tell the truth

REVIEW

Now that you have studied the vocabulary, re-read or re-skim the passage.

Cultural Survey: What Is "The Columbus Controversy"?

Today Christopher Columbus has become a *controversial* figure—that is, some people think he was a great man, while others think he was one of the worst people in history. Using English, ask one or more people to explain this controversy to you. The next time your class meets, you will freewrite about what you learned.

FREEWRITING

Write what you learned about why Columbus has become a controversial figure.

After you finish writing, form a group with two or three classmates and tell each other what you wrote. Did your partners have any information that was different from yours?

Charting Columbus's Good and Bad Sides

Turn a piece of paper sideways (horizontally) and write the title "The Columbus Controversy" at the top. On the left side under the title, write the heading "The Good Side"; on the right, write "The Bad Side." Work with a partner to list what you learned from Reading One. Then compare your list with another group's.

READING TWO

As we all know, finally Columbus's ships did reach land. The following account of that memorable day was made by Bartolomé de las Casas, a Catholic priest who knew Columbus personally and who spent many years in the "New World." In this passage de las Casas refers to Columbus as "the admiral."

LEARNING STRATEGY

Understanding and Using Emotions: Focusing on what you *can* understand in a reading helps you develop a positive attitude and increases your comprehension.

Reading process: Look at the Comprehension Questions at the end of this reading. First try to locate the paragraph where each answer is found. Then read the passage carefully.

LAND AT LAST

1   *Friday, October 12:* Two hours after midnight land appeared, at a distance of about two leagues from them. They . . . kept . . . waiting for day, . . . on which they reached a small island of the Lucayos, which is called in the language of the Indians "Guanahaní." Immediately they saw naked people, and the admiral went ashore in the armed boat, and Martin Alonso Pinzón and Vicente Yañez, his brother, who was captain of the *Niña*. . . . When they had landed, they saw very green trees and much water and fruit of various[1] kinds. The admiral called the two captains and the others who had landed, . . . and said that they should bear witness and testimony how he, before them all, took possession of the island . . . for the King and Queen. . . . Soon many people of the island gathered[2] there. What follows are the actual words of the admiral, in his book of his first voyage and discovery of these Indies.

2   "I," he says, "in order that they might feel great amity towards us, because I knew that they were a people to be delivered and converted to our holy faith rather by love than by force,[3] gave to some among them some red caps and

some glass beads, which they hung round their necks, and many other things of little value.[4] At this they were greatly pleased and became so entirely[5] our friends that it was a wonder to see. Afterwards they came swimming to the ships' boats, where we were, and brought us parrots and cotton thread in balls, and spears and many other things, and we exchanged[6] for them other things, such as small glass beads and hawks' bells,* which we gave to them. In fact, they took all and gave all, such as they had, with good will, but it seemed to me that they were a people very deficient in everything.

3   "They all go naked as their mothers bore[7] them, and the women also, although I saw only one very young girl. And all those whom I did see were youths, so that I did not see one who was over thirty years of age; they were very well built, with very handsome bodies and very good faces. Their hair is coarse almost like the hairs of a horse's tail and short; they wear their hair down over their eyebrows, except for a few strands behind, which they wear long and never cut. Some of them are painted black, and they are the colour of the people of the Canaries, neither black nor white, and some of them are painted white and some red and some in any colour that they find. Some of them paint their faces, some their whole bodies, some only the eyes, and some only the nose.

4   "They do not bear arms or know them, for I showed to them swords and they took them by the blade and cut themselves through ignorance. They have no iron. Their spears are certain reeds, without iron, and some of these have a fish tooth at the end, while others are pointed in various ways. They are all generally fairly tall, good looking and well proportioned. I saw some who bore marks of wounds on their bodies, and I made signs to them to ask how this came about, and they indicated to me that people came from other islands, which are near, and wished to capture[8] them, and they defended[9] themselves. And I believed and still believe that they come here from the mainland to take them for slaves.[10]

5   "They should be good servants and of quick intelligence, since I see that they very soon say all that is said to them, and I believe that they would easily be made Christians, for it appeared to me that they had no creed. Our Lord willing, at the time of my departure I will bring back six of them to Your Highnesses, that they may learn to talk. I saw no beast of any kind in this island, except parrots." All these are the words of the admiral.

---

*Hawks' bells were small bells that European people of that time tied onto the bodies of hawks, which were hunting birds that they used for sport. The little bells that Columbus mentions here will become very important in the next reading passage.

Upon contact, Europeans and Americans began a lively exchange. From the Americas came chocolate, hot peppers, peanuts, tomatoes, and potatoes; from Europe came horses, pigs, cattle, goats, sheep, honey bees, and wheat. But they also exchanged deadly diseases: the Europeans introduced malaria, measles, smallpox, tetanus, and typhus, which killed large numbers of native Americans who had no resistance to them. The Native Americans, in turn, sent a strain of syphilis back to Europe.

After You Read

COMPREHENSION QUESTIONS

Instructions: Answer the questions and write the numbers of the paragraphs where you found the information.

¶ number

_____ **1.** How long did Columbus wait between the time that he first saw the land and the time that he went ashore to it?

_____ Why did he wait?

_____ **2.** What was the Indian name for the island?

_____ **3.** Were the Indians friendly or unfriendly to the Spaniards?

_____ **4.** What did the Spaniards give to the Indians?

_____ What did the Indians give in exchange?

_____ **5.** Tell three things that Columbus noticed about how the Indians looked.

_____ **6.** What plans did Columbus have for the Indians?

_____ **7.** What did Columbus mean when he said, "I will bring back six of them to Your Highnesses, *that they may learn to talk*" (¶2)?
• Does that mean that these people had no language of their own?
• Why do you suppose that Columbus didn't say, "that they may learn to speak our language"?
• Did Columbus express any interest in learning to speak the Indians' language?
• What do the answers to these questions tell you about Columbus's attitude toward the Indians?

Vocabulary

KEYWORDS

Now look at the new words in the passage. Choose ten of them that seem central to a general understanding of it. Discuss your choices with your teacher; s/he will help you decide how important they are. Then write new vocabulary cards for them.

In addition to your ten words, write entries for these keywords:

1. various* ¶1
2. gather ¶1
3. force ¶2
4. value* ¶2
5. entirely ¶2
6. exchange* ¶2
7. bore (past tense of bear) ¶3
8. capture ¶4
9. defend* ¶4
10. slave ¶4

KEYWORD EXERCISE

1. *EXAMPLE:* When they had landed, they saw . . . fruit of *various* kinds.

   Name some *various* supplies that you might need if you were going to go scuba-diving.

2. *Gathered* can be an intransitive verb (with no direct object) . . .

   EXAMPLE: Soon many people of the island *gathered* there.

   . . . or a transitive verb (with a direct object):

   EXAMPLE: In the autumn people go into the forest to *gather* wild mushrooms.

   NOTE: Don't confuse *gather* with *collect*. People *gather* things that they want to use; they *collect* things that they want to have and to show to people. *Collecting* things can be a hobby, but not *gathering* things.

   Finish the sentences:
   If you were in the forest and you wanted to build a fire, you would

   gather ———————————————————————————— .

   Collecting ———————————————————— is a popular hobby.

3. Which of the following words are connected with the idea of *slavery*?
   sell   rent   *force*   property   work   salary

   EXAMPLE: I . . . believe that they come here from the mainland to take them for *slaves*.

4. *Meanings:*
   • Something which is *of value* is worth more than a little money.

     QUESTION: Look around you and name something of *value* and something of little *value*.

   • The *values* of a person are the beliefs that they have about how they should act and what is important to them.

     QUESTION: Name a *value* that is important to you personally or to people of your culture in general.

   • Explain the similarities between the two meanings.

5. Which one of the following words does not mean the same thing as the others?
   partially   *entirely*   completely   totally

   EXAMPLE: They . . . became so *entirely* our friends that it was a wonder to see.

6. *Exchange students* are students from different nations who go to study in each other's countries for a year or so.
   Name three other words that people can use the word *exchange* with.

7. *Meanings:*

   • A woman who *bears* children gives birth to them.

   QUESTION: How many children did your two grandmothers *bear?*

   • When we say that someone *bears* arms, we mean that they carry a weapon such as a gun or a knife.

   QUESTION: Name another arm that a person might *bear.*

   • If something *bears* the weight of something else, it carries the weight of that thing.

   QUESTION: What parts of your body *bear* your weight when you are walking?

   • Explain the similarities among the three meanings.

   NOTE: *Bear* is an irregular verb; the three principal parts are *bear, bore, borne.* The mother has *borne* the children; but the baby has been *born.* Note the difference in spelling and that the sentence about the baby is passive, not active.

8. What are the two most important elements of meaning in the word *capture*?
   take   give away   call   *force*   notice

   EXAMPLE: . . . people came from other islands . . . and wished to *capture* them, and they defended themselves.

9. In which of the following situations might you *defend* yourself?
   a courtroom   a boxing ring   a war
   a police station   a dark, lonely street

REVIEW

Now that you have studied the vocabulary, re-read or re-skim the passage.

CONTINUING YOUR CHART

Using information from Reading Two, add to your lists of Columbus's good side and bad side.

Writing: Two News Stories from Different Points of View

Write a short news story summarizing Columbus's arrival and first meeting with the native population. Choose one of these imaginary newspapers to write it for: either *The Daily News of Spain* (from the point of view of the Spaniards) or *The Daily News of Guanahaní* (from the point of view of the Guanahaní Indians). Try to write the kind of information, and in the kind of style, that you would expect to find in a newspaper. When you finish, meet with your classmates to compare the differences between the Spanish and the Guanahaní points of view.

Threads

I do not much wish well to discoveries, for I am always afraid they will end in conquest and robbery.

Samuel Johnson

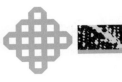

WHAT ELSE DID COLUMBUS DO?

1   Until recently, most American school textbooks told only part of Columbus's story, and that part made him look like a brave hero.[1] He was presented as the man who discovered the "New World." But a more balanced[2] presentation[3] would have shown another side to the story: It would have described some values and beliefs that Columbus shared with most European travelers of that time and with the kings and queens of their nations in the "Old World." First of all, (they) were hungry for gold, and were willing[4] to do anything to get it. Second, they believed that they had the right to claim other people's land for their own European nations (especially if the inhabitants of those lands were not Christians, were "uncivilized,"[5] and looked very different from them). Finally, they believed that they had a right[6] to do anything they pleased with the native inhabitants of those lands. Let us see what part Columbus played in the history of early European contacts with the people of the Americas.

2   On his first voyage, Columbus claimed all the lands that he found for the king and queen of Spain. He gave Spanish names to many of the islands that he "discovered" (such as Hispaniola), though he kept the native names for other islands (such as Cuba and Jamaica). He took ten Indians captive and forced them to return to Spain with him, but four of them died on shipboard. During their captivity (the remaining six) were taught Spanish, and Columbus took them back to America on his second voyage to serve as interpreters.

3   From the very first voyage, Columbus suggested the possibility of enslavement of the Indians to the king and queen of Spain. He wrote in his journal, "But, should Your Majesties command it, all the inhabitants could be taken away to Castile [in Spain], or made slaves on the island. With fifty men we could . . . make them do whatever we want." He repeated this idea in the report that he wrote at the end of this voyage: "I will bring back . . . as many slaves as [you] ask."

4   On the second voyage he put this idea into practice in the most brutal[7] way possible. Author Hans Koning describes the scene in his book *Columbus: His Enterprise:*

5   We are now in February 1495. Time was short for sending back a good "dividend" on the supply ships getting ready for the return to Spain. Columbus therefore turned to a massive slave raid as a means for filling up these ships. The brothers rounded up fifteen hundred Arawak [Indians]—men, women, and children—and imprisoned them in pens in Isabela, guarded by men and dogs. The ships had room for no more than five hundred, and thus only the best specimens were loaded aboard. The Admiral then told the Spaniards they could help themselves from the remainder to as many slaves as they wanted. Those whom no one chose were simply kicked out of their pens. Such had been the terror of these prisoners that (in the description by Michele de Cuneo, one of the colonists) "they rushed in all directions like lunatics, women dropping and abandoning infants in the rush, running for miles without stopping, fleeing across mountains and rivers."

6   Of the five hundred slaves, three hundred arrived alive in Spain, where they were put up for sale in Seville . . . "As naked as the day they were born," the report . . . says, *"but with no more embarrassment[8] than animals."*

*   *   *

Threads

Sunday, 28 October, 1492. **At sunrise I approached the coast of Cuba. I am now certain that Cuba is the Indian name for Japan.**

From Columbus's journal

> "Hispaniola is a miracle. Mountains and hills, plains and pastures, are both fertile and beautiful . . . the harbors are unbelievably good and there are many wide rivers of which the majority contain gold. . . . There are many spices, and great mines of gold and other metals."
>
> —*From Columbus's report to the king and queen of Spain at the end of his first voyage. Why did he say this about the spices and the gold mines?*

7   The slave trade immediately turned out to be "unprofitable, for the slaves mostly died." Columbus decided to concentrate on gold, although he writes, "Let us . . . go on sending all the slaves that can be sold."

Koning adds that the only reason the slave trade was stopped by the king and queen of Spain was because there was no money to be made in it, since the slaves soon died of such treatment. But by then it was too late to save the Arawak Indians.

8   Columbus always believed that the lands he had "found" were in Asia, and that they were rich in gold, even though he never saw much of (it) and was never able to locate the source[9] of it. The natives wore a few small ornaments of gold in their noses, and they occasionally used it to make parts of masks. But Columbus wanted gold so much that he believed that it was there even when it was not. He actually wrote false reports of great amounts of gold to the king and queen of Spain so that they would continue to send him back to these new lands. During his second voyage, he was governor of the Spanish colony on the island of Hispaniola (which today contains the nations of Haiti and the Dominican Republic). He was so sure that the gold existed[10] that he set an impossible task[11] for the native people to carry out, and punished[12] them with extreme[13] cruelty[14] when they were unable to give him (what he wanted.) He required[15] every Indian over the age of about fourteen years to bring him a hawk's bell full of gold dust, one every three months. In return for the gold, he gave the Indian a piece of copper stamped with the month. If an Indian was found without a copper token—or with an outdated token—his or her hands were cut off.

9   Because there really was almost no gold on the island, some of the Indians tried to escape into the mountains, but the newcomers followed them, caught them, and burned them to death or hanged them. In response, many of the Indians committed suicide rather than wait for the white settlers to kill them. By the end of two years, about half of the native population of Hispaniola had died either at their own hands or at the hands of the colonists.

10   Because the natives were not able to bring in gold, Columbus decided to make use of them in a different way. He divided up the island among his men. Any Indians who were living on a settler's land belonged to (him) and could be used—or misused[16]—any way he wished. Such uses included forced labor and forced sex. Many Indians were killed for sport, and there are even reports that their bodies were sold to the colonists as food for their dogs. By 1540 the entire native population of Hispaniola was dead.

11   For obvious reasons, then, native American Indians do not see Columbus as a hero, nor do they see any reason to celebrate "Columbus Day," October 12, as a holiday in the same way that many white Americans celebrate it. To them Columbus was an extremely cruel man whose coming marked the end of their freedom and traditional way of life—and marked the beginning of many millions of native deaths at the hands of the Europeans in North America, Central America, the Caribbean area, and South America. In fact, today many Americans from all ethnic groups, including European-Americans, have begun to question the one-sided way that Columbus has traditionally been presented in school textbooks, and are insisting that a more balanced picture be given. No one

Threads

Before returning to Spain from his second voyage, Columbus forced his crews to sign a paper stating that Cuba was part of the mainland of Asia.

questions his accomplishments[17] in sailing across the Atlantic and in opening up contact between Europe and the Americas, but many people want their children to learn the whole story in school—the ugly side as well as the good.

> The Spanish government set aside $500 million to celebrate the 500th anniversary of Columbus's landing in America—a million dollars for every year since the first voyage. In contrast, native Americans from Alaska and Peru met at the Teotihuacan pyramids in Mexico and celebrated "500 years of survival." In Mexico City, people went to a public statue of Columbus and hung around its neck a sign that read "Five centuries of massacre." Thousands of native Americans demonstrated in Bolivia and Chile, and in Argentina, a three-day hunger strike was timed to end on "Columbus Day," October 12. Visitors to Managua, Nicaragua, were confronted with a poster proclaiming Christopher Columbus as "a great thief, murderer, racist, torturer, oppressor of native people, and instigator of the great lie." Instead of celebrating "Columbus Day" on October 12, Uruguayan author Eduardo Galeano recommended celebrating October 11 as "the last day of Indian independence."

After You Read

Identify the circled reference words.

IN WHICH PARAGRAPH CAN YOU FIND:

1. a description of a "slave raid"? _____

2. a punishment for not bringing in gold? _____

3. a description of Columbus's values? _____

COMPREHENSION QUESTIONS

1. The American continents have existed for as long as Europe has. Why do you think they were called the "New World" and Europe the "Old World"?

   _____

   • Who called them that? _____

   • Who didn't? _____

2. In ¶5, who was "the Admiral"? _____

3. What uses did Columbus have for the Indians that he found?

   _____

4. Why did Columbus believe there was a great deal of gold on the island of Hispaniola even though there was no evidence of it?

   _____

5. What lie did Columbus tell to the king and queen of Spain?

   _____

6. What "impossible task" did he require the natives to do?

_____

• Why was it impossible? _____

• What was the punishment for not doing it? _____

7. How many Arawak Indians are living on the island of Hispaniola today?

_____

8. In what ways was Columbus a brave hero? _____

• In what ways wasn't he? _____

9. Why do you suppose that children's history books used to tell only one side

of the story? _____

Whose side did they tell? _____

TRUE-FALSE QUESTIONS

Circle "True" or "False" and tell the number of the paragraph where you found your answer.

¶ number

1. Columbus had the same values as most European travelers and kings and queens of his time.　　T　　F　　_____

2. Columbus changed the names of all of the islands that he "discovered" from Indian languages into Spanish.　　T　　F　　_____

3. 200 of the 500 Indians died on the voyage to Europe.　　T　　F　　_____

DISCUSSION: A CONFLICT IN VALUES

Working with a classmate or two, contrast Columbus's values with the Arawak Indians' values. What was important to Columbus? What was important to the Arawaks? Can you think of a way that their differences could have been respected so that each side could have gotten something of what they wanted? In the best of all possible worlds, what should have happened?

LEARNING STRATEGY

Remembering New Material: You can remember information better if you think of new ways to organize and present it.

TAKING NOTES FROM YOUR READING: REORGANIZING INFORMATION

What are the three main points of this reading, and what examples are given for each point? (The main points of a reading passage are often given in the first paragraph.) Make an "outline" summarizing the information, like this:

Point One: Point Two: Point Three:

Desire
for
gold
_____   _____   _____
Examples: *Examples:*   *Examples:*

COMPLETING YOUR CHART

Using information from Reading Three, complete your lists of Columbus's good side and bad side. Then compare your lists with a small group of classmates. You will use this information in a paper that you are going to write later.

FREEWRITING OR DISCUSSION: THE WHOLE STORY

Did you learn any of the information from this passage when you studied Columbus in school? If so, what? If not, can you imagine why it was not taught? Do you think that it is important for people to know it? Of all the actions mentioned in the passage, which seems the worst to you?

Vocabulary

KEYWORDS

1. hero ¶1
2. balanced ¶1
3. presentation ¶1
4. willing* ¶1
5. uncivilized ¶1
6. right ¶1
7. brutal ¶4
8. embarrassment ¶6
9. source* ¶8
10. exist* ¶8
11. task ¶8
12. punish ¶8
13. extreme, extremely* ¶8
14. cruelty, cruel ¶8
15. require* ¶8
16. misuse ¶10
17. accomplishment* ¶11

KEYWORD EXERCISE

1. A *hero* is a man who is brave and good and is admired by people. Such a woman is called a *heroine*. Children and young people usually have heroes and heroines whom they admire greatly. Nations and cultures also have them.

    Name a hero or heroine you used to have (or still do), or one of your nation or culture.

    What did this person do to become so admired?

2. *Meanings*:

    • If you *balance* two things with each other, each of the things has equal weight.

    QUESTION: When the reading passage speaks of "a more *balanced* presentation" of Columbus in ¶1, what are the two elements that would be *balanced*?

    • If you *balance* your checkbook, you count the money you have spent in order to be sure that you have not spent more than you had.

    QUESTION: Name a career that would require a person to *balance* records of money received and spent.

    • Explain the similarities between the two meanings.

3. *Meanings*:

    • A society that is *civilized* has a highly developed society, culture, and technology.

    • If you call a person *civilized,* you mean that they seem polite and reasonable to you.

    • People who describe others as *uncivilized* have a low opinion of them and generally think that they are better than these others.

    QUESTION: Why did Columbus believe that the Arawak Indians were *uncivilized*?

4. If you have a *right* to do or have something, it means no one should stop you from doing it or having it. *Rights* are things that people want to do or have, not things that they have to do but don't want to.

    Name an activity that only citizens of a country have the *right* to do.

5. *Brutal* and *cruel* are very similar in meaning. They can be used to describe people, governments, actions, crimes, punishments, etc.

    Can you think of two adjectives that mean the opposite of *brutal* and *cruel?*

    a _____ person   a _____ act

6. In the reading passage, a Spaniard suggests that the Indian slaves are like animals because they don't feel *embarrassment* at being naked. To the Spaniards, the Indians' custom of wearing no clothing is a sign that they are uncivilized.

    Is there a custom in this country that is *embarrassing* to you because people in your country would never do it?

7. *Meanings:*

• The *source* of something is where it comes from.

QUESTION: Name a country that is a major *source* of diamonds.

• A *source* is a person or book that gives information.

QUESTION: If you wanted information about English vocabulary, what two kinds of books would be good *sources?*

• Explain the similarities between the two meanings.

8. EXAMPLE: Columbus believed that the gold *existed* because he wanted it to be true.

Name a word whose meaning *exists* in English but not in your language, or that *exists* in your language but not in English.

9. A *task* is a piece of work that must be done. It could be at home, on a job, or anywhere. You might enjoy it or you might not.

EXAMPLE: Columbus set the Indians an impossible *task.*

What are some *tasks* that you enjoy doing at home? That you don't enjoy?

10. EXAMPLE: Columbus *punished* the Indians with extreme cruelty when they failed to bring him enough gold.

What is a common way in your culture that parents *punish* their children for doing something wrong?

11. EXAMPLE: Most governments *require* their citizens to pay taxes.

Finish the sentences:
Most parents require their children to . . .
Most schools . . .
Most religions . . .

12. *Matching:*

_____ 1. *willing*

_____ 2. *presentation*

_____ 3. *extremely*

_____ 4. *misused*

_____ 5. *accomplishments*

a. synonym: very
b. something important that someone has done
c. giving information formally, as in a book or speech
d. ready to agree to do something
e. used badly or wrongly

REVIEW

Now that you have studied the vocabulary, re-read or re-skim the passage.

Many books for children have been written about Christopher Columbus. Some of them tell a balanced story—both the good and the bad sides of the man. Others leave out all the ugly facts. Still others change the facts so that other men do the bad things, but Columbus is not responsible. Read the following passage from a children's book called *Christopher Columbus and His Brothers,* and then answer the questions that follow. The first conversation takes place on Columbus's second voyage. He is talking with his brothers Bartholomew and Diego, who went with him.

CHRISTOPHER COLUMBUS AND HIS BROTHERS

1   "Why not take back some of these Carib savages that I have locked up in prison?" Bartholomew asked. "They are not like the other natives. They are cannibals and can never be Christianized."

2   "You mean to sell them for slaves?" Christopher was shocked.

3   "Why not? The Portuguese sell those from Africa."

4   "What do you think, Diego?"

5   "I think it would be wrong," Diego replied promptly. "True, they probably never will become Christianized, yet that is no reason to make slaves of them."

6   "Then I'd rather not take them," Columbus decided.

7   Bartholomew was angry and sat scowling at Christopher and Diego. "You are both too soft and weak!" he stormed. "We need the money that the slaves would bring to build the colony. . . ."

8   Christopher finally agreed, though unwillingly, to his brother's proposals. "Have it your own way, Bartholomew. . . ."

[In the next scene, Columbus has returned to Spain and is talking with Queen Isabella.]

9   One day Isabella sent for Columbus. "What is this I hear, *Don* Columbus? You have been selling Indians for slaves?"

10   It was true. Both Bartholomew and Hojeda had insisted that selling the unruly Caribs was necessary and that the money could be spent to build up the colony.

11   "That was against my own judgment, Your Majesty." Columbus flushed with embarrassment as he replied, for he did not wish to blame Bartholomew. "I was persuaded to do so because these natives are cannibals and can never be Christianized and made to have souls like ourselves. The Portuguese . . ."

12   "The Portuguese," Isabella broke in sharply, "may practice slavery if they will, but that is something which I forbid. It shall never be done in Spain with my consent."

13   Columbus promised that no more natives from Hispaniola would be sold as slaves.

Before the return voyage the men seized hundreds of Indians, torturing and executing them, and then kidnaped thirty, including the chieftain. . . . The prisoners were naked, cold, packed in unbearable conditions, and almost starving. Their suffering knew no end. Food was scarce for all, and some of the Christians went so far as to suggest killing the Indians and eating them, but that was not done. Most died en route anyway, Columbus's friend Michele de Cuneo wrote, and were "cast into the sea." The few who survived in Spain were sold into slavery.
    —*Nancy Smiler Levinson, Chistopher Columbus: Voyager to the Unknown*

This is a drawing from the children's book *Columbus*, by Ingri and Edgar Parin D'Aulaire. What kind of impression does it give of the Native Americans?

After You Read

COMPARING INFORMATION FROM TWO SOURCES

Compare the content of this passage with the content of Reading Three. Answer the following questions according to the information given in each source.

1. Who first suggested enslaving the Indians?

   • Reading Three, ¶3 _____

   • Reading Four, ¶1 _____

2. When was this suggestion first made: on the first voyage, or the second voyage?

   • Reading Three, ¶3 _____

   • Reading Four, Introduction _____

3. What is the name of the ethnic group of Indians that was enslaved?

   • Reading Three, ¶5 _____

   • Reading Four, ¶1 _____

4. Why was enslavement of the Indians discontinued?

   • Reading Three, ¶7 _____

   • Reading Four, ¶12 _____

5. This is the most important question: If children read *Christopher Columbus and His Brothers,* what kind of person will they believe that Columbus was?

   • Is this picture accurate and balanced? _____

   • Why do you suppose that the author wrote the book in this way?

   _____

Writing an Essay: National Heroes

Choose one of these topics:

1. What should we teach our children about our national heroes? Should we give them the whole story (both the good and the bad sides), or would that just confuse them? What should American history books teach children about Christopher Columbus? Whose hero is he—all Americans', or just some Americans'?

2. Describe both the good and the bad results of Columbus's voyages. Do you think that it would have been better if he had not made them? Explain.

Managing Your Learning: After you try out new learning strategies, evaluate them and find ways to keep using the ones that match your needs and your learning style.

Evaluating Learning Strategies

In this chapter you have been presented with several learning strategies. Think for a moment about the strategy of making vocabulary cards. Was this helpful for you? Do you think that you will want to keep using it? If not, can you revise or simplify it to make it more useful?

Look back over the chapter at the other learning strategies that were presented. Were there any that weren't very helpful to you? What wasn't helpful about them? Which ones did you find especially helpful? Think about times and ways that you can keep using them in your future reading. If you know of other strategies that were not suggested in this chapter, tell your classmates about them.

Evaluating Your Learning

Look at the following list of items that you practiced in this chapter. How did you do on each one? Check your answers (√).

	Very little	*Quite a bit*	*A lot*
You know some new vocabulary.	——————	——————	——————
Your comprehension is stronger.	——————	——————	——————
Your writing has improved.	——————	——————	——————
You can pick out the most important words in a passage.	——————	——————	——————
You learned about the Columbus controversy.	——————	——————	——————

Verbs
anticipate*
bear
capture
deceive*
defend*
exchange*
exist*
gather
misuse
punish
require*
resemble*

Adjectives
accurate
balanced
brutal
confidential
cruel
extreme
numerous*
suicidal
uncivilized
useless
various*
willing*

Nouns
accomplishment*
ambition
cruelty
embarrassment
force
hero
insanity
presentation
right
slave
source*
task
value

Adverbs
entirely
extremely*

The First North Americans

PLANNING YOUR LEARNING

Review your overall goal statement. How much progress did you make toward it in the last chapter? Do you want to change it? Think about how you can work to meet your goal as you study this new chapter.

- How many words do you want to learn? (minimum 69, the number of keywords in the chapter)
- What grade would you like to make on the vocabulary section of the exam at the end of the chapter?
- What grade would you like to make on the reading comprehension section of the exam?
- What are you going to read outside of class?

PREVIEWING THE CHAPTER

- Think about the title of this chapter. Who were "the first North Americans"?
- Look in the Table of Contents at the titles of the eight readings in this chapter. Look through the chapter at the pictures and the maps. What are some things that you would like to learn about?
- Which reading looks the most interesting?

FREEWRITING: AMERICAN INDIANS

- What do you know about American Indians? Take a few minutes to make a list. If you're unsure about something, write it and put a question mark after it. Make your list as long as you can in the time your teacher gives you.
- After you finish writing, show your list to two or three of your classmates. Do you and your partners have any differences of information or opinion? Where did you get your information? How could you find out if it's accurate?

LEARNING STRATEGY

Managing Your Learning: As you skim, forming questions that you expect a reading to answer will improve your learning.

PREPARING TO READ: CONTENT

Look at the title, subheadings, box, and map from the following passage. What kinds of information do you expect to read in it? Make a list of at least five items.

1. _____
2. _____
3. _____
4. _____
5. _____

PREPARING TO READ: VOCABULARY

Working alone, list ten vocabulary items that you might expect to find when reading about American Indians. If you know some words in your native language but not in English, look them up in your bilingual dictionary and write the English equivalents. This "vocabulary preview" will make your reading easier when you encounter these words and concepts.

1. _____   6. _____
2. _____   7. _____
3. _____   8. _____
4. _____   9. _____
5. _____   10. _____

READING ONE

As you read the following article, look for information that tells more about what you already knew, or that differs from what you had heard.

Reading process: You have already done the first step in skimming, which is to look at the title and the subheadings. Now skim each section quickly. Then as you read it more carefully, highlight whatever new vocabulary you wish. As you finish reading each section, skim it again for review.

An Introduction to North American Indian Cultures

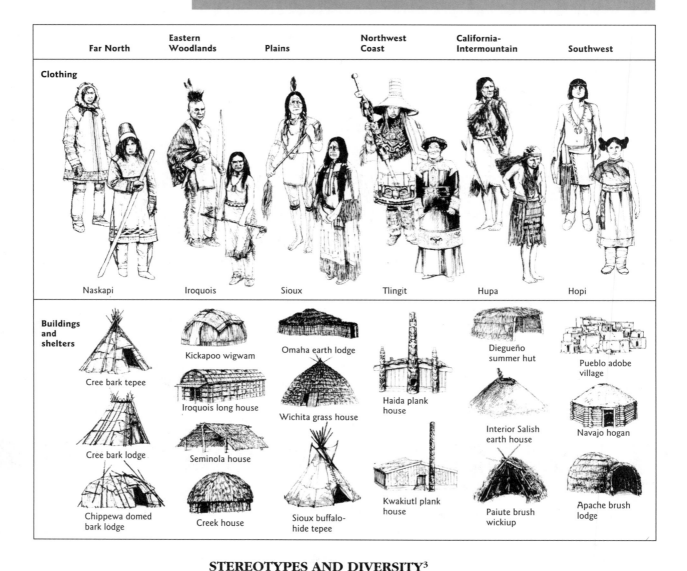

Far North	Eastern Woodlands	Plains	Northwest Coast	California-Intermountain	Southwest

Clothing

Naskapi — Iroquois — Sioux — Tlingit — Hupa — Hopi

Buildings and shelters

Cree bark tepee
Cree bark lodge
Chippewa domed bark lodge

Kickapoo wigwam
Iroquois long house
Seminola house
Creek house

Omaha earth lodge
Wichita grass house
Sioux buffalo-hide tepee

Haida plank house
Kwakiutl plank house

Diegueño summer hut
Interior Salish earth house
Paiute brush wickiup

Pueblo adobe village
Navajo hogan
Apache brush lodge

STEREOTYPES AND DIVERSITY[3]

1   American Indians are one of the most famous ethnic groups in the world, yet people have usually gotten their impressions of them from comic books, television, and cowboy films. Such sources may lead people to believe that all Indians were bloodthirsty savages, or on the other hand that they were "children of nature" who never did anything wrong. Some believe that Indians never lied, that their languages were very simple and had limited vocabularies, that they were lazy, or that they couldn't adapt to modern life. All these views are what we call *stereotypes* of Indians.

2   The problem with stereotypes is that they are either untrue or only partly true. The members of any group may be similar in some ways, but they are never all the same. Some Indians were/are cruel, some kind; some warlike,

Threads

A stereotype is a generalized belief that all members of a group are the same in some way.

some peaceful; some quiet, some talkative; some lazy, some hardworking; some today prefer traditional life, while others have left traditions behind. Believing stereotypes about American Indians keeps us from appreciating the richness and complexities[1] of their cultures.

3   In fact it's difficult to talk about "Indians" because it is a mistake to view American Indians as one large culture. That's because there are hundreds of tribal cultures in the western hemisphere, and the Native population of North America alone stands at about three million today. Before Europeans settled in the Americas, members of the Native populations thought of themselves as Iroquois or Navajo or Comanche—never as members of a larger group that included the entire population of the two continents. Remember, it was Columbus who gave the one name *Indians* to all the Natives he found; and later European settlers followed his example with all the ethnic groups from the northernmost part of Canada to the southern tip of South America. In reality there are countless variations[2] in values, religious beliefs, customs, and life styles among such diverse[3] peoples as the Apache of the Southwestern United States, the Sioux of the Great Plains, the Seminole of the Southeast, the Huron of the Eastern Woodlands, the Ute of the Great Basin, the Nez Percé of the Northwest Plateau, the Kwakiutl of the Northwest Coast, the Yurok of California, the Cree of the Subarctic. Before white settlement changed the face of the land, there were specialized hunting-gathering cultures, farming cultures, fishing cultures. Different economies influenced the development of different social systems, housing styles, religious beliefs.

4   Why, then, should we study such diverse cultures in one chapter called "The First North Americans"? The answer is that once Columbus had opened the door to the millions of Europeans who would come to the Americas over the next 500 years, suddenly the Native peoples all had something in common for the first time: (they) were more like each other than they were like the Europeans (or the Africans or the Asians who followed). The various tribes or bands also experienced similar treatment at the hands of these newcomers. This encounter between the European newcomers and the first Americans led—on both sides—to great misunderstanding and mistrust and to the shedding of rivers of blood.

5   So it is possible to generalize[4] about Indians, as long as we keep in mind that generalizations[4] don't cover all members of all groups. Please remember this as you continue to read in this chapter. Note also that the terms *Indian, Native American* (used in the United States), and *Native peoples* (used in Canada) will be used interchangeably. Other interchangeable terms will be *tribe* (United States), *band* (Canada), *nation,* and *ethnic group* to refer to various groups of Native Americans.

6   The map on page 44 groups North American Native cultures into ten regions. Within each region, despite many variations, we find certain similarities due to common climate,[5] vegetation, and game; due to common ancestors and intermarriage in some cases; and due to trade among the tribes in that particular area. For example, the peoples who inhabited the western part of the Great Plains centered their culture on the most important game[6] animal there: the American bison or buffalo. Because the buffalo moved from place to place, so did they; consequently, they needed housing that could be carried with them. All of the cultures that inhabited this region used the tipi, a house made from buffalo hides and long poles; it could easily be taken down, carried by horses, and set up again in another place. The different Plains tribes shared a number of other features[7] also. But we must keep in mind that there were also many differences among these groups, and the existence of some similarities does not mean that they were similar in everything.

44

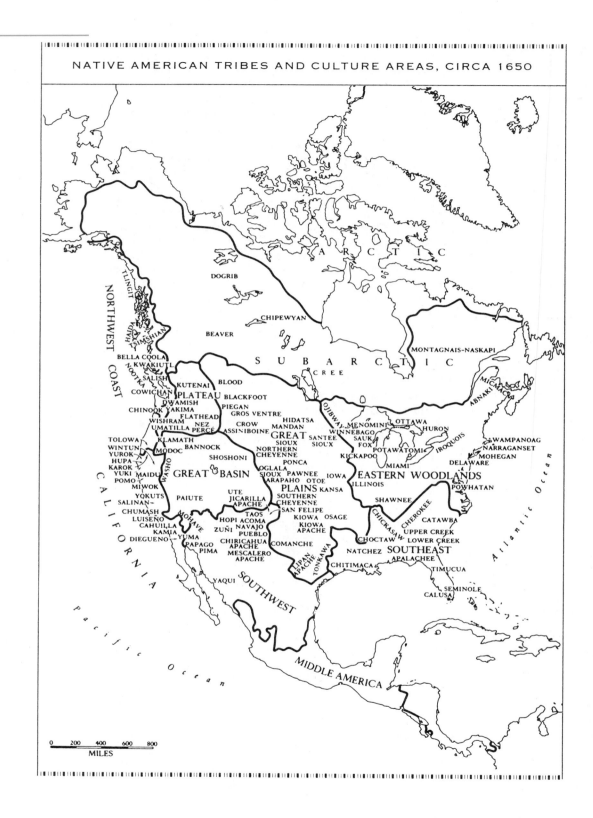

NATIVE AMERICAN TRIBES AND CULTURE AREAS, CIRCA 1650

NATIVE AMERICAN TRADITIONAL CULTURES

7   American Indian tribes depended on nature, whether they were farming or hunting or fishing communities. As a result they believed in the importance of living in harmony with nature and with all its parts. They saw all nature as interconnected: its life forms, both animals and plants; geological features such as mountains, rocks, and rivers; and weather—the four winds, rain, snow. Nature for them was filled with spiritual forces[8] that affected their lives. People were not the most important beings, but only one part of the larger network, neither more nor less important than the other parts. Destroying[9] the balance of nature would bring misfortune, illness, and death to the tribe.

> The earth is your mother,
> she holds you.
> The sky is your father,
> he protects you.
> Sleep,
> sleep.
> Rainbow is your sister,
> she loves you.
> The winds are your brothers,
> they sing to you.
> Sleep,
> sleep.
> We are together always
> We are together always
> There never was a time
> when this
> was not so.
>   *—Traditional lullaby, Laguna Pueblo*

8   Religious ceremonies[10] were performed to mark important stages of life (births, marriages, deaths) and to ask the spirits[8] for help or to thank them. It was common for individual people to believe that they each had one particular spirit that helped them personally; often this spirit was associated with a particular type of animal such as the bear or the wolf.

9   In family life, men and women generally performed separate tasks. In most nations the men did the hunting or farming; the women prepared food, tanned the animal hides, and made clothing. Marriage came early; in some tribes it might be arranged by the families, in others the couple might choose for themselves. Usually an extended family (several generations, including aunts and uncles) lived together or near each other, and everyone helped with work and with children. There was much variation in childrearing. In some tribes children were never punished; in others they were controlled very strictly. Children played games and imitated the adult roles that they would take for themselves when they grew up. Special ceremonies marked a young person's passage from childhood into adulthood.

10   The food they ate depended on the climate, the customs, and what could be found. Many tribes gathered wild nuts, berries, roots, seeds, and herbs for teas and for medicines. Hunters brought home deer, antelope, buffalo, rabbits, birds, seals, turtles, or other game that might exist in their region. Farming communities lived on whatever their mixture of soil and climate allowed— mainly beans, corn, and squash in the dry Southwest. Fishing tribes caught and smoked fish and ate shellfish.

11   Before the Europeans arrived, most Native Americans wore clothing made from animal hides. Some wove cotton and woolen cloth, and along the Northwest Coast, they wove cloth made from strips of tree bark. The amount of clothing worn depended largely on the climate. For shoes some wore sandals, some soft leather moccasins.

12   Housing varied greatly, depending on climate, available materials, and customs. Nomads[11]—people who move from place to place—used housing that could be broken down and carried with them. Peoples who stayed in one place might build from stone, wood, earth, or brick, whichever was common in their area. In some tribes many families lived together in large houses; in others, each family had its own dwelling place.

> May it be beautiful, my house;
> From my head may it be beautiful;
> To my feet, may it be beautiful;
> All above me, may it be beautiful;
> All around me, may it be beautiful.
> —*Traditional Navajo prayer*

NOMADS OF THE GREAT PLAINS REGION

13   Let's look more closely at the inhabitants of one particular area: the nomadic tribes of the western and central Great Plains area, which included the Blackfeet, Crow, Sioux, Kiowa, and some smaller nations. These peoples lived a simple and rather poor life until around 1740, when two European introductions came their way: the horse and the gun. (These) made their traditional way of life much easier and permitted their cultures to grow strong for the next 150 years, until the disappearance of the buffalo around 1890.

14   For these cultures were totally dependent on the buffalo. They did not farm and did little fishing or gathering. The buffalo provided them with meat for food, hides for clothing and for their tipis, and bones and horns to make into tools. They burned dried buffalo dung for fuel. The people followed the great herds[12] on foot and hunted them in very simple ways until the horse and the gun suddenly made life richer and easier. More meat could be killed with a gun from the back of a horse than on foot with a spear or bow and arrow, and more of it could be carried home. Tipis could be larger with horses to carry the hides and poles that they were made from. Hunters, warriors, and villages could move farther than they had been able to move before.

15   These nations were warlike, and their warfare was also greatly changed by the horse and the gun. They raided villages of other tribes to steal horses, which were a measure of wealth. In addition to the number of horses he had, a man's importance in his tribe was measured by his bravery in war and by the number of enemies he had killed, though also by his wisdom or his abilities at healing and communicating with the spirits.

16   The spiritual life was very important to the Plains tribes. People took dreams and visions[13] very seriously and believed that (these) could predict the future and should guide their actions. Young men left the village and went

alone into the wilderness for a time, during which they fasted and prayed in hopes that a personal spirit would visit them in a dream. This spirit would advise and teach them and would become their protector for the rest of their lives. It often took the form of an animal, and the young man might then think of the bear, or the mountain lion, or the eagle as his own special guide. The belief in visions was so strong that young men might go without food for days and might actually cut their bodies in hopes that doing so would bring them into communication with the spirit world. In the Sun Dance, young Blackfeet men sometimes pushed sharpened sticks through the skin of their chests. These sticks were tied to a tall pole with leather thongs. Then the young men sang, prayed, and danced until their movements tore the sticks out of their bodies. This ceremony was believed to lead to visions and to spiritual guidance.

17   The tribes traveled in small bands, coming together in larger groups once a year to exchange news, have games and competitions, and hold important ceremonies. Important decisions were made by councils of the men during these yearly gatherings. Because survival[14] in hunting, warfare, and village life depended on people's cooperating[15] with each other, decisions were generally made by discussion and group agreement. Public shame and disapproval were very strong methods of controlling people's behavior. The most serious punishment that a person could receive was exile from the tribe, because a lone Indian would readily be killed by enemy tribes. When possible, exiled men banded together in small groups of outlaws and they no longer followed the rules or advice of the other members of the tribe.

18   But this way of life did not last forever. With the destruction[9] of the buffalo herds by white hunters around 1890, the tribes lost their source of food and the central feature of their culture. Nothing was the same after that.

After You Read

Identify the circled reference words.

COMPREHENSION QUESTIONS

1. In the first section of the reading, which paragraphs talk about stereotypes?

_____

Which paragraphs talk about diversity? _____

2. Give an example of a stereotype of American Indians. _____

How could you find out if it were true or not? _____

_____

3. Who gave the name "Indians" to Native Americans? _____

_____

4. Look at the map on page 44. Name one tribe or nation from any four of the regions:

Subarctic: _____

Northwest Coast: _____

Plateau: _____

California: _____

Great Basin: _____

Southwest: _____

Great Plains: _____

Eastern Woodlands: _____

Southeast: _____

• Which of the tribes on the map had you heard of before? Highlight or underline them.

• Are you living in one of these regions now? If so, which one?

_____

• Study the names of the tribes in your region. Remember them and try to learn something about them.

5. In the second section of the reading, identify the topic of each paragraph.

¶7 _____

¶8 _____

¶9 _____

¶10 _____

¶11 _____

¶12 _____

6. What did the white people bring to the Plains Indians that greatly changed their way of life?

a. _____   b. _____

7. What was the most important feature of Plains Indian life? _____

_____

8. Why did the Plains cultures grow weaker around the end of the nineteenth

century? _____

_____

TRUE-FALSE QUESTIONS

¶ number

1. People were more important than nature to   T   F   _____
   Native Peoples.
2. Indians never punished their children.   T   F   _____
3. Ceremonies were very important in Native   T   F   _____
   cultures.
4. Food was variable, depending on the climate   T   F   _____
   and customs.
5. Most Indians were vegetarians.   T   F   _____
6. Cloth was unknown to the Native Americans   T   F   _____
   until the arrival of Europeans.
7. Each Indian family lived in a separate tent   T   F   _____
   made from animal skins.

LEARNING STRATEGY

Remembering New Material: Thinking about what you have learned from a reading makes you remember it better and longer.

FREEWRITING: REVIEWING WHAT YOU HAVE READ

What did you learn from this reading passage that you didn't already know? List one or two things and comment on them. Did you find anything that contradicted information you had heard? Did anything surprise you? What interested you most?

LEARNING STRATEGY

Overcoming Limitations: Knowing good readers' habits and practicing them helps you become a stronger reader.

Developing Good Habits During Reading

What goes through a good reader's mind as she or he reads? In addition to thinking about the content, a good reader thinks about the reading process in the following ways:

1. Good readers make predictions about what's coming next.
2. Good readers form pictures in their heads as they read.
3. Good readers make connections between the content and their own experience, or with things that they already knew.
4. Good readers recognize problems that they are having and they think about them as they read.
5. Good readers know some strategies for solving their reading problems.

Your own reading will become stronger if you use these thought processes as you read. Your teacher will demonstrate each one, using material from the Columbus chapter as examples. Listen carefully to what she or he says: she's or he's thinking aloud, showing you what your own thoughts can be as you read. Imitate these ways of thinking as you look back on the passage that you just read in this chapter. Then in future readings, practice them until they have become habitual to you too.

Vocabulary

VOCABULARY IN CONTEXT

1. Look at ¶s 11 and 14. What do you suppose *hides* and *poles* are? What clues make you think so?
2. Look at ¶8. What do you suppose it means by *stages* of life? What makes you think so?
3. Look at ¶9. What do you think *extended family* might mean? What makes you think so?

VOCABULARY STUDY: CHOOSING THE MOST IMPORTANT NEW WORDS

As you learned in the Columbus chapter, good readers don't look up every new word in the dictionary. They select only those which (1) are most important and which (2) they can't figure out from the context.

Look at the new words that you highlighted as you read. Make careful decisions about which ones you want to look up. Choose no more than fifteen.

KEYWORDS

1. complexities ¶2
2. variation ¶3
3. diverse,* diversity ¶3, title
4. generalize, generalization ¶5
5. climate ¶6
6. game ¶6
7. feature* ¶6
8. spiritual force, spirit ¶s7, 8
9. destroy,* destruction ¶s7, 18
10. ceremony ¶8
11. nomad ¶12
12. herd ¶14
13. vision ¶16
14. survival ¶17
15. cooperate* ¶17

KEYWORD EXERCISE

1. *Complexities* are the interconnected parts that make something *complex,* which is an antonym for *simple.* We can use the word to talk about physical objects, ideas, or relationships between people. For example, human relationships—even good ones—are very *complex.*
Name a *complex* machine.

   EXAMPLE: Believing stereotypes about American Indians keeps us from appreciating the richness and *complexities* of their cultures.

2. If you wanted to eat soup for dinner, you could choose from many *variations* of it. What are some of them?

   EXAMPLE: There are countless *variations* in values and customs among American Indian tribes.

   NOTE: In the Columbus chapter you learned the adjective *various.* Note that *variations* is a noun form related in meaning.

3. The population of North America is very *diverse.* Can you name four of the largest ethnic groups that live there?

   a. _____   c. _____

   b. _____   d. _____

   EXAMPLE: *Diverse* ethnic groups populated North America before the arrival of the Europeans.

4. The following statement is a *generalization:*
                   Chinese people never let their feelings show.
   • What's dangerous about *generalizations* in general?
   • About this one in particular?

   EXAMPLE: *Generalizations* don't cover all members of all groups.

5. Which of the following are elements of the *climate* of a country?
   population   total square kilometers   wind
   temperature   yearly rainfall

   EXAMPLE: Some flowers grow well in cold, wet *climates,* while others prefer hot, dry ones.

6. Which of the following are examples of *game?*
   horses   buffalo   deer   sheep   ducks

   EXAMPLE: Native Americans hunted *game* for food, skins, and feathers.

7. Are there some *features* of homes in your culture that are different from most homes that you have seen in North America?

    EXAMPLE: Certain tribes shared *features* with other tribes.

8. Does your culture believe in *spirits?* If so, what do you call them, and what can they do?

    EXAMPLE: They each had one particular *spirit* that helped them personally.

9. Which of the following can cause the most *destruction?*
    floods   earthquakes   hurricanes (= typhoons)
    tsunamis   wars

    EXAMPLE: White hunters *destroyed* the buffalo herds that the tribes depended upon.

10. What *ceremony* have you attended most recently, either in your own country or in another?

    EXAMPLE: Religious *ceremonies* were an important part of the life of each tribe.

11. You have read that the *nomadic* tribes of the Great Plains lived in tipis. What are some other kinds of housing that other *nomads* live in, and why?

    EXAMPLE: *Nomads* are people who move from place to place.

12. The word *herd* generally applies to a group of animals that have feet (called "hooves") like buffaloes' feet. Which of the following groups of animals would not be called a *herd?*
    dogs   horses   sheep   snakes   cattle   goats

    EXAMPLE: The people followed the great buffalo *herds* on foot.

13. *Meanings:*
    • A *vision* is like a dream that you have, only you're awake, not asleep.

        EXAMPLE: Religious leaders may have *visions* in which they can see the future.

    • Your *vision* is the quality of your eyesight.

        EXAMPLE: She has better *vision* in her right eye than in her left.

    • What's the similarity between the two meanings?

14. If you got lost in the forest, what are some things that you could do to help yourself *survive?*

    EXAMPLE: People had to cooperate in order to *survive.*

15. Which of the following activities requires the most *cooperation?*
    building a house   earning a university degree   raising a child

REVIEW

Now that you have studied the vocabulary, re-read or re-skim the passage.

NOTE: This reading is also on the tape.

Storytelling was one of the most common ways of passing along the history, values, and traditions of many Native American ethnic groups. Folk stories were often told around the evening fire. Some people knew hundreds of stories, and they were considered important historians and guardians of the tribal way of life. They usually chose one or two younger people as students and taught them the stories so that they could continue to be passed down from generation to generation.

In the following story, look for the answers to these two questions:

- What did the White Buffalo Calf Woman bring?
- What did she teach?

Reading process: Skim the story before you read it carefully. After you read it, skim it again and mark the answers to the two questions above.

THE WHITE BUFFALO CALF WOMAN AND THE SACRED PIPE

1   It was a time when there was little food left in the camp and the people were hungry. Two young men were sent out to scout for game. They went on foot, for this was a time long before the horses . . . were given to the people. The two young men hunted a long time but had no luck. Finally they climbed to the top of a hill and looked to the west.

2   "What is that?" said one of the young men.

3   "I cannot tell, but it is coming toward us," said the other.

4   And so it was. At first they thought that it was an animal, but as the shape[1] drew closer they saw it was a woman. She was dressed in white buffalo skin and carried something in her hands. She walked so lightly that it seemed as if she was not walking at all, but floating with her feet barely[2] touching the Earth.

5   Then the first young man realized that she must be a Holy Person and his mind filled with good thoughts. But the second young man did not see her that way. He saw her only as a beautiful young woman and his mind filled with bad thoughts. She was now very close and he reached out to grab her. As soon as he did so, though, there was a sound of lightning and the young man was covered by a cloud. When it cleared away there was nothing left of the second young man but a skeleton.

6   Then the White Buffalo Calf Woman spoke. "Go to your people," she said, holding up the bundle in her hands so that the first young man could see it. "Tell your people that it is a good thing I am bringing. I am bringing a holy thing to your nation, a message from the Buffalo People. Put up a medicine lodge for me and make it ready. I will come there after four days have passed."

7   The first young man did as he was told. He went back to his people and gave them the message. Then the crier went through the camp and told all the people that something sacred was coming and that all things should be made ready. They built the medicine lodge and made an earth altar which faced the west.

8   Four days passed and then the people saw something coming toward them. When it came closer, they saw it was the White Buffalo Calf Woman. In her hands she carried the bundle and a bunch of sacred sage. The people welcomed her into the medicine lodge and gave her the seat of honor. Then she unwrapped the bundle to show them what was inside. It was the Sacred Pipe. As she held it out to them she told them what it meant.

9   "The bowl of the pipe," she said, "is made of the red stone. It represents the flesh and blood of the Buffalo People and all other Peoples. The wooden stem of the Pipe represents all the trees and plants, all the things green and growing on this Earth. The smoke that passes through the Pipe represents the sacred wind, the breath that carries prayers up to Wakan Tanka, the Creator."

10   When she finished showing them the Pipe, she told the people how to hold it and how to offer[3] it to Earth and Sky and the Four Sacred Directions. She told them many things to remember.

11   "The Sacred Pipe," said the White Buffalo Calf Woman, "will show you the Good Red Road. Follow it and it will take you in the right direction. Now," she said, "I am going to leave, but you will see me again."

12   Then she began to walk toward the setting sun. The people watched her as she went, and they saw her stop and roll once on the Earth. When she stood up she was a black buffalo. Then she went farther and rolled again on the Earth. This time when she stood up she was a brown buffalo. She went farther and rolled a third time and stood up. Now the people saw that she was a red buffalo. Again she walked farther and for a fourth and final time she rolled upon the Earth. This time she became a white buffalo calf and continued to walk until she disappeared[4] over the horizon.

13   As soon as the White Buffalo Calf Woman was gone, herds of buffalo were seen all around the camp. The people were able to hunt them and they gave thanks with the Sacred Pipe for the blessings they had been given. As long as they followed the Good Red Road of the Sacred Pipe and remembered, as the White Buffalo Calf Woman taught them, that all things were as connected[5] as parts of the Pipe, they lived happily and well.

—Lakota (Sioux), Great Plains

Before talking of holy things, we prepare ourselves by offerings. If only two are to talk together, one will fill his pipe and hand it to the other, who will light it and offer it to the sky and earth. Then they will smoke together, and after smoking they will be ready to talk of holy things.
    —*Chased-by-Bears, Santee-Yanktonai Sioux, northern Great Plains*

After You Read

COMPREHENSION QUESTIONS

1. What did the White Buffalo Calf woman bring? _____

   _____

   What did she teach? _____

   _____

   (These are the two most important elements of the story.)

2. In ¶6, what does the woman mean when she says "your nation"? _____

   _____

3. In ¶9, the White Buffalo Calf Woman refers to "the Buffalo People and all

   other Peoples." What is her definition of *peoples?* _____

   _____

Charting Cultural Values

What information does the story give you about Sioux values? Take a piece of
paper and divide it in half vertically. Write two titles: Native American Values on
one side, and Euro-American (White) Values on the other. List the Sioux values that
you just noted, and write "(Sioux)" after them. You'll add more to this list later, and
you'll use the information in a paper that you're going to write.

Vocabulary

VOCABULARY IN CONTEXT

Look at ¶9 and re-read the three sentences that contain the word *represents*.
What do you think it means? What clues make you think so?

VOCABULARY STUDY

Look at the new vocabulary that you marked. Some of it is *not* necessary to
an understanding of the story. Don't bother with those words. Working with one
or two partners, identify five new words that are not worth looking up.

Now work with your partners to identify words that you think you *do* need
to understand in order to comprehend the story. Make cards for them.

KEYWORDS

1. shape ¶4
2. barely* ¶4
3. offer* ¶10
4. disappear ¶12
5. connected ¶13

KEYWORD EXERCISE

1. Which of the following are examples of *shapes?*
   large   small   round   flat   square

   EXAMPLE: As the *shape* drew closer they saw that it was a woman.

2. *EXAMPLE:*   I can *barely* hear you because of the noise from the radio.

   Finish the sentences:
   That child is so small that it can barely . . .
   We have barely enough gasoline to . . .
   My grandmother can barely . . .

3. *EXAMPLE:*   The Lakota *offered* the sacred pipe to the Earth and the Sky before they smoked it.

   Finish the sentences:
   When friends come to visit you, you should offer them . . .
   On the airplane the stewardess offered me . . .
   An old man got on the bus, so I offered him . . .

4. Some people believe that thousands of years ago, a whole continent *disappeared* beneath the Atlantic Ocean. What was the name of it?

   EXAMPLE: The woman continued to walk until she *disappeared* over the horizon.

5. How are the problems of overpopulation and pollution *connected?*

   EXAMPLE: All things in life are as *connected* as the parts of the sacred pipe.

REVIEW

Now that you have studied the vocabulary, re-read or re-skim the passage.

READING THREE

There are many interesting histories of the first encounters between the European-Americans and various Indian nations. You read one from the European point of view when you read a page from Columbus's journal in the last chapter. The following encounter, from the point of view of Native Americans, took place in the early nineteenth century on the coast of the Gulf of Mexico.

THE WHITE PEOPLE WHO CAME IN A BOAT

1   My grandmother used to tell this story; she told it to my mother. It is about the time when they lived near the gulf. She says that they lived at a place called "Beside the Smooth Water." They used to camp there on the sand. Sometimes a big wave would come up and then they would pick up many seashells. Sometimes they used to find water turtles. They used to find fish too and gather them and eat them. . . .

2   One day they looked over the big water. Then someone saw a little black dot over on the water. He came back and told that he had seen that strange thing. Others came out. They sat there and looked. It was getting larger. They waited. Pretty soon it came up. It was a boat. The boat came to the shore. The Indians went back to the big camp. All the Indians came over and watched. People were coming out. They looked at those people coming out. They saw that the people had blue eyes and were white. They thought these people might live in the water all the time.

3   They held a council[1] that night. They were undecided whether they should let them live or kill them.

4   One leader said, "Well, they have a shape just like ours. The difference is that they have light skin and hair."

5   Another said, "Let's not kill them. They may be a help to us some day. Let's let them go and see what they'll do."

6   So the next day they watched them. . . .

7   Some still wanted to kill them. Others said no. So they decided to let them alone.[2]

8   The Lipan went away. After a year they said, "Let's go back and see them."

9   They did so. Only a few were left.[3] Many had starved[4] to death. Some said, "Let's kill them now; they are only a few." But others said, "No, let us be like brothers to them."

10   It was spring. The Lipan gave them some pumpkin seed and seed corn and told them how to use it. The people took it and after that they got along all right.[5] They raised a little corn and some pumpkins. They started a new life. Later on the Lipan left for a while. When they returned, the white people were getting along very well. The Lipan gave them venison. They were getting along very well. After that, they began to get thick. The Lipan were coming toward the west then. The Lipan never did go back to the coast.

—Percy Bigmouth, Lipan Apache, Southwest

After You Read

Identify the reference words: Beginning with ¶3, identify each mention of *they* and *them*. If it means the Lipan, write "L"; if it refers to the white people, write "W."

COMPREHENSION QUESTIONS

1. What event does this passage tell about? _____

2. In your own words, list the main events that happened in the passage.

1 _____

2 _____

3 _____

4 _____

5 _____

6 _____

7 _____

3. In the last paragraph, what does it mean when it says "They began to get thick"? _____

_____

CONTINUING YOUR CHART OF CULTURAL VALUES

Can you find anything in this reading to add to your list of Native American values? (Look in ¶s 3–7.)

Vocabulary

KEYWORDS

1. hold a council ¶3
2. let them alone ¶7
3. were left* ¶9

4. starve ¶9
5. get along all right ¶10

KEYWORD EXERCISE

1. Which of the following are elements of a *council?*
   native   advice   meeting   group   decisions   hero

   EXAMPLE: The members of the *council* listened thoughtfully to our questions and then told us what we should do.

2. Name an animal that you would *let alone.*
   Why? Is it for a different reason than the reason the Lipan decided to *let* the white people *alone?*
   Why did they decide to do that?

3. A farmer had seven sheep. All but three of them died. How many *were left?*

4. Which of the following are elements of the verb *starve?*
   hunger   capture   die   discover   claim

   EXAMPLE: Many of the white people *starved* during the winter.

5. What did the Lipan do that helped the white people to *get along all right?*

REVIEW

Now that you have studied the vocabulary, re-read or re-skim the passage.

Reading process: As usual, begin by reading the title, reading the first paragraph, skimming the rest, and then reading the last paragraph. Then read everything carefully. When you finish, follow the instructions given at the end of the reading.

Contact And Beyond

PART ONE: _____

Notes

1   The history of Indian-white relations[1] is a bloody one. The problems that arose were a result of misunderstanding, mistrust, and—most important—great differences in values between the European and the Native cultures. Conflict[2] began as soon as Columbus landed in the New World. In most cases the Indians were friendly and helpful to the strangers at first, giving them food and showing them how to make a living off lands that were new to them. But relations turned ugly as the whites began cutting down the forest, plowing up the land to make farms, putting up fences. Perhaps most of all, the whites claimed personal possession of land and believed that they had the right to keep other people off of it. This was a complete contradiction[3] of the Native attitude[4] toward land, which was that it belonged to all the forms of life that lived on it. No one had the right to claim it for their own.

> Our land is more valuable than your money. It will last forever. . . . It was put here for us by the Great Spirit and we cannot sell it because it does not belong to us.
> —*A Blackfeet chief, northern Great Plains*

2   As more and more settlers arrived needing more and more land, relations between the two groups worsened. The United States and Canadian governments' solution for this conflict was to make treaties with the Natives, just as they would with any other foreign government. These treaties were agreements, signed by both sides, that met the white people's interests and that made certain promises to the Indians. In most of (them,) the whites claimed the right to use particular areas of land and the Indians agreed to give (them) up and to move away, sometimes to other land that the whites agreed to give them in exchange. This other land was not their ancestral[5] homeland and was generally land that neither they nor the whites wanted to live on. In addition, the Indians were usually required to agree to keep peace with the whites and to recognize[6] the power of the white government. In return, the whites usually agreed to pay money and goods to the Indians and to protect them.

Treaties
Whites agreed to

_____

Indians agreed to

_____

3   The Indians' problem with the treaties was that their attitude toward land ownership and use was totally different from the whites'. (They) often did not realize that in giving the white people the rights to the land, they were giving up[7] their own rights to use it. In the eyes of the whites, they were buying the land from the Indians, but the very idea of buying and selling land was foreign to Indian cultures. But if they didn't sign, it soon became clear that the whites would take the land anyway and might make war on them.

Problems

1.

2.

3.

4   A third problem was that the whites broke most of the treaties. As the years passed and the white population grew, more and more settlers moved onto Indian lands, pushing the Indians further and further west. A tribe might sign a treaty and move onto less desirable land, only to be forced to sign another treaty and move again several years later. The Cherokee people of the eastern United States were moved to 36 different locations by treaties signed between 1721 and 1835. This or that tribe often went to war with the settlers, but the population of any one tribe was small and their weapons were no match for the guns of the white men.

PART TWO: _____

History

1.

2.

5   By 1830 the whites had settled much of the land east of the Mississippi River, which runs north and south and divides the eastern third of the United States from the western two-thirds. In that year the government decided that they would simply remove most of the Indians from the eastern part of the country and force them to live west of the river, where few whites wanted to live at that time. By 1840 more than 70,000 Indians had been torn from their homelands and forcibly moved. Many of them died on the journey. The Indian name for this removal is the Trail of Tears.

> The whites were always trying to make the Indians give up their life and live like white men—go to farming, work hard and do as they did—and the Indians did not know how to do that, and did not want to anyway. . . . If the Indians had tried to make the whites live like them, the whites would have resisted, and it was the same way with many Indians.
>
> —*Wamditanka (Big Eagle), Santee Sioux, northern Great Plains*

The Trail of Tears

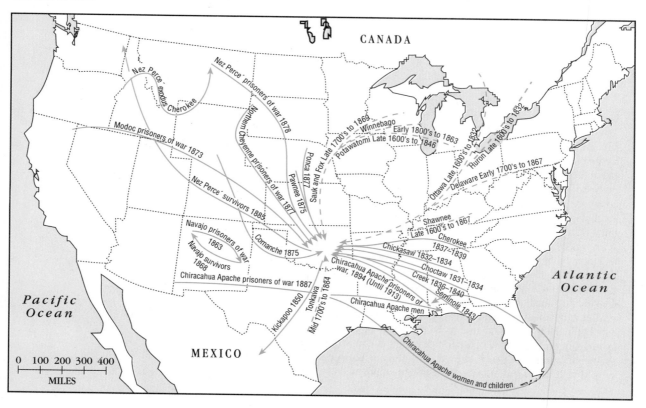

6   But that wasn't the end of the story. In 1848 gold was discovered in California, attracting[8] a movement of whites all the way across the continent. Once in California, they killed the game and pushed the Indians off their homelands there. A few years later, after the United States Civil War ended in 1864, thousands of white families began to make their way across the Mississippi River north and west along the Oregon Trail to "new" lands. Meanwhile in Canada, whites were attracted by the trade in furs and by the availability of lands for farming and ranching in the western territories. Of course these lands were already occupied by Indian tribes. Of course the Indians resisted.[9] And as before, they were eventually defeated and new treaties were signed—most of which were broken, as before.

7   Some of the Indian nations were traditionally warlike; others were peaceful by nature. Either way, they lost. But in the meantime thousands of people were killed on both sides, and many of them were not soldiers or warriors, but innocent men, women, and children who were in the wrong place at the wrong time, or whose only offense was that they were white, or were Indian. Each case of bloodshed became a reason for revenge[10] in some people's minds, continuing the cycle on and on.

3.

4.

5.

PART THREE: _____

8   The reason that it finally stopped was not because the two groups were finally wise enough to sit down, talk, and develop respect for each other—it was because the whites had better weapons, more power, and greater numbers. Furthermore, (they) acted as one large group against small Native bands that were divided, not united. The Indians' food source had lessened as the whites cleared the land, destroying the homes of the game that (they) depended on. Within a ten-year period white hunters had killed off the millions of buffalo on the Great Plains, partly because buffalo hides had become popular among white people, but partly just because they knew that the destruction of the herds would destroy the power of the Plains Indians. The Europeans also brought with them diseases that were new to the Indians and that took many lives. When Columbus arrived in 1492, the Indian population of the present United States was somewhere between one and two-and-a-half million people, in present Canada about 350,000; by 1900 it had been reduced to less than a quarter of a million in the U.S. and to under 100,000 in Canada.

Reasons for _____

1.

2.

3.

> I have heard that you intend to settle us on a reservation near the mountains. I don't want to settle. I love to roam over the prairies. There I feel free and happy, but when we settle down we grow pale and die.
> —Satanta, Chief of the Kiowas, southern Great Plains

9   Most of the remaining Indians were herded onto *reservations* (United States) or *reserves* (Canada), land set aside for their use by the government. Most of these areas are not on the tribes' ancestral homelands, though some are. But life on the reservations was not at all like life had been before. The traditional way of life no longer seemed possible and continued to be attacked[11] in reserve schools, which attempted[12] to replace Indian customs, values, and languages with white customs, values, and English. The Indians were caught between the old way of life and a new one that they did not want. For many years the only power was held by white government agents, leaving the Natives no real power in their communities or in their own personal lives. Not surprisingly, alcohol and depression[13] became serious problems on the reservations, as well as unemployment,[14] poverty,[15] and poor health. The future looked unpromising for Native Americans as recently as the middle of the twentieth century.

Problems of reservation life

1.

2.

3.

4.

10 Today there are about 285 Indian reservations in the United States. (They) range in size and population from less than one acre (0.4 hectare) and fewer than ten Indians to about 14 million acres (six million hectares) and about 150,000 Indians. The land they occupy may be desert, forested, mountainous, plains. Just under half of the Indian population lives on them, while in Canada, about 59 percent of the Native peoples live on reserves. The most common jobs on the reservations are in farming, ranching, and manufacturing. Some reservation Indians live well, but on the whole they have high unemployment rates, low incomes, little education, and poor health.

After You Read

Identify the circled reference words.

COMPREHENSION: NAMING THE PARTS OF THE READING

For each part of the reading, write a heading that tells what it is about.

LEARNING STRATEGY

Forming Concepts: Writing brief notes of the most important ideas in a reading helps you review and remember the material.

TAKING NOTES AS YOU READ

Now review the reading passage, focusing on comprehension. In the right-hand margin you'll notice that there are some incomplete lists and diagrams; once you have completed these, they will serve you as good notes of the most important information and as a study guide. This is a model of a useful way to take marginal notes in your textbooks.

In order to take good notes, you have to understand not only the content, but also how it's organized. Turn to the Appendix on page 256. This lists some of the most common ways to organize written material, and it also tells you some common *markers* or *signals* that help you recognize the organization. What are the organizational patterns that are mentioned in this appendix?

1. Look at ¶s 3 and 4. Find the words in each paragraph that tell you they're organized around a description of problems. Circle these markers. Then complete the notes.
2. Look at ¶s 5 and 6. Find the markers that tell you the organization is chronological. Circle them. Then complete the notes.
3. Complete the rest of the marginal notes. When you finish, compare your work with a partner.

   Useful tips for notetaking:
   • Don't use complete sentences
   • Abbreviate and use symbols
   What do you think these abbreviations and symbols mean? Inds & whs signed trts
   Can you read this sentence? Gold disc in CA; attracted whs to Ind lands

TRUE-FALSE QUESTIONS

¶ number

1. Native Americans believed that land could not be bought or sold because it did not belong to people.   T   F   _____

2. The white people honored most of the treaties.   T   F   _____

3. The United States government asked the Native peoples if they would like to move west across the Mississippi River.   T   F   _____

4. Whites and Indians wanted the same land, though often for different purposes.   T   F   _____

5. Native Americans have to live on reservations today.   T   F   _____

DISCUSSION AND WRITING: REWRITING HISTORY

Working in groups, discuss why there was so much conflict and bloodshed between the European-Americans and the Native Americans. Make suggestions as to how this conflict could have been avoided.

Then choose one of the following writing assignments:

1. If you could rewrite history, tell the story of how the Native Americans and the European newcomers learned to live peacefully.
2. Where did these problems begin? What could have been done to prevent them?

Vocabulary

KEYWORDS

1. relations ¶1
2. conflict ¶1
3. contradiction ¶1
4. attitude* ¶1
5. ancestral ¶2
6. recognize ¶2
7. give up* ¶3
8. attract* ¶6
9. resist* ¶6
10. revenge ¶7
11. attack ¶9
12. attempt* ¶9
13. depression ¶9
14. unemployment ¶9
15. poverty ¶9

KEYWORD EXERCISE

1. *Meanings:*
   • *Relations* between people are ways in which they behave toward each other.

     EXAMPLE: *Relations* between Indians and whites soon turned ugly.

   • Your *relations* are your family, both immediate (parents, children) and extended (uncles, aunts).

     EXAMPLE: Most of her *relations* live in Texas.

   • Explain the similarities between the two meanings.

2. Think of a *conflict* that is happening somewhere in the world today. Who are the groups of people who are having the conflict? What is it about? How could it be solved?

3. What was the *contradiction* between the white and the Native attitudes toward ownership of land?

   EXAMPLE: The white attitude was a complete *contradiction* of the Native attitude toward land.

4. What was the difference between the white and the Native American *attitudes* toward land? Toward nature?

5. *Ancestral* is the adjective form of the noun *ancestors*. Which of the following are not your *ancestors*?

   cousins   parents   aunts   grandparents   great-grandparents

   EXAMPLE: Indians generally preferred to live on their *ancestral* homelands.

6. *Meanings:*
   • When you *recognize* someone, you know who they are because you have seen them before.

     EXAMPLE: I didn't *recognize* you in those dark glasses.

   • When you *recognize* the power of a government, you accept its power over you and you agree to let it have that power.

     EXAMPLE: The treaties said that the Indians had to *recognize* the white government.

   • Explain the similarities between the two meanings.

7. *EXAMPLES:* The treaties required the Indians to *give up* their lands.
   I've just *given up* smoking.
   Finish the sentences:
   When he became a Muslim, he had to give up . . .
   My husband lost his job, so we had to . . .

8. *EXAMPLES:* The discovery of gold *attracted* settlers to California.
   Finish the sentences:
   Magnets attract . . .
   If you put a lamp outside, it will attract . . .
   The good-looking . . .

9. In many parts of the world, individuals or groups of people *resist* what their governments want them to do. Name some of those countries.
   How many different ways of *resistance* can you think of?

   EXAMPLE: When white people moved onto their lands, the Indians generally *resisted.*

10. An English proverb says, "Living well is the best *revenge.*" What do you think that means?

    EXAMPLE: Each case of bloodshed became a reason for *revenge* in some people's minds.

11. *EXAMPLE:* In the discussion that followed, the manager *attacked* my suggestion.
    Finish the sentences:
    The soldiers attacked . . .
    The mountain lion . . .

12. *EXAMPLE:* The settlers *attempted* to make a new life in the strange land.

  Finish the sentences: '

  For the first time, I attempted to . . . recently.

  When she got lost in the woods, she . . .

13. Which of the following are elements of *depression?*

  supplies   surprise   force   sadness   disappointment

  EXAMPLE: His *depression* led to alcoholism, which only made the *depression* worse.

14. Which of the following problems can be connected with *unemployment?*

  homelessness   divorce   pollution   overpopulation   crime

  EXAMPLE: *Unemployment* is a serious problem in towns where large factories have had to shut down.

15. List three common causes of *poverty.*

REVIEW

Now that you have studied the vocabulary, re-read or re-skim the passage.

READING FIVE

NEVER SELL THE BONES OF YOUR FATHER AND YOUR MOTHER

1   Soon after this my father sent for me. I saw he was dying. I took his hand in mine. He said: "My son, my body is returning to my mother earth, and my spirit is going very soon to see the Great Spirit Chief. When I am gone, think of your country. You are the chief of these people. They look to you to guide them. Always remember that your father never sold this country. You must stop your ears whenever you are asked to sign a treaty selling your home. A few years more, and white men will be all around you. They have their eyes on this land. My son, never forget my dying words. This country holds your father's body. Never sell the bones of your father and your mother." I pressed my father's hand and told him I would protect his grave with my life. My father smiled and passed away to the spirit land.

2   I buried him in that beautiful valley of winding waters. I love that land more than all the rest of the world. A man who would not love his father's grave is worse than a wild animal.

—Heinmot Tooyalaket (Chief Joseph), Nez Percé, Northwest Plateau

> **Threads**
>
> One does not sell the earth upon which the people walk.
>
> Tashunka Witko (Crazy Horse), Oglala Sioux, western Great Plains

The earth was created by the assistance of the sun, and it should be left as it was. . . . The country was made without lines of demarcation, and it is no man's business to divide it.

—*Heinmot Tooyalaket (Chief Joseph), Nez Percé, Northwest Plateau*

After You Read

COMPLETING YOUR CHART

Using information from Reading Five, complete your chart of cultural values. Then compare your chart with a small group of classmates.

READING SIX

NOTE: This reading is also on the tape.

Reading process: As you read the following passage, try to decide whether it is historical fact or is a folktale.

THE END OF THE WORLD: THE BUFFALO GO

1   Everything the Kiowas had came from the buffalo. Their tipis were made of buffalo hides, so were their clothes and moccasins. They ate buffalo meat. Their containers were made of hide, or of bladders or stomachs. The buffalo were the life of the Kiowas.

2   Most of all, the buffalo was part of the Kiowa religion. A white buffalo calf must be sacrificed in the Sun Dance. The priests used parts of the buffalo to make their prayers when they healed people or when they sang to the powers above.

3   So, when the white men wanted to build railroads, or when they wanted to farm or raise cattle, the buffalo still protected the Kiowas. They tore up the railroad tracks and the gardens. They chased[1] the cattle off the ranges. The buffalo loved their people as much as the Kiowas loved them.

4   There was war between the buffalo and the white men. The white men built forts in the Kiowa country, and the woolly-headed buffalo soldiers [the Ninth and Tenth Cavalries, made up of black troops] shot the buffalo as fast as they could, but the buffalo kept coming on, coming on, even into the post cemetery at Fort Sill. Soldiers were not enough to hold them back.

A pile of 40,000 buffalo hides at a Dodge City, Kansas, railroad depot. The meat was left uneaten on the plains.

5   Then the white men hired[2] hunters to do nothing but kill the buffalo. Up and down the plains those men ranged, shooting sometimes as many as a hundred buffalo a day. Behind them came the skinners with their wagons. They piled the hides and bones into the wagons until they were full, and then took their loads[3] to the new railroad stations that were being built, to be shipped east to the market. Sometimes there would be a pile of bones as high as a man, stretching[4] a mile along the railroad track.

6   The buffalo saw that their day was over. They could protect their people no longer. Sadly, the last remnant of the great herd gathered in council, and decided what they would do.

7   The Kiowas were camped on the north side of Mount Scott, those of them who were still free to camp. One young woman got up very early in the morning. The dawn mist was still rising from Medicine Creek, and as she looked across the water, peering through the haze, she saw the last buffalo herd appear [5] like a spirit dream.

8   Straight to Mount Scott the leader of the herd walked. Behind him came the cows and their calves, and the few young males who had survived. As the woman watched, the face of the mountain opened.

9   Inside Mount Scott the world was green and fresh, as it had been when she was a small girl. The rivers ran clear, not red. The wild plums were in blossom, chasing the red buds up the inside slopes. Into this world of beauty the buffalo walked, never to be seen again.

—Old Lady Horse, Kiowa, southern Great Plains

After You Read

Identify the circled reference words.

COMPREHENSION QUESTIONS

The title of this reading has two parts: "The End of the World" and "The Buffalo Go." What's the connection between them?

Identify three folktale elements from the story, and three historical facts.

Folktale:

1. _____

2. _____

3. _____

History:

1. _____

2. _____

3. _____

LEARNING STRATEGY

Forming Concepts: *Paraphrasing,* **or rewriting information in your own words, makes you think carefully about the information and helps you to master it.**

PARAPHRASING

Paraphrase:

1. In the old days: _____

2. Then something happened: _____

3. As a result, first this happened: _____

4. But then later, this happened: _____

5. Finally, this happened at the end: _____

Vocabulary

KEYWORDS

1. chase ¶3
2. hire ¶5
3. loads ¶5

4. stretch ¶5
5. appear* ¶7

KEYWORD EXERCISE

1. Why did the buffalo *chase* the white people's cattle?
2. Which of the following verbs means the same thing as *hire?*
   fire   establish   employ   salary   work

   EXAMPLE: The white men *hired* hunters to kill the buffalo.

3. Which *load* would be easier to carry: ten kilograms of iron or ten kilograms of feathers? Why?

   EXAMPLE: The wagons carried the *loads* to the railroad stations.

4. *Meanings:*
   • When you *stretch,* you hold your arms and legs out straight and make them as long as you can.

     EXAMPLE: I did some *stretching* exercises before I started to ski.

   • Something that *stretches* over a distance goes from one end to the other of it.

     EXAMPLE: The Sahara Desert *stretches* across most of northern Africa.

   • Explain the similarities between the two meanings.
5. From what direction does the moon *appear?*

REVIEW

Now that you have studied the vocabulary, re-read or re-skim the passage.

Look at the following title. Given what you have already learned about their traditional ways of life and about the history of Native-white relations, how do you think that Native Americans probably live today? Write three questions that you hope will be answered in the following reading passage.

Reading process: For this reading you'll use skimming to build up your speed as well as your comprehension. Your teacher will give you exactly three minutes to skim the passage very quickly. Be sure to go all the way to the end in this period of time. Your purpose is just to catch some of the vocabulary and phrasing as a way of establishing the topic in your mind. Then you'll be given five minutes to skim again. Remember, it's skimming; don't try to read every word or sentence. Finally, you'll read the passage carefully.

NATIVE AMERICANS TODAY

1   In the 450 years between Columbus's arrival and the mid-twentieth century, the Native population of what is now the United States sank from one or two million to less than 250,000. There were people who believed that the Indian nations were going to "go the way of the buffalo." But in recent years the Indian population has risen greatly, to almost two million inhabitants again. The same trend of lessening and then growing populations has taken place in Canada, where the current Native population is estimated at somewhere between 700,000 and one million, depending on how it is figured. One reason for this increase is that the Indian birth rate is higher than the average: between 1980 and 1990 the total U.S. population grew at a rate of 10 percent, the white population at 6 percent, but the Native American population at a rate of 38 percent. Half of the Native population in the United States today lives in five states: California, Oklahoma, Arizona, New Mexico, and North Carolina. Just under half live on reservations, with the rest in cities, small towns, and the countryside.

2   The Indians who remain on the reserves often do so because they want to live in a community of others like themselves, where they can follow tribal customs. But some of the drawbacks[1] of reservation life are that unemployment is high, incomes[2] are low, health is poor, and social problems such as alcoholism are fairly common. Other Indians have moved to the cities or towns, hoping for better employment and perhaps looking for a different kind of life. And today a growing number are entering professions such as education, law, medicine, and engineering. Some of these professionals return to the reservations to provide advice and leadership to their tribes and to make their expertise[3] available[4] to the whole community.

3   Although living conditions on most of the reservations are difficult, a number of success stories can be told. On some reservations business corporations have been set up that employ local tribespeople in manufacturing jewelry or clothing, electronics parts, car parts, and cement. Other businesses include agriculture, hydroelectric generators, services, fish-packing, construction, airlines, forestry, mining, and four-star tourist resorts. Some Plains tribes are raising buffalo herds. Although these success stories are not frequent, they serve as encouragement[5] to other bands that Indians can establish[6] and operate their own businesses, providing employment and income for individual tribespeople and benefits[7] for the entire reserve community.

> When I was inducted into the service, one of the commitments I made was that I was willing to die for my country—the U.S., the Navajo Nation, and my family. My language was my weapon.
>
> —*David Patterson, Navajo Code Talker, 4th Marine Division, United States Marine Corps*

4   Interestingly enough, many Indians are very proud to consider themselves citizens[8] of the United States or Canada. During World War II, for example, more than 25,000 Indians served in the United States armed forces, and 30,000 more worked in war-related industries. The "Navajo Code Talkers" became famous: radio communications in the Pacific depended on using codes that could not be translated by outsiders. Navajo servicemen broadcast messages in their native language which were translated back into English by other Navajos on the receiving end. Thus their native language was valuable to the country's war effort.[9]

5   Remember that it was the white settlers who grouped all Native populations under the single name "Indians"? The "Indians" thought of themselves only as members of their own band, and not as a part of the overall Native population. But in recent years they have found it useful to have not only individual identities as Crow, Blackfeet, Mohawk, but also a larger identity that joins them to all other Native American groups. By cooperating with other tribes, they gain power through numbers, power that can lead to improvements[10] in their lives. In the 1960s certain Native Americans joined forces to form a movement[11] which they called *Indian Power.* They forced the public to pay attention to the way they were treated by the government and by white society. Members of the

American Indian Movement joined forces with certain members of the Oglala Sioux tribe, and armed with rifles, they took over the village of Wounded Knee, South Dakota, where U.S. soldiers had killed a large number of Sioux in 1890. Some Indians were for (this movement) and others were against it, but everyone had to agree that it focused the public's attention on some changes that needed to be made. And since the 1970s in both Canada and the United States, Indians have been given more and more control over their lands and their own future. Today the reserves are managed largely by the bands, not by white government agents. The local reservation communities have a greater voice in policy-making.[12] And certain bands have talked the government into returning some lands to tribal control, particularly in Canada. The most notable example of (this) is the Canadian government's agreement to turn over a huge segment of the Northwest Territories to the Inuit peoples, who have renamed the area "Nunavut" ("Our Land"). This is by far the largest land settlement to date by either government.

6   In the 500 years between the coming of the Europeans and the end of the twentieth century, Native cultures were very badly treated. Their way of life was not valued: (it) was attacked, its economic base was destroyed, its traditions were belittled. But although some tribes completely disappeared, (many) have responded by becoming very adaptive in order to survive: that is, they have borrowed new ways and used them in their traditional lives without giving up some of the features that make them Indians. Their dress, their languages, their economic activities, their forms of housing, even their religions have changed in some cases, but they remain clearly and recognizably Indian. Many of them continue in some of their traditional beliefs and customs, and even those who live off the reservation may return to (it) periodically to attend ceremonies and to renew ties with their people.

7   One example of this cultural survival is a renewed interest in Native languages. Originally about 300 different Indian languages were spoken in what are now the United States and Canada. Sadly, almost half of these have completely disappeared. On many reservations in the past, children were taken away from their families to boarding schools where they were punished if they spoke their native tongues, so many children grew up never knowing their tribal languages. But today on many reservations they are being instructed in these languages from a very young age, and it is hoped that soon some of the (less common ones) will be spoken in the home and will become children's first languages again. On other reservations the Native languages are widely spoken, as on the Navajo reservation in New Mexico and Arizona. Locals can tune in to a Navajo radio station, and bookstores sell *The Oxford Picture Dictionary* in Navajo/English.

8   Other areas in which traditions remain strong include keeping family and kinship ties and patterns, following the old ceremonies, joining tribal societies, eating native foods, and bringing up children in traditional ways. Tribal ceremonies, songs, dances, arts and crafts are valued and are taught, not only within the tribe, but from one tribe to another. There is a Native American Church which has about 140,000 members from many tribes. Some of its teachings are similar to Christian ones, but its ceremonies and rituals are distinctly Indian, including the importance attached to dreams and visions.

9   And what is the status[13] of American Indians in the larger society today? It must be said that stereotyping and discrimination[14] still exist, but there is also a more open and interested attitude toward Indians and their culture on the parts of many whites and in the media.[15]

After You Read

Identify the circled reference words

IN WHICH PARAGRAPH CAN YOU FIND MENTION OF:

1. the land of Nunavut? _____

2. renewed interest in Native American languages? _____

3. the Navajo Code Talkers? _____

4. the return of buffalo herds? _____

5. the Native American Church? _____

IDENTIFYING TOPICS AND MAIN IDEAS

Reading Seven can be divided into the following sections. Each of these sections discusses a particular *topic,* or subject. Identify the topics.

Each section also has a *main idea,* which is what it says about the topic. The main idea can best be expressed in a complete sentence. Identify the main ideas.

	TOPIC	MAIN IDEA
¶1	Population	After decreasing for many years, the Native American population is now growing again.
¶s 2–3	_____	_____
¶4	_____	_____
¶5	_____	_____
¶s 6–8	_____	_____
¶9	_____	_____

Vocabulary

KEYWORDS

1. drawback ¶2
2. income ¶2
3. expertise ¶2
4. available ¶2
5. encouragement ¶3
6. establish ¶3
7. benefit* ¶3
8. citizen ¶4
9. effort* ¶4
10. improvement ¶5
11. movement ¶5
12. policy ¶5
13. status ¶9
14. discrimination ¶9
15. the media ¶9

KEYWORD EXERCISE

1. Almost every decision has advantages (results that you like) and *drawbacks*. Think about your decision to come to North America to study. What were some advantages, and what were some *drawbacks?*

2. Divide the word *income* into its two parts, and then explain the connection between the parts and the meaning of the whole.

   EXAMPLE: Most people who live on the reservations have low *incomes.*

3. Name three different kinds of *expertise* that a medical doctor needs.

4. If you were trying very hard to learn something for a class but you were having a hard time, what's something that your teacher might say to you that would give you *encouragement?*

5. Which of the following are elements of the verb *establish?*
   discover   create   locate   begin   business

   EXAMPLE: Many Indians *establish* and operate their own businesses.

6. Which invention of the twentieth century has *benefited* human life the most?

7. Name two things that only *citizens* of a country are allowed to do.

   EXAMPLE: Many Indians are proud to be *citizens* of the United States or Canada.

8. *Meanings:*
   • *Movement* is the act of moving.

   EXAMPLE: The cat saw a sudden *movement* in the grass and jumped on it.

   • A *movement* is a group of people who share the same beliefs and who work together to get what they want.

   EXAMPLE: The Indian Power *movement* succeeded in improving the treatment of Native Americans.

   • Explain the similarities between the two meanings.

9. Choose a world leader, and briefly explain his or her *policy* about something.

   EXAMPLE: Today local reservation communities have a greater voice in *policy* making.

10. Which of the following are examples of the *media?*
    cinema   books   television   radio   newspapers

11. *Matching*:

_____ **1.** *available*   **a.** position or level in society

_____ **2.** *effort*   **b.** better conditions

_____ **3.** *improvements*   **c.** unfair treatment

_____ **4.** *status*   **d.** possible to get or use

_____ **5.** *discrimination*   **e.** attempt

REVIEW

Now that you have studied the vocabulary, re-read or re-skim the passage.

Reading a Table of Information

Look carefully at the following table. Then answer the questions that follow.

LIFE EXPECTANCY AT BIRTH, BY SEX, AMERICAN INDIANS AND ALASKA NATIVES AND U.S. WHITE POPULATION, 1940-1980						
	American Indians and Alaska Natives			**U.S. White Population**		
Year	**Both Sexes**	**Male**	**Female**	**Both Sexes**	**Male**	**Female**
1980	71.1	67.1	75.1	74.4	70.7	78.1
1970	65.1	60.7	71.2	71.6	67.9	75.5
1960	61.7	60.0	65.7	70.7	67.6	74.2
1950	60.0	58.1	62.2	69.0	66.3	72.0
1940	51.0	(51.3)	51.9	64.9	62.8	67.3

1. Does this table give information about Indians throughout North America?

   _____

2. Who lives longer: Native Americans or white Americans? _____

   _____

3. Compare the difference in life expectancy between the two groups from 1940 to 1980. Then write a sentence about how the difference has changed over this period of time.

   _____

4. Look at the circled figure. Write a sentence expressing this information.

   _____

5. The table does not explain the reasons for the differences in life expectancy. Can you think of three factors that might shorten the life expectancy of Native peoples?

   _____

   _____

   _____

Not too many years ago in the United States and Canada, Native American children on the reservations were sent away from their families to live at government boarding schools. In those days the boys' long hair was cut off, all the children had to wear white people's style of uniforms, and they were not permitted to speak their native languages. The books that they learned to read English from had nothing to do with their traditional lives: they described middle-class white children who lived in white people's housing in white people's towns. Everything they learned taught them that the white values and lifestyle were what was normal and good. The following passage describes a six-year-old Pueblo boy's first encounter with this strange culture and the conflicts that he felt as a result.

AND THEN I WENT TO SCHOOL

1   Values in life style were dictated in various ways. The Dick and Jane reading series in the primary grades presented me pictures of a home with a pitched roof, straight walls, and sidewalks. I could not identify with these from my Pueblo world. However, it was clear I didn't have these things, and what I did have did not measure up.[1] At night, long after grandmother went to sleep, I would lie awake staring at our crooked adobe walls casting uneven shadows from the light of the fireplace. The walls were no longer just right for me. My life was no longer just right. I was ashamed of being who I was, and I wanted to change right then and there. Somehow it became very important to have straight walls, clean hair and teeth, and a spotted dog to chase after. I even became critical of, and hateful toward, my bony fleabag of a dog. I loved the familiar and cozy[2] environment at grandmother's house, but now I imagined it could be a heck of a lot better if only I had a whiteman's house with a bed, a nice couch, and a clock. In school books, all the child characters ever did was run at leisure after the dog or kite. They were always happy. As for me, all I seemed to do at home was go for buckets of water and cut up sticks for a lousy fire. Didn't the teacher say drinking coffee would stunt my growth? Why couldn't I have nice tall glasses of milk so I could have strong bones and white teeth like those kids in the books? Did my grandmother really care about my well being[3]?

[At the age of seven, Joe was sent away to boarding school. He was very homesick for his family and his village, Cochiti. Three months later he came home for the Thanksgiving holidays. At the end of the weekend he had to say goodbye and return to school.]

2   Leaving for the boarding school the following Sunday evening was one of the saddest events in my entire life. Although I had enjoyed myself immensely the last few days, I realized then that life would never be the same again. I could not turn back the time just as I could not do away with school and the ways of the whiteman. They were here to stay and would creep more and more into my life. The effort to make sense of[4] both worlds together was painful,[5] and I had no choice but to do so. The schools, television, automobiles, and many other outside ways and values had chipped away at the simple cooperative life I began to grow in. The people of Cochiti were changing. The winter evening gatherings, the exchanging of stories, and even the performing of certain ceremonies were already only a memory that someone commented about now and then. Still, the two worlds were very different and the demands of both were ever present.[6] The whiteman's was flashy, less personal, but very comfortable. The Cochiti were both attracted and pushed toward these new ways which they had little to say about. There

75

was no choice left but to compete with the whiteman on his terms for survival. To do that I knew I had to give up part of my life.

3   Determined not to cry, I left my home that dreadfully lonely night. As I made my way back to school, my right hand clutched tightly the mound of cornmeal grandmother had placed there and my left hand brushed away a tear.

—Joe Suina, Pueblo, Southwest

[Today Native peoples in both Canada and the United States have more control over policy making in their schools, and children on the reserves grow up in a way that combines traditional social and spiritual values with the white culture's technology, clothing, etc.]

After You Read

TRUE-FALSE QUESTIONS

¶ number

1. Young Joe learned to read from books whose culture was foreign to him.   T   F   _____
2. The books made him begin to feel dissatisfied with his traditional life.   T   F   _____
3. But when he went away to boarding school, he felt very homesick for that traditional life.   T   F   _____
4. When he returned home for a visit, he realized that the old world was changing even in his village and would never be the same again.   T   F   _____
5. Knowing that he would have to give up part of his life made him dreadfully lonely.   T   F   _____

Vocabulary

KEYWORDS

1. measure up ¶1
2. cozy ¶1
3. well being ¶1
4. make sense of ¶2
5. painful* ¶2
6. ever present ¶2

KEYWORD EXERCISE

1. In what ways did young Joe believe that his traditional world did not measure up to the white world?
2. *Matching*:

_____ **1.** *cozy*   **a.** comfortable and warm

_____ **2.** *well being*   **b.** unpleasant and hurting

_____ **3.** *make sense of*   **c.** always there

_____ **4.** *painful*   **d.** a healthy and happy condition

_____ **5.** *ever present*   **e.** understand

REVIEW

Now that you have studied the vocabulary, re-read or re-skim the passage.

> I think we will still win, I think there are enough people who wish to understand the Indian mind, that we are not going to harm anyone, that we are peaceful people, we are not aggressive people. In this lies our strength and from here we will pick up. I believe that we will survive, I still believe we will survive. That is our dream.
> —*An Indian grandfather*

FREEWRITING: WHAT HAVE YOU LEARNED ABOUT NATIVE AMERICANS?

What are the most interesting or important things you've learned about Native Americans in this chapter? Identify information that you hadn't known before, or that you hadn't known much about.

Writing an Essay: The Best of Both Worlds

Look at your chart of cultural values again. Which ones from both sides do you most admire? How might a Native American or a non-Native American today combine some values from both sides in their life?

Evaluating Learning Strategies

Look back over the chapter at the learning strategies that were presented. Were there any that weren't especially helpful for you? What wasn't helpful about them? Which ones did you find especially helpful? Think about times and ways that you can keep using them in your future reading. If you know of other good strategies that were not suggested in this chapter, tell your classmates about them.

Evaluating Your Learning

	Very little	Quite a bit	A lot
You know more vocabulary.	_____	_____	_____
Your comprehension is stronger.	_____	_____	_____
You can read unsimplified passages.	_____	_____	_____
You can guess vocabulary from context.	_____	_____	_____
You can take notes from your reading.	_____	_____	_____
You learned about Native Americans.	_____	_____	_____

Verbs
appear*
attack
attempt*
attract
chase
cooperate*
destroy*
disappear*
establish
generalize
get along all right
give up*
hire
hold a council
let someone alone
make sense of
measure up
offer*
recognize
resist*
starve
stretch

Nouns
attitude*
benefit*
ceremony
citizen
climate
complexity
conflict
contradiction
depression
destruction
discrimination
diversity
drawback
effort*
encouragement
expertise
feature*
game
generalization
herd
improvement
income
loads
media
movement
nomad
policy
poverty
relations
revenge
shape
spirit
status
survival
unemployment
variation
vision
well being

Adjectives
ancestral
available
connected
cozy
diverse*
ever present
be left*
painful

Adverb
barely*

Alternative Education

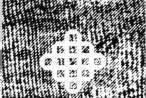

INTRODUCTION

PLANNING YOUR LEARNING

Review your overall goal statement. How much progress did you make toward it in the last chapter? Do you want to change it? Think about how you can work to meet your goal as you study this new chapter.

- How many words do you want to learn? (minimum 58, the number of keywords in the chapter)
- What grade would you like to make on the vocabulary section of the exam at the end of the chapter?
- What grade would you like to make on the reading comprehension section of the exam?
- What are you going to read outside of class?

PREVIEWING THE CHAPTER

- Think about the title of this chapter. What do you think "alternative education" is?
- Look in the Table of Contents at the titles of the five readings in this chapter. Look through the chapter at the pictures. What are some things that you expect to learn about?
- Which reading looks the most interesting?

DISCUSSION OF CARTOON: HOW EDUCATION WORKS

- What's the connection between the first nine pictures and the last picture? In other words, what's this cartoon about?
- What does each of the first nine pictures have to say about school? Does any one of these pictures describe your own feelings?
- What did (or do) you like about school? What didn't (or don't) you like? Either draw a picture of your own, or freewrite for about ten minutes.

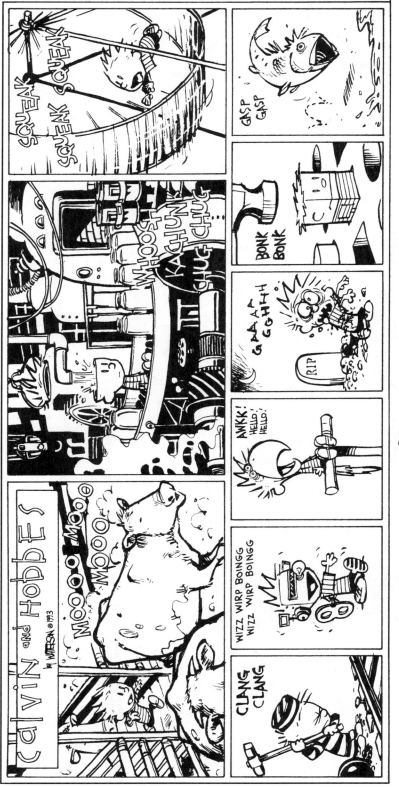

FREEWRITING AND/OR DISCUSSION: THE PURPOSE OF EDUCATION

1. In your own personal opinion, what is the most important purpose of education? (√)

	Most Important	Important	Not So Important
To train students for future careers	_____	_____	_____
To prepare them to be good citizens	_____	_____	_____
To make them better persons	_____	_____	_____
To teach them information about things	_____	_____	_____
To teach them how to do things	_____	_____	_____
To teach them how to think for themselves	_____	_____	_____
To teach them how to learn	_____	_____	_____
To encourage and develop their creativity	_____	_____	_____
To develop an understanding of their own cultures	_____	_____	_____
To teach them how to get along together	_____	_____	_____
Other: _____	_____	_____	_____

2. Think about your own experience in education. Did/does it serve the purposes that you believe are "most important," or did/does it serve other ones?
3. Did you study anything in school that you don't think was useful for you?
   • If so, what was it?
   • Do you think you should have had to learn it?
   • If so, why?

First Alternative for a Longer Project: Observing a Traditional Class

In this chapter, your teacher may assign you to choose a longer project that you could spend two or three weeks working on. Three of these projects will be described, but if you think of something else that you would rather work on, discuss it with your teacher. Here is the first alternative:

1. You will visit a traditional class at a level of your choice: kindergarten, elementary, secondary, or college/university. As you observe, answer the following questions:
   a. What method is the teacher using? (lecture, discussion, individual reading/writing/problem solving, group or paired work, lab experiments, etc.)

b. Does the teacher expect the students to have completed homework or readings before the class?

c. Does the teacher conduct the class formally, or casually? Do the students behave formally, or casually? Give examples.

d. Do the students ask questions and give opinions during the class? If so, how does the professor react? (Is s/he pleased, or annoyed?)

e. What else do you notice that is interesting to you?

f. Which of the "purposes of education" list do you think that this class fulfills?

g. In what ways does this class differ from a traditional class in your country?

2. If you wish, interview some students from the class that you visited. Beforehand, make a list of two or three questions that you wish to ask them. Write your questions here:

_____

_____

_____

3. Write up a report of your observation. Include an introductory paragraph telling what you did and what your purpose was. In the next paragraph, tell what you observed. If you interviewed students, in the third paragraph summarize what you learned from them. Then in the last paragraph, give your conclusions about the whole experience, your reactions and opinions, and any comments that you wish to make.

PREPARING TO READ: VOCABULARY

The following questions practice basic vocabulary used to discuss education. Work with a partner. If you don't know an answer, use your dictionary or skip that question, but fill it in later when you compare your work with the rest of your classmates'.

1. What is the name for the school that children attend at:

• around the age of five? _____

• around ages 6–12? _____

• 13–18? _____

2. What's the way of teaching in which the teacher does all the talking, giving information to the students?

_____

3. What's another word for *way* of teaching?

_____

4. What's the name for the list of all the courses that are taught at a particular school?

_____

5. What do you call schools that are operated by the state or the city?

_____

What about the schools that are operated by another group, for instance, religious schools?

_____

6. At the end of the course each student receives a _____, e.g. A/B/C/D/F. A good one means the student _____; a poor one means the student _____ the course.

7. The person in charge of an elementary or secondary school is called the

_____ .

8. _Academic_ subjects are (for example) _____,

_____, _____. _____ is a _non-academic_ subject.

9. _____ tests are tests that all students in the state, province, or country take at a certain point in their education.

READING ONE

Sometimes people have an experience that suddenly teaches them something very important, something they'll remember all their lives. Usually these experiences take place outside the classroom. The following reading describes such a "learning moment" for one of the little boys in the story. Thirty years later he still remembered it so clearly that he told the story to Joseph Bruchac, an Abenaki Indian educator, who thought it was a perfect example of how the Native American approach to education differs from the Euro-American one.

THANKING THE BIRDS

1   One day thirty years ago, Swift Eagle, an Apache man, visited some friends on the Onondaga Indian Reservation in central New York. While he was out walking, he heard sounds of boys playing in the bushes.

2   "There's another one. Shoot it!" said one of the boys.

3   When he pushed through the brush to see what was happening, he found that they had been shooting small birds with a BB gun. They had already killed a chickadee, a robin and several blackbirds. The boys looked up at him, uncertain[1] what he was going to do or say.

4   There are several things that a non-Indian bird lover might have done: given a stern lecture[2] on the evil[3] of killing birds; threatened to tell the boys' parents on them for doing something they had been told not to do; or even spanked them. Swift Eagle, however, did something else.

5   "Ah," he said, "I see you have been hunting. Pick up your game and come with me."

6   He led the boys to a place where they could make a fire and cook the birds. He made sure they said a thank-you to the spirits of the birds before eating them, and as they ate he told stories. It was important, he said, to be thankful to

the birds for the gifts of their songs, their feathers, and their bodies as food. The last thing he said to them they never forgot—for it was one of those boys who told me this story many years later: "You know, our Creator gave the gift of life to everything that is alive. Life is a very sacred thing. But our Creator knows that we have to eat to stay alive. That is why it is permitted to hunt to feed ourselves and our people. So I understand that you boys must have been very, very hungry to kill those little birds." . . .

7   As the anecdote about Swift Eagle shows, children were taught the values of their culture through example and stories. Instead of scolding or lecturing them, Swift Eagle showed the boys how to build a fire and cook the game they had shot, giving the songbirds the same respect he would have given a rabbit or deer. He told stories that pointed out the value of those birds as living beings. The ritual activity of making the fire, thanking the spirits of the birds, hearing the stories, and then eating the game they had killed taught the boys more than a hundred stern lectures would have done, and the lesson stayed with them all their lives. Western education today tends[4] to be didactic. Children are told—in books, lectures, film scripts and movies—*about* things, but rarely do they experience them. Adults then test the children by having them answer questions about what they have "learned." There is good reason for (this method,) of course. The world our children must know about is too broad[5] to allow them to learn everything through a hands-on approach. However, as many educators have observed, the result of such a method is too often learning that is more a conditioned reflex than a true understanding. Furthermore, the artificial[6] divisions between fields of study—with natural science alone being divided into botany, zoology, geology, astronomy, and hundreds of other areas—can lead to knowledge that is fragmented.[7] It is like what you learn by dissecting a frog: you know the parts, but you cannot put them together to understand the animal. And, in cutting the frog apart, you have killed it.

8   Native American education, in contrast, has always been experiential[8] and holistic.[9] If you wish to know how to make baskets, you go to a basket maker and watch that person at work. If you are patient and watch long enough, eventually the basket maker may ask you to do something—to hold onto this coil of sweetgrass here, to help shave down that strip of ash. If you return the next day, and the next, and the next, then one day you discover that you, too, know how to make a basket.

Threads

What is the task of all higher education? To make man into a machine. What are the means employed? He is taught how to suffer being bored.

F. W. Nietzsche

After You Read

Identify the circled reference words.

COMPREHENSION QUESTIONS

1. Why did Swift Eagle force the boys to cook and eat the songbirds?

_____

_____

2. What did he want the boys to learn from the experience?

_____

_____

Forming Concepts: Summarizing a reading in your own words requires you to think actively about the main ideas and helps you to remember them.

SUMMARIZING

1. Using your own words, summarize the first six paragraphs (the anecdote about Swift Eagle) into three sentences with a total of not more than 40 words.

_____

_____

_____

_____

_____

_____

2. If you were going to summarize ¶7, highlight not more than four sentences that contain the main points.

3. If you were going to summarize ¶8, which sentence contains the main idea?

_____

What is the purpose of the other sentences? _____

DISCUSSION AND FREEWRITING: "LEARNING MOMENTS"

1. Discuss with a partner: Have you learned more inside the classroom, or outside of it? Give examples of some of the most important things you've learned. Where did you learn them? Who did you learn them from?

2. Freewrite: Write about a "learning moment" of your own. What happened, and what did you learn?

DISCUSSION: HOW PEOPLE LEARN BEST

How do you learn best? How do you think most people learn best? (Through lectures, discussion, lab or field work, trial and error, observation, working with a partner, independent reading, etc.) Which of these methods are used in the style of education described in ¶7? In ¶8?

Vocabulary

VOCABULARY IN CONTEXT

Look at the following sentences from ¶7:

"It is like what you learn by dissecting a frog: you know the parts, but you cannot put them together to understand the animal. And, in cutting the frog apart, you have killed it."

Given the context, what do you think *dissecting* means?

LEARNING STRATEGY

Remembering New Material: Recording new words in a vocabulary notebook reserved for that purpose helps you remember them.

KEYWORDS

1. uncertain* ¶3
2. lecture ¶4
3. evil ¶4
4. tend ¶7
5. broad ¶7

6. artificial ¶7
7. fragmented ¶7
8. experiential ¶8
9. holistic ¶8

KEYWORD EXERCISE

1. Choose the synonym for *uncertain* from the following:
   sure   confident   doubtful   definite   positive

   EXAMPLE: The boys looked up at him, *uncertain* what he was going to do or say.

2. *Meanings:*
   - A *lecture* is a speech that someone gives in order to teach something.

     EXAMPLE: Our professor gave a *lecture* on the causes of the conflict in Northern Ireland.

   - If someone *lectures* you about something, they point out a bad thing you did and tell you how you should behave.

     EXAMPLE: Swift Eagle didn't *lecture* the boys.

   - Explain the similarities between the two meanings.

3. The following adjectives are all related to "bad," but some are worse than others. Rank them from the least bad (1) to the worst (6).
   evil   wrong   unpleasant   poor   naughty   harmful
   (1)   (2)   (3)   (4)   (5)   (6)

   EXAMPLE: Many religions teach about the difference between good and *evil* behavior.

4. **EXAMPLE:** Today North Americans *tend* to pay with checks or credit cards instead of carrying cash.

   Finish the sentences:
   • On rainy weekends I tend to . . .
   • One stereotype of politicians is that they tend . . .
   • Cats . . .

5. If you define the word "family" in a *broad* way, whom does it include? If you define it in a narrow way, whom does it include?

   EXAMPLE: An educated person has a *broad* knowledge of the world.

6. Which of the following materials are not *artificial?*

   cotton   wool   nylon   wood   plastic   gold   stone   vinyl

   EXAMPLE: Computers make use of *artificial* intelligence.

   What word is a good antonym for artificial?

7. *Meanings:*
   • Something that is *fragmented* is made of a lot of different parts that seem unconnected with each other.

   EXAMPLE: My family moved around so often that my childhood is made up of *fragmented* memories of different cities, schools, and friends.

   • A *fragment* is a small broken-off piece of something.

   EXAMPLE: When he dropped the cup, he had to sweep up all the *fragments* so no one would step on them and be cut.

   • Explain the similarities between the two meanings.

8. The word *experiential* may not be in your dictionary. It's the adjective form of the noun *experience.* In ¶8, Bruchac says that Native American education has always been *experiential* and holistic. Swift Eagle educated the boys through an experiential method. In what ways was his method related to the word *experience?*

9. *Holistic* is a word that may not be in your dictionary either. If you look at something *holistically,* you look at all of it in a connected way instead of just looking at separate parts of it. For instance, a holistic approach to medical practice considers not just the patient's temperature and pains, but also his or her eating habits, emotional condition, amount of regular exercise, etc.

   Look at Bruchac's example of basketmaking in ¶8. In what ways is it *experiential?* In what ways is it *holistic?*

REVIEW

Now that you have studied the vocabulary, re-read or re-skim the passage.

READING TWO

Reading process: As you read the following passage, look for the answers to the following questions (often called "journalists' questions"):

Who?   Why?   Where?
What?   How?   When?

Mountainview
ACADEMY
An alternate education for grades K through 8.

At Mountainview you may be assured of an absolutely dedicated staff of qualified instructors. You will be pleased to know that we have made every effort to design an educational facility and course of study which bring out the best of every student.

Culver
INTERNATIONAL

A fully integrated K through 5 education in a home-based atmosphere. Our facility is located in a peaceful setting inducive to creativity and intellectual pursuits. We strive to conduct an educational curriculum responding to modern-day needs for a well-rounded student body.

EDUCA

In an
with
of g
since Te
to the edge
when Delbert
Since its inception
schooling of unequal

St. Ann's
Christian Academy

Your child's education is largely shaped by the start he or she is offered. Here at St. Ann's, we offer individual attention designed to meet your child's K through 8 needs. Our experienced staff is eager to meet with you and explore your child's educational future.

If you would like to further your understanding of what we have to offer please contact our educational planner

ALTERNATIVE SCHOOLS IN THE UNITED STATES

1   [An] alternative school is any public or private school that differs from traditional schools in curriculum, purpose, or teaching methods. Most alternative schools attempt to establish a less formal relationship between pupils and teachers. They also try to make greater use of community facilities outside the school and to involve[1] parents in the educational process. Alternative schools developed because of dissatisfaction[2] with the quality[3] and aims of traditional schools.

2   Alternative schools have voluntary enrollments. A typical alternative school has from 30 to 40 students. A school of this size can easily adjust[4] its program to fit individual needs and desires. Some alternative schools work only with children of elementary-school age, and others accept only teen-agers. Many alternative schools put students of several ages into classes based on[5] subject interest.

3   Many alternative schools in the United States operate independently of the public school system. These schools, which are privately run, are usually called free schools. The word free refers to the independence of such schools. It also describes the emphasis[6] of these schools in allowing students to make their own decisions in various matters. Other alternative schools operate as part of the public school system. Such schools may be located in one area of a public school building or in a separate building provided by the school system. The separate buildings are often called *magnet schools* or *specialty schools.* They attempt to attract students from throughout[7] the school system.

4   The basic[8] principle[9] followed by alternative schools is that not all children have the same goals and the same ways of learning. Many of the people involved in operating these schools do not want to convert[10] the whole school system to their methods. They want to provide the opportunity for a different kind of education for children who would benefit from (it.)

5   The major feature of many alternative schools is the *open classroom*. The teacher of an open classroom, instead of lecturing most of the time, helps students find interesting ways to learn on their own.[11] Many kinds of educational materials are kept in the classroom. The students work with these materials alone or in groups. The teacher gives the students individual help. . . .

6   Many forms of alternative schools have developed in response to various needs. *Street academies* and *dropout centers,* which function in the poor sections of big cities, help high-school dropouts continue their education. *Storefront schools* have developed from child-care and kindergarten facilities. *Work schools* hold classes part of the day, and the students work at regular jobs the rest of the day.

7   The *school without walls* plan, used in some large cities, takes advantage of the educational opportunities[12] provided by businesses and institutions of the community. Students may spend part of the day at an artist's studio, a factory, a museum, a newspaper office, a repair shop, a theater, or a government or private agency. The purpose of (this method) is to make learning more realistic and enjoyable, and to broaden the experiences offered high-school students.

8   Some alternative schools emphasize[6] the study of the culture and history of a certain minority group.[13] Some accept only students from (one such group.) Others seek students from several cultures and races.

9   A number of alternative schools have been designed[14] for children from middle- or upper-class families. Usually such schools are in suburban or rural areas. Most of them stress[15] the independence of each student and have no required subjects.

10   A trend[16] in the development of alternative schools has been the establishment of such schools within the public school system. One plan offers a variety of learning environments from which students, parents, and teachers may choose. At the elementary school level, parents can choose to place their children in a traditional classroom or in one of several kinds of open classrooms. High-school students decide whether to enter a free school with few course requirements, or one of several programs in the regular high-school program.

Threads

In a natural learning environment a child is permitted to pursue whatever direction his curiosity takes.

Jane Williams, alternative educator

After You Read

Identify the circled reference words.

> What makes all this "alternative" is that the American public school system is not oriented to the fullest human development of students, but to preparing them to be loyal, obedient citizens, employees, and consumers. The social history of American education makes it clear that mass schooling, in the form we know it, was created to meet the needs of industrial capitalism. While many individual teachers are devoted to the needs and interests of their students, the system is mainly interested in sorting and controlling them.
>
> —*Ron Miller, alternative educator*
>
> Do you agree with this view of traditional schooling?

COMPREHENSION QUESTIONS

1. In ¶1 the authors tell why some people wanted to develop alternative schools. What might have dissatisfied them in traditional schools?

   _____

   _____

   _____

2. Based on the information in the reading, would it be accurate to say that alternative schools have a lot in common with each other?

   _____

3. According to the article, alternative schools can operate either within or

   outside of _____ .

4. Re-read the first sentence of ¶4. Who are the children who would want to attend alternative schools?

   _____

   • In your experience, what goals and ways of learning would traditional schools serve?

   _____

   _____

   _____

5. Can you find anything in the article that suggests that the author believes that alternative schools are better—or are worse—than traditional schools?

   _____

   _____

   _____

   _____

TRUE-FALSE QUESTIONS

¶ number

1. Most alternative schools are very small.   T   F   _____

2. *Free schools* cost the students nothing.   T   F   _____

3. *Magnet schools* are public schools.   T   F   _____

4. In an *open classroom,* students study independently instead of all together.   T   F   _____

5. In the *school without walls* plan, classes are held out-of-doors.   T   F   _____

Second Alternative for a Longer Project: Observing an Alternative Class

Your teacher will take you to visit an alternative school in your community, and/or will invite an alternative educator to your class to be interviewed. If you visit a class, fill out the answers to these questions:

1. What method is the teacher using? (lecture, discussion, individual reading/writing/problem solving, group or paired work, lab experiments, etc.)
2. Does the teacher expect the students to have completed homework or readings before the class?
3. Does the teacher conduct the class formally, or casually? Do the students behave formally, or casually? Give examples.
4. Do the students ask questions and give opinions during the class? If so, how does the professor react? (Is she or he pleased, or annoyed?)
5. What else do you notice that is interesting to you?
6. Which of the "purposes of education" list do you think that this class fulfills?
7. In what ways does this class differ from a traditional class in your country?

If an alternative educator comes to your class to be interviewed, work with your classmates to prepare a list of questions in advance. Each student should be responsible for asking one question. Advance preparation will help you to plan good questions and to make sure that questions aren't repeated.

Write up a report on what you have learned. In the first paragraph, summarize what you did and tell your purpose. In the second, tell what you observed or summarize what the educator said. (If you both observed a class and interviewed an educator, devote a separate paragraph to each.) In your last paragraph, give your conclusions about the whole experience, your reactions and opinions, and any comments that you wish to make.

Vocabulary

VOCABULARY IN CONTEXT

1. Find the word *dropout* in ¶6. (It's used twice.) You can figure out the meaning in two ways: (1) by looking at the context, and (2) by dividing the word into its two parts and thinking about them. What do you think it means?
2. Find the phrase *learning environments* in ¶10. The context gives you several examples of learning environments. Name two.

    a. _____

    b. _____

KEYWORDS

1. involve ¶1
2. dissatisfaction ¶1
3. quality ¶1
4. adjust* ¶2
5. based on* ¶2
6. emphasis, emphasize* ¶s 3, 8
7. throughout* ¶3
8. basic ¶4
9. principle ¶4
10. convert ¶4
11. on their own* ¶5
12. opportunity ¶7
13. minority group ¶8
14. design ¶9
15. stress ¶9
16. trend ¶10

KEYWORD EXERCISE

1. *EXAMPLES:* Most alternative schools try to *involve* parents in their children's schooling.

   My roommate wants to *involve* me in all of his personal problems.

   Finish the sentences:
   Should religious leaders be involved . . .
   A good teacher will become . . .

2. You studied the prefix *dis-* in the last chapter. It is often used to form the antonym of a word, as with *satisfaction/dissatisfaction.* Look in your dictionary and find three other words that you already know that form antonyms by adding *dis-.*

   a. _____

   b. _____

   c. _____

   EXAMPLE: Alternative schools developed because of *dissatisfaction* with the quality and aims of traditional schools.

3. List four features that a high-*quality* school would have.

   a. _____

   b. _____

   c. _____

   d. _____

4. When you travel, list four things that you might need to *adjust* to.

   a. _____

   b. _____

   c. _____

   d. _____

   EXAMPLE: A small school can easily *adjust* its program to fit individual needs and desires.

5. When a scientist makes a discovery, what might it be *based on?*

    EXAMPLE: Many alternative schools put students of several ages into classes *based on* subject interest.

6. Which of the following words are elements of *emphasis* or *emphasize?*
    appear barely generalize strong important true

    EXAMPLES: Native American education *emphasizes* teaching through stories.
          My high school put a lot of *emphasis* on examination scores.

7. *EXAMPLES:* It rained *throughout* the night.
          Spanish is spoken *throughout* most of Latin America.

    Finish the sentences:
    The soldiers kept watch throughout . . .
    Around this time of year, students . . .

8. Which of the following are elements of the word *basic?*
    the most important the simplest the most available
    the most diverse

    EXAMPLE: The *basic* elements of good art are imagination and technique.

9. *Meanings:*
    • A *principle* is a general belief that you have about the way you should behave. This principle governs your behavior. An example: "Friends should always have time for each other."
    • A *principle* is also a general rule about how something should be done, or a general scientific law that explains how something happens or works.
    • Which meaning is used in this sentence from ¶4?

    "The basic *principle* followed by alternative schools is that not all children have the same goals and the same ways of learning."

10. *EXAMPLE:* She won't marry him if he doesn't *convert* to her religion.

    Finish the sentences:
    After I left home, my parents converted my bedroom to . . .
    The children converted the large cardboard box . . .

11. Which of the following is an antonym for *on their own?*
    independently alone without help cooperatively

    EXAMPLE: The teacher helps students find interesting ways to learn *on their own.*

12. Which of the following is the best representation of an *opportunity?*
    money a good friend a prison an open door a key

    EXAMPLE: Businesses and institutions in the community also provide educational *opportunities.*

13. Name some *minority groups* that live in North America.
    Name some *minority groups* that live in your country.

    EXAMPLE: Some alternative schools emphasize the study of the culture and history of a certain *minority group.*

14. Which of the following is not an element of the word *design?*

accidental   plan   prepare   decide   details

    EXAMPLE: A number of alternative schools have been *designed* for children from middle- or upper-class families.

15. In ¶8, find a synonym for the verb *stress.*

    EXAMPLE: Some alternative schools *stress* the independence of each student and have no required subjects.

16. One synonym for *trend* is *fashion,* a popular style that people are doing (or wearing) these days. We can speak of *trends* in clothing, in cars, in eating or exercise habits, in television and films, and also in education, government, medical practice. Choose one of these areas and describe some recent trends. Remember, if it's a trend, it must be something that wasn't happening several years ago.

REVIEW

Now that you have studied the vocabulary, re-read or re-skim the passage.

LEARNING STRATEGY

Managing Your Learning: Every evening, organize your handouts and pages of notes from that day. These papers can't help you if you can never find them. Review them every week or two.

READING THREE

Reading process for Readings Three and Four: Your teacher will ask half of the class to read Reading Three, and the other half to read Reading Four. If you read Reading Three, you will answer questions that a partner who hasn't read it will ask you. Then you will ask your partner questions about Reading Four, which she or he will have read. The questions follow the readings.

    When each of you has finished, read the other passage.

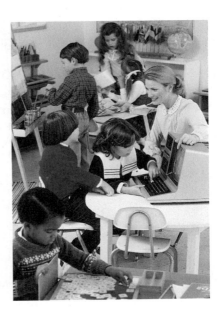

THE MONTESSORI METHOD

1   The Montessori method of education, used worldwide today, was developed by Dr. Maria Montessori (1870–1952). She was the first woman in Italy to receive a medical degree, but found it difficult to practice medicine because Italians at that time were not ready to accept female doctors. So she turned to education, working with children who had been locked away in mental institutions because they were considered[1] unable to learn. Through her thoughtful observations[2] and through her experience with these children, she developed a method of educating them that was so successful that

Threads

Maria Montessori believed that education begins at birth, and that the first few years of life are especially important.

Mark and Helen Hegener, alternative educators

Threads

In a classic Montessori school four areas of development are addressed: care of self and the environment, sensory and motor education, reading and writing skills, and premath teaching.

Mark and Helen Hegener, alternative educators

they were able to pass reading and writing examinations designed for normal children. She wrote several books about her methods, the best-known of (which) is entitled *The Absorbent Mind.* These books form the basis for[3] "the Montessori method" which is still in use today in Montessori schools.

2   Montessori schools do not group children as traditional schools do. Instead of all the six-year-olds studying together in the first grade, taking examinations, receiving grade reports, and then either passing to the next grade or repeating the first grade, Montessori children are grouped in larger age groups—say, three- to five-years olds together, six- through nine-year-olds together in one classroom. The teachers keep careful records of each child's development[4] and activities, but they do not grade the children. If a child is having difficulty with an activity, the teacher will spend extra time with her until she succeeds[5] in learning it. Parents are welcome to observe classes at any time, and parents and teachers meet to discuss the child's development at regular intervals throughout the year.

3   Children are carefully taught how to do things, beginning at the earliest ages. For example, in kindergarten, each day a different child may be in charge of preparing a snack for all the children. The child would be taught how to cut up apples safely and how to pour and serve glasses of milk without spilling them. If a Montessori school has any space around it, the children will usually be taught how to plant and care for a garden. There are often small animals in the classroom: maybe fish, birds, white mice, guinea pigs, kittens. Even the smallest children are taught how to respect and care for these pets. But children are also taught traditional academic subjects. Part of their course of study is independent research into topics of their choice, which they write papers and give oral reports on.

4   Dr. Montessori based her method on observing each child to see when he was ready to learn a new concept[6] or process[7] instead of making the whole class do the same thing at the same time. She believed that children begin to learn best when they can see and touch something, can experience it through their senses. Concepts are always taught by exposing the children to a real-life, concrete[8] experience first, before the abstract[9] idea is introduced. For instance, when learning about mathematics, the children begin by counting and arranging colored beads or other small objects, then later move on to working with abstract numbers on paper. Everything they learn should be made real.

After You Read

Identify the circled reference word.

> One of the objectives of Montessori is to assure that the child does not fail when attempting new tasks. Montessori believes that failure can have negative effects on the child, so Montessori instructors do everything they can to assure that this doesn't happen.
>
> —*Jane Williams, alternative educator*

COMPREHENSION QUESTIONS

1. Who was Maria Montessori?

_____

_____

2. Why didn't she practice medicine, as she was trained to do?

_____

_____

3. Identify two features of the Montessori method.

_____

_____

4. Would you have enjoyed learning this way? Would you have liked it better than the way that you learned in school?

_____

_____

IN WHICH PARAGRAPH CAN YOU FIND . . .

1. a description of the principles that the Montessori method is based on?
2. a description of what children learn in a Montessori school?
3. a history of how the Montessori method developed?
4. a description of the organization and policies of a Montessori school?

TAKING NOTES AS YOU READ

In the last chapter (on pages 59–62) you made notes of the important points in the reading passage. Now practice this again, in a slightly different way.

1. Look at ¶1. Pick out the three most important pieces of information in this paragraph, and highlight or underline them.
   • How is ¶1 organized: chronology, examples, cause and effect, comparison/contrast, or problem/solution? (See the Appendix on page 246, for a list of markers that will help you answer this question.)
   • Circle the markers that tell you the organization.
2. Pick out the three most important pieces of information in ¶2.
   • How is it organized?
   • Circle the markers.
3. What are the two most important pieces of information in ¶3?
   • What's the organization?
   • The markers?
4. What are the three most important parts of ¶4?
   • The organization?
   • The markers?
5. Now make notes on a piece of paper. Use abbreviations and symbols instead of writing complete sentences. For instance:

   Maria Montessori: MM
   children: chdrn
   learn: lrn
   school: schl
   students: sts

6. Choose one of these graphic formats for each paragraph:

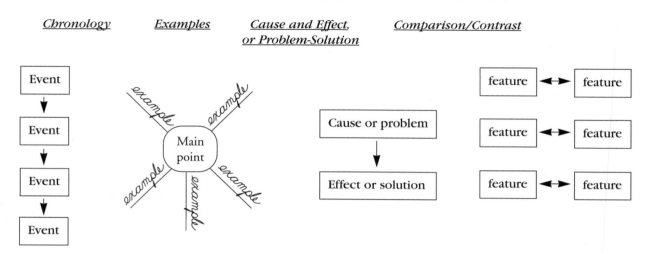

Chronology   *Examples*   *Cause and Effect,*   *Comparison/Contrast*
or Problem-Solution

Use the appropriate format to make notes of the most important points and details on a separate piece of paper. When you finish, compare your work with a classmate's and then show it to your teacher.

Vocabulary

VOCABULARY IN CONTEXT

1. ¶2 says, "Parents and teachers meet to discuss the child's development at *regular intervals* throughout the year." What do you think *intervals* are? If you can't think of a definition, give an example.
2. ¶3 says that children are taught how to pour and serve glasses of milk without *spilling* them. Using your arms and hands, show what happens when you *spill* milk.
3. ¶4 says that Dr. Montessori "believed that children begin to learn best when they can see and touch something, can experience it through their *senses*." What can you understand about the word *senses*?

KEYWORDS

1. consider ¶1
2. observation ¶1
3. form the basis for ¶1
4. development ¶2
5. succeed* ¶2
6. concept ¶4
7. process ¶4
8. concrete ¶4
9. abstract ¶4

KEYWORD EXERCISE

1. *EXAMPLES:* Those children were *considered* (to be) unable to learn.
   We *consider* these figures to be accurate.

   Finish the sentences:
   Some people consider Columbus to have been . . .
   This tourist resort is . . .

2. Which of the following are elements of the word *observation?*
   offer   watch   think   learn   notice

   EXAMPLE: Dr. Montessori made thoughtful *observations* of the children she was working with.

3. *Meanings:*
   • If something *forms the basis for* a method or decision, it provides the reasons for doing it.

   EXAMPLE: Maria Montessori's books *formed the basis* for her educational methods.

   • We say that the most important and simplest parts of something are its *basics.*

   EXAMPLE: Children are not ready to learn algebra until they have mastered the *basics* of arithmetic.

   • Explain the similarities between the two words.

4. Which of the following are elements of the word *development?*
   slow   sudden   step by step   growth   change

   EXAMPLE: The teachers keep careful records of each child's *development.*

5. *EXAMPLE:* The teacher worked patiently with the little boy until he *succeeded* in learning to tie his shoes.

   Finish the sentences:
   After many attempts, the athlete finally succeeded in . . .
   I hope to . . .

6. Remember when you were a child, how it took you a long time to understand the idea, the *concept,* of time? At an early age you had no clear idea of how long a year would be, nor a week, nor even the hour that your parents asked you to be quiet so they could take an afternoon nap. An understanding of those *concept*s came with experience.

   What are some other *concepts* that children have difficulty understanding? Can you remember any from your own experience?

   EXAMPLE: Dr. Montessori introduced children to new *concepts* and processes as they became ready to learn them.

7. What are the steps in the *process* of winning an Olympic gold medal in your favorite event?

   a. _____

   b. _____

   c. _____

   (etc.)

8. Divide the following words into *concrete* and *abstract* nouns.

diary   ambition   knowledge   belief   hero   controversy
inhabitants   report   value   loads   encouragement   nomads

Concrete	*Abstract*
_____	_____
_____	_____
_____	_____
_____	_____
_____	_____
_____	_____

REVIEW

Now that you have studied the vocabulary, re-read or re-skim the passage.

READING FOUR

AN AFRICAN-CENTERED PUBLIC SCHOOL
IN DETROIT, MICHIGAN

1   The Paul Robeson Academy in Detroit, Michigan, is a public elementary
school that combines instruction in traditional subjects such as math, science,
and history with a special focus on African cultures and history. African values
and methods of education are emphasized throughout. The original purpose of
the school was to serve the needs of young African-American boys, aged four to
eight years; however, the school does accept some African-American girls and
some white children as well.

2   Principal Ray Johnson puts great emphasis on involving parents in their children's education. The parents actually sign a contract promising to help their children at home, and to attend meetings and put in volunteer[1] time at the school when possible. One father volunteered to teach a class how to build a traditional Tanzanian house, (a project) that not only taught the students Tanzanian culture and construction techniques,[2] but also developed their spirit of cooperation and responsibility.[3] Johnson refers to an "African village model," where "everyone in the school is a teacher, parents being the primary teachers."

3   Students' responsibilities extend beyond the classroom walls and into the community. All of them, from the oldest to the youngest, are required to perform some community service, such as helping the elderly, each week. They are not just taught traditional school subjects, but also are trained[4] to become responsible[3] citizens.

4   The school is controversial even among African-Americans, some of whom fear that in focusing on African cultures and values, the curriculum[5] doesn't pay enough attention to more traditional subjects and points of view. But Johnson responds that all the basics are taught, only with added emphasis on the African heritage[6] of his students. In spite of[7] the doubts of (some,) there seems to be plenty of interest from the community: there's a long waiting list of parents who want to enroll their children.

After You Read

Identify the circled reference words.

COMPREHENSION QUESTIONS

1. Who are the students at the Paul Robeson Academy?

_____

_____

2. Identify two ways in which this approach differs from traditional education.

_____

_____

3. Why did the founders of this school want to establish a school with such an approach?

_____

_____

4. How similar or different is the parental involvement at P.R.A. from the parental involvement in the elementary school you went to?

_____

_____

TAKING NOTES AS YOU READ

Each of the paragraphs in this reading contains what's called a *topic sentence:* a single sentence that identifies the main idea of the paragraph. Can you find them?

HINT: The most common place it might appear is at the beginning of the paragraph. The second most common place is the last sentence. The third would be somewhere in the middle. And finally, many paragraphs don't have an actual topic sentence, although they do have a main idea or purpose.

Everything else in the paragraph *supports* the topic sentence by giving details about it. As you did with the reading on the Montessori Method, look at each paragraph and identify the way this information is organized: chronology, examples or features, cause and effect, comparison/contrast, or problem/solution.

Paragraph 1: _____

Paragraph 2: _____

Paragraph 3: _____

Paragraph 4: _____

Make notes of the most important points and details in the margin, using one of the formats from page 98 for each paragraph. When you finish, compare your work with a classmate's and then show it to your teacher.

Vocabulary

VOCABULARY IN CONTEXT

1. In ¶2, "the parents actually sign a *contract* promising to help their children at home. . . " What do you suppose a *contract* is?
   Why do you think so?
2. In ¶4, "There seems to be *plenty* of interest in the community: there's a long waiting list of parents who want to enroll their children." What might *plenty* mean?
   What words are the clues?

VOCABULARY STUDY: A CONFUSING PAIR

Here's a sentence from the article on "Alternative Schools in the United States" from page 90:

"The basic *principle* followed by alternative schools is that not all children have the same goals and the same ways of learning."

This one is from the article on the Paul Robeson Academy:

"*Principal* Ray Johnson puts great emphasis on involving parents in their children's education."

You looked up the word *principle* earlier, so you know what it means. From the context, what can you tell about the word *principal*?

Notice that Ray Johnson is the only person mentioned by name in the article. What do you suppose this word means?

Is there any difference in pronunciation? Look them up and pronounce them both.

KEYWORDS

1. volunteer ¶2
2. technique ¶2
3. responsibility, responsible ¶s 2, 3
4. train* ¶3
5. curriculum ¶4
6. heritage ¶4
7. in spite of* ¶4

KEYWORD EXERCISE

1. Students at the Paul Robeson Academy have to perform some kind of community service each week, such as helping the elderly. Name two other examples of community service that they might *volunteer* to do.

   a. _____

   b. _____

2. Think about the kinds of *techniques* involved in painting a picture, cooking something, performing a particular sport. Explain to a partner the features or *techniques* of one of these activities, or of another activity of your own choice.

   EXAMPLE: One volunteer taught the students Tanzanian construction *techniques.*

3. What are some things that you are *responsible* for doing now, but which you didn't use to be *responsible* for doing? Write them here:

   _____

   _____

   _____

   EXAMPLE: Students are trained to become *responsible* citizens.

4. The following are some educational methods. Rank them from best to worst as ways to *train* someone to do something.
   lectures   practice   discussions
   reading assignments   demonstrations

   (*best*)   **a.** _____

   b. _____

   c. _____

   d. _____

   (*worst*)   **e.** _____

5. The *curriculum* of a school is the list of courses that are taught there. The *curriculum* also refers to the goals and objectives of each course. Ask your teacher to identify some of the goals of this course for you (although she or he no doubt did so at the beginning of the term).

   EXAMPLE: The Robeson Academy's *curriculum* also includes the usual basic subjects.

6. Look back at the reading passage and find an example of African *heritage*. Give an example of your own cultural or familial *heritage*.

   EXAMPLE: The curriculum emphasizes the African *heritage* of the students.

7. *EXAMPLE:* *In spite of* the doubts of some, there seems to be plenty of interest in the community.

   Finish the sentences:
   He finished the race in spite of . . .
   In spite of the icy roads, . . .

VOCABULARY REVIEW

Now that you have studied the vocabulary, re-read or re-skim the passage.

We are students of words: we are shut up in schools, and colleges, and recitation-rooms, for ten or fifteen years, and come out at last with a bag of wind, a memory of words, and do not know a thing.

—*Ralph Waldo Emerson*

READING FIVE

The time was the late 1960s. A young man named Eliot Wigginton was just starting his teaching career. He had accepted a job at a rural high school in the Appalachian mountains of Georgia, far from the nearest large city. The school included both boarding students from outside the area and day students from the local community. Wigginton was feeling very discouraged because none of his students took his classes seriously. He was using the traditional methods and curriculum that he had been taught to use, but they weren't working. He wrote a letter to a friend about his experience:

> One class in particular grates. It has about four . . . dorm students, and twenty-four . . . community ones who can't pass a thing they are taking. They enter my class, turn off their ears, turn on their mouths, and settle down for a period of socializing. Every time I think I've gotten through to some of them, one of two things happens—either someone belches and breaks the spell, or the period ends and they are out in the free world again where the last fifty minutes evaporate like mist from dry ice. They really do *not* see why they should have English, and in a sudden revelation several days ago I suddenly realized that I couldn't see why they should have it either. Lots of them will never leave this area of the country except perhaps to go to war—they will never read or write—they will help with a gas station and love it—that's all they need. . . . so why am I here? I keep trying to think of something that will wake them up that they may also find useful someday, and I can't.

What was Wigginton feeling depressed about? Do you think he was right in deciding that his students shouldn't really have to develop their English skills, or was he just discouraged when he said that? Given what he said in the last two sentences, do you think that students with these interests and ambitions should be excused from having to study a traditional curriculum?

Wigginton knew he had to do something about his problem class. They were driving him crazy, and he believed that he wasn't meeting their needs. What do you think he should have done?

*   *   *

The Appalachian Mountains run northeast to southwest, parallel to the Atlantic coast of the United States but several hundred miles inland. The stereotype of people who live in the southern Appalachian area is that they are poor and uneducated, very traditional, and closed to outsiders, though of course this is an overgeneralization. As an outsider to the area, Eliot Wigginton wasn't able to force his curriculum or methods onto his students. He was going to have to try something completely different in order to find common ground on which they could all meet each other.

Reading process: As you read, use the "Good Habits During Reading" methods that you learned about on page 50. If you need to, review the procedure before you start. Remember, these are the steps:

- Make predictions
- Form mental pictures
- Make connections with your own experience, or with something you already know
- Recognize your reading problems
- Solve these problems

When you finish, fill out the chart on the handout that your teacher gave you earlier.

NOTE: This reading is also on the tape.

FOXFIRE TURNS 25 AS RECORD OF FOLKLIFE

1   Twenty-five years ago, rookie teacher Eliot Wigginton was trying desperately to get his students interested in English class. So he asked them: Just what would they be willing to do to learn? After a lengthy debate,[1] the students decided. "They chose to put out a magazine," he recalled.[2] "They chose the title and they chose the contents." The result was *Foxfire,* a magazine on mountain folklife. . . . [T]he publication was wildly successful—both as a teaching tool and as a magazine that made the region's heritage of self-sufficiency known[3] to an interested nation.

2   Wigginton's original students at Rabun Gap School belonged to two distinct[4] groups. About half of them were budding juvenile delinquents from Atlanta, 100 miles to the southwest. They were sent to the private school for discipline[5] or as an escape from family problems. The rest were poor children living in the hills and hollows of the southern Appalachian Mountains, above the broad valley where the school's red brick buildings were clustered. . . . The boarding students and the locals had little in common except a healthy disrespect for school and no plans for college. They saw little use for the literature and grammar lessons that Wigginton had on the agenda.

3   "I was just trying to get them to cooperate so we'd have a chance to learn English," Wigginton recalled.

4   For teachers today, the word Foxfire has come to mean a democratic and cooperative approach to education at all grade levels. Foxfire teachers allow students to choose how they will learn in order to pass the standardized tests and graduate. For those interested in mountain folklife, the still-thriving magazine has preserved[6] evidence of a dying lifestyle among the independent, isolated people of the southern Appalachians. "It's unique," said Ellis Bateman, head of Partners in Education, a state program linking[7] local businesses with public schools. "It's a teaching technique that grew into a business within the school itself."

5   *Foxfire* magazine articles basically are transcriptions of interviews the high-school students conduct with their grandparents and neighbors about their lives and pasts. The topics range from[8] how (they) made lye soap to how they butchered hogs, from how they celebrated Christmas to why they chose to sell the family land to developers. "It uses the resources[9] of the community to help the youngsters learn about their community and at the same time learn reading, writing and arithmetic," Bateman said. "And (they)'re doing a real service to the community by documenting it and preserving its heritage." . . .

6   Just what is a "Foxfire" class? Wigginton describes it as "intensely collaborative,[10] democratic, problem solving, analytical and reflective." In a Foxfire classroom, all the work flows from student desire and student concerns. The teacher is a collaborator, team leader and guide, rather than a boss. The process emphasizes peer teaching, small group work and teamwork. Foxfire makes clear connections between the classroom work and surrounding communities and the real world. There must be an audience beyond the teacher for students' work. And Foxfire projects include time for reflection on the aesthetic experience, as well as an ongoing evaluation for skills and content, and changes in students' attitude.

7   Wigginton's English students at Rabun County High still publish a quarterly magazine on their community. Tenth-grader Tammy Henderson called the magazine class "the highlight[11] of my day. It's a place I know I can be creative," she said. "I don't have to feel like I'm just going to be lectured." She and other students learn grammar, spelling, letter writing, composition and interviewing techniques, as well as a variety of business skills, while publishing the magazine. . . .

8   Wigginton, meanwhile,[12] is much the same person who solved his rookie teaching dilemma[13] by asking his students for help. Now 48 years old, he still teaches English. He still lives in a log cabin he built in 1971 with the help of volunteers seeking escape from the Rabun Gap School dormitories on weekends. And he still writes about his work, as he did in the early years when he was trying to drum up donations to keep the magazine afloat. . . .

9   Twenty-five years after his teaching debut at Rabun Gap School, Wigginton recalls the start of Foxfire as "basically an act of desperation on the part of a teacher trying to survive." He attributed the phenomenal public interest in the magazine and books initially to the back-to-the-earth, back-to-the-roots movements of the 1970s. But Foxfire continues to work as a teaching technique, he said, because "we had stumbled across some essential[14] truths by trial and error."[15] . . .

Threads

The important thing is not so much that every child should be taught, but that every child should be given the wish to learn.

John Lubbock, Lord Avebury

After You Read

Identify the circled reference words.

PARAPHRASING AND SUMMARIZING THE MAIN IDEAS

First, identify the most important information in each paragraph. It may be one topic sentence, or it may be just parts of two sentences. Compare your choices with a partner's.

Now summarize the article by writing a sentence that contains the main idea of each paragraph. Don't just copy the author's sentences; paraphrase them in your own words. When you finish, compare your work with your partner's and make whatever changes you think would improve both. Your teacher can help you too.

Paragraph 6 has been done for you as an example.

¶1: _____

_____

_____

¶2: _____

HINT: Is the part about the two groups of students a main idea?

_____

_____

¶4: _____

_____

_____

¶5: _____

_____

_____

¶6: Foxfire classes are highly democratic and teach skills that are related to the world outside the classroom.

¶7: _____

_____

_____

¶8: _____

_____

_____

¶9: _____

_____

_____

TWO DIFFICULT SENTENCES

From ¶2:

"The boarding students and the locals had little in common except *a healthy disrespect* for school and no plans for college. They saw *little use* for the literature and grammar lessons that Wigginton had on the agenda."

In the first sentence, the word *healthy* refers not to the students, but to their *disrespect.* It means that their disrespect was very strong.

If you changed the second sentence to read "They saw *a little use* for the literature and grammar lessons that Wigginton had on the agenda," how would the meaning be different?

What does the original sentence mean, then?

FREEWRITING: YOUR OPINION OF FOXFIRE

What do you think of Wigginton's "solution"? If you were in the Foxfire class, would you take it as seriously as you would a traditional class? What do you think of an approach to education in which the students have the power to make decisions like this? Does it have more advantages, or more disadvantages, than a traditional teacher-directed class?

Vocabulary

KEYWORDS

1. debate ¶1
2. recall ¶1
3. made known ¶1
4. distinct ¶2
5. discipline ¶2
6. preserve* ¶4
7. link ¶4
8. range from* ¶5
9. resource ¶5
10. collaborative ¶6
11. highlight ¶7
12. meanwhile* ¶8
13. dilemma ¶8
14. essential ¶9
15. trial and error ¶9

KEYWORD EXERCISE

1. *EXAMPLE:*   So he asked them: Just what would they be willing to do to learn? After a lengthy *debate,* the students decided.

   Imagine that you are Wigginton's students. What are some of the specific things you might say in this *debate?*

2. You can divide the word *recall* into its two parts, *re-* + *-call.* What's the connection between the meaning of the two parts and the meaning of the whole word?

   Meaning of the two parts: _____

   Meaning of the whole word: _____

   EXAMPLE: Wigginton *recalled* how the students made their decision to start a magazine.

3. How did Wigginton and his students *make* the area's traditions *known* to the rest of the country?

_____

_____

4. In what way were Wigginton's two groups of students *distinct?*

_____

_____

   EXAMPLE: Wigginton's original students belonged to two *distinct* groups.

5. Which of the following are elements of *discipline?*
   flexible   strict   punishment   control   rules   free   obey

   EXAMPLE: Some students were sent to the private school for *discipline.*

6. *EXAMPLE:* *Foxfire* magazine has helped to *preserve* information about traditional ways of life in the Appalachian Mountains of north Georgia.

   Finish the sentences:

   _____ is a way of preserving foods.

   The carpenter _____ the table in order to preserve the wood.

7. *EXAMPLE:* Satellites help to *link* people by telephone from continent to continent.

   Finish the sentences:
   Police linked the murder to . . .
   Charles Darwin linked human beings . . .

8. *EXAMPLE:* The topics *ranged from* how they made lye soap to how they butchered hogs.

   Finish the sentences:
   My interests range from . . .
   Causes of the war . . .

9. Which of the following could be called a country's natural *resources?*
   petroleum   people   water   gold   agriculture

   EXAMPLE: The magazine uses the *resources* of the community to help the students learn.

10. Give an example of a project that you and a partner or partners *collaborated* on in the past, or any project that persons would need to *collaborate* on.

    EXAMPLE: The teacher is the *collaborator,* team leader and guide, rather than the boss.

11. *Meanings:*
    • To *highlight* words on a page is to mark them with color so that they will be noticeable.

      EXAMPLE: I *highlighted* the main ideas of the article.

    • The *highlight* of something is its most interesting or exciting part.

      EXAMPLE: The *highlight* of the evening was the fireworks.

    • What are the similarities of the two meanings?

12. *Finish the sentences:*

The old man sat at home all day counting his money. *Meanwhile,* his son . . .

Today the weather is _____ here. Meanwhile, at my family's home, . . .

The master criminal was planning the perfect crime. Meanwhile, the police . . .

13. In a *dilemma,* you have to make a difficult choice between two or more alternatives. In English this is sometimes called "being caught between a rock and a hard place." What's the connection between this quotation and the meaning of *dilemma?*

Give an example of a *dilemma* that you or someone you know has been in.

EXAMPLE: Wigginton solved his teaching *dilemma* by asking his students for help.

14. Is the ability to use English *essential* to your future? If so, how?

EXAMPLE: Wigginton believes that giving the students a voice in decision-making is *essential* to successful education.

15. *Trial and error* is a kind of experiential learning without benefit of a teacher. What is something that you have learned by *trial and error?*

EXAMPLE: Wigginton developed his methods of education by *trial and error.*

REVIEW

Now that you have studied the vocabulary, re-read or re-skim the passage.

Third Alternative for a Longer Project: Doing an Oral History

Find an older person in your community, and do an oral history of something interesting that that person can tell you about. Here are some ideas:

- How _____ was different when she or he was a child (education, childhood, daily life, etc.)
- Something she or her parents learned how to do that isn't often done today
- Personal or family values when he was young
- Hard times in her life
- Celebrations when he was young

Once you and the person have decided on a topic, make a tape recording of the person talking. Feel free to record your own questions and comments as you go along.

Later, listen to the recording and write down anything that you want to include, *but you must write it down exactly as the person said it.* If you want to leave anything out, write three spaced periods . . . (this is called an *ellipsis*) to indicate that something was omitted. When you finish, listen to the recording as you read along, and make corrections as needed. This word-for-word written copy is called the *transcript* of the recording.

For your final report, write an introduction telling what you did, what your purpose was, and who the person was. Then give the transcript. Finally, write a concluding paragraph telling what you learned, your opinions, and/or your comments.

Writing an Essay: How Would You Have Learned Best?

Write an essay on the following topic:

Compare the way that you were educated with one of the three ways described in this chapter:

1. The Montessori method
2. The Paul Robeson Academy method
3. The Foxfire method

Do you think that you would have gotten a better education if you had gone to one of these three schools? Or on the other hand, do you think that the education you received was better? Explain your opinion, giving specific examples of what you are talking about.

LEARNING STRATEGY

Managing Your Learning: Reading on your own outside of class improves your reading skills.

Evaluating Learning Strategies

Look back over the chapter at the learning strategies that were presented. Were there any that weren't especially helpful for you? What wasn't helpful about them? Which ones did you find especially helpful? Think about times and ways that you can keep using them in your future reading.

Evaluating Your Learning

	Very little	*Quite a bit*	*A lot*
You've increased your vocabulary.	————	————	————
Your comprehension is stronger.	————	————	————
You can identify the topic sentences of paragraphs.	————	————	————
You can take good notes from your reading.	————	————	————
You've learned something about alternative education.	————	————	————

Verbs
adjust*
consider
convert
design
emphasize*
involve
link
make known
preserve*
range from*
recall
stress
succeed*
tend*
train*
volunteer

Adjectives
abstract
artificial
based on*
basic
broad
collaborative
concrete
distinct
essential
experiential
fragmented
holistic
responsible
uncertain*

Nouns
basis
concept
curriculum
debate
development
dilemma
discipline
dissatisfaction
emphasis
evil
heritage
highlight
lecture
minority group
observation
opportunity
principle
process
quality
resource
responsibility
technique
trial and error

Adverbs
in spite of*
meanwhile*

Prepositions
on one's own*
throughout*

Wolf Children

PLANNING YOUR LEARNING

Review your overall goal statement. How much progress did you make toward it in the last chapter? Do you want to change it? Think about how you can work to meet your goal as you study this new chapter.

- How many words do you want to learn? (minimum 37, the number of "keywords" in the chapter)
- What grade would you like to make on the vocabulary section of the exam at the end of the chapter?
- What grade would you like to make on the reading comprehension section of the exam?
- What are you going to read outside of class?

PREVIEWING THE CHAPTER

- Think about the title of this chapter. What do you think a "wolf child" is?
- Look in the Table of Contents at the titles of the three readings in this chapter. Look through the chapter at the pictures. What are some things that you would like to learn about?
- Which reading looks the most interesting?

PREPARING TO READ: CONTENT (DISCUSSION)

1. How are human beings different from animals?
2. Which of these human characteristics are "learned" (for example, from our parents), and which are truly "biological" (automatic to all humans, not dependent on being taught)?
3. If we wanted to find out which are learned and which are biological, how might we do this?

PREPARING TO READ: CONTENT (FREEWRITING)

1. Think about your own childhood before you read the following story. Who taught you to do the human behaviors that you listed above in Item 2?
2. If you had been brought up by wolves instead of humans, how would you be different? What could you do that you can't do now, and what couldn't you do that you can do now?
3. Do you believe stories about animals "adopting" human babies?

PREPARING TO READ: VOCABULARY

You will encounter these words in this chapter's readings. Work with a partner. If you don't know an answer, use your dictionary or skip that question.

1. Horses, cattle, sheep, and goats are called *tame* or *domestic* animals. What's the adjective used to describe animals that aren't tame?

   w_____

2. If humans wanted to bring a wolf child back into human society, they would probably have to catch it and force it to come. What's another verb for this

   action? c_____

3. A wolf child would b_____ more like a wolf than like a

   human. What's the noun form of this verb? _____

4. A wolf child would have to l_____ to do all the things that normal humans are taught by their parents when they are very young.

5. Learning to walk, to talk, to laugh, etc., is part of the process of human

   d_____.

6. Parents teach their children to live comfortably in human society. This process

   is called s_____. (It's the verb form of the noun *society.*)

 READING ONE

Reading process: This reading has been divided into four parts. Everyone will read the first part, but then your teacher will assign each of you to read Part Two, Three, or Four in a limited time. When you finish, you will meet with two students who read the other parts, and you'll tell each other what you learned.

NOTE: Parts of Mr. Singh's journal are on the tape.

KAMALA, A WOLF-GIRL OF INDIA

Part One

In the year 1920, in an isolated part of India, a missionary named J. A. L. Singh was visiting some isolated villages. One of the inhabitants complained to him of an evil spirit, a "man-ghost" that was living nearby with a family of wolves. The villagers were very frightened of this creature. Singh asked to see it, so they took him to the place late one afternoon. In the half-light of evening he saw a group of wolves emerging one by one from their "home," a hole in a mound of earth. Singh counted three adult wolves and two young cubs. Then he saw the "man-ghost," which did indeed have the body of a small human, but whose head "was a big ball of something

Amala and Kamala asleep overlapping

covering the shoulders," as he later wrote in his journal. Immediately after it came another, smaller version of the same kind of creature. Singh immediately realized that these two beings were human children, even though they acted exactly like the wolves, looking around to the right and left before coming out of the hole and walking on all fours. The villagers wanted to shoot them, but Singh stopped them from doing this. Instead, he suggested that they frighten the wolves away and capture the man-ghosts. This they did, but not easily; the human children were wilder than the wolves, and tried to attack the people.

Part Two

2   The two "man-ghosts" turned out to be two little girls, one around one and a half and the other about eight years of age. Mr. Singh took the children home with him to the city of Midnapore, where he directed an orphanage. He and his wife

Kamala receiving biscuits from Mrs. Singh's hand

named the younger "Amala" and the older "Kamala." They were a terrible sight, covered with dirt and sores. After the Singhs bathed them and cut off their filthy matted hair, the children looked more human, although they certainly did not behave[1] in any human way. They could not stand up at all. They moved around mostly on their elbows and knees; when they "ran" on their hands and feet, it was almost impossible to catch them. The only food they would eat was raw meat and raw milk; they chased chickens and tried to eat the bodies of any dead animals that they found on the grounds of the orphanage. Their tongues hung out through their thick red lips, and they growled and showed their teeth when anyone came near them. During the day they stayed in the darkest corners of the room with their backs to the other children, showing not the least interest in anything that was going on. It was obvious[2] that they wanted nothing to do with human company. They repeatedly tried to escape, and they bit any of the other children who tried to stop them. Clearly they missed the company of wolves and wanted nothing more than to rejoin their "family." At night they livened up, howling and barking noisily like wolves, but they were unable[3] to speak or to understand human speech.

> They had a powerful instinct and could smell meat or anything from a great distance like animals. On the fifteenth of September, 1922, Kamala smelled meat from a distance of seventy yards and ran quickly to the kitchen veranda, where meat was being dressed. With a ferocious look, she tried to grab it, her eyes rolling, jaws moving from side to side, and teeth chattering while she made a fearful growling sound, neither human or animal.
>
> —From the journal of J. A. L. Singh

3   Amala and Kamala had very sharpened senses[4], as wolves and some other animals do. They could see perfectly well on the darkest night when humans could see nothing. Their sense of smell was very sensitive, especially for raw meat, which they could detect from a long distance away. Like wolves, they always used to smell their food carefully before they would eat it. They also had very sharp hearing. When they were fed, they would not sit at the table; they ate from dishes set on the ground or the floor. When they were thirsty, they would crouch in front of their bowls on the floor and lap up the milk or water with their tongues, like dogs. They seemed insensitive to heat or cold. Singh wrote in his diary, "In cold in winter we used to make them wear clothing, but they resented it very much and used to tear it to pieces as soon as they were left alone. We tried to cover them up with

blankets at night, but they threw (them) away, and if repeated, they used to tear them off. They did not feel cold at all, and used to love to be without any covering or clothing on their body, even in the coldest weather. They were never seen shivering in the most chilly season, nor perspiring in the hottest day or night." Like animals, they feared fire. They hated being given baths.

Part Three

4   Coming to the orphanage was a traumatic[5] experience for the little girls, but a worse one followed about a year later. They both became very ill, and Amala died. At first Kamala did not appear[6] to understand what had happened, but eventually[7] she seemed to comprehend that her "sister" was gone, and a single drop of water fell from each eye. They were the only tears she ever shed. Afterwards she seemed to be very lonely, and she began to keep company with the animals of the orphanage. She first developed[8] an affection for the kid goats, then for the cat and for the dogs, with (whom) she ate from the same plate at feeding time. The Singhs then removed the animals to a farm, leaving Kamala with no other choice but human company. At this point she seemed in danger of going crazy from loneliness, but still she wanted nothing to do with humans.

Kamala standing up for the first time

5   The Singhs thought hard about how to win Kamala over. Mr. Singh believed that her human nature[9] had been replaced by wolf-nature so early in her life that she really thought of herself as a wolf. In order to become human, she would have to unlearn (that whole first nature) and replace it with (something very foreign to her.) This could only happen if she came to want to do it. It seemed to the Singhs that the person with the best chance of getting through to her was Mrs. Singh, a loving and motherly woman. She worked with incredible patience to build a feeling of trust in Kamala. This unbelievably slow process involved eliminating[10] some of her wolf habits and replacing them with human ones, but (she) fought so bitterly against the change that it took years to happen. When she came to the orphanage, Reverend Singh noted, it was as though "she had to begin life from her very infancy over again."

6   One of the ways which Mrs. Singh used to try to awaken a sense of trust and affection in Kamala was by massaging her, a common practice by Indian mothers with their children. She also talked with her tenderly and patiently. The first time that Kamala indicated[11] an understanding of what she said was about three months after Amala's death. Kamala approached[12] Mrs. Singh, who asked her if she was hungry, and she nodded yes and stayed by her side instead of trying to move away. At this point Kamala must have been around nine years old, but in terms of human development she behaved like a child of one and a half.

Part Four

7   As the years passed, Kamala very gradually[13] began to behave in a more human way, taking food with her hand instead of with her teeth, drinking from a glass, bathing herself. She seemed to be intelligent, and the adults who observed her concluded that her odd behavior was the result not of stupidity, but of growing up with the wolves instead of with human models of behavior. As Reverend Singh wrote in his journal,

> First of all, her dislike to all that was human presented itself in a very strong form, as we have seen before, and then gradually and very very slowly, it changed into a liking, and then the pleasure in that liking attracted

Threads

Every man has a wild animal within him.

Frederick the Great

her to new things and actions so that she acquired new knowledge and new practice to the making up of a different life altogether. All this came to pass during her stay with us during those years from 1920 to 1929.

Within three years she no longer wanted to go outside at night; indeed, she came to fear the night and preferred to be inside. At around the same time she first stood up on her two legs, but it took about three more years for her to learn to walk, and she never was able to run upright[14] like a human child. By 1925 she had developed a taste for salt with her food. A year later the Singhs noticed that she seemed to be enjoying her baths. She developed a strong preference for the color red, both of toys and of clothing. She would pick red toys out of all the rest and would run away with them in her mouth.

8   Over the years she began to understand language more and more. By 1923 she could nod and shake her head to indicate "yes" or "no," though she could not speak yet. Within another year she had learned to say a number of words which meant *yes, no, rice, all right, red, I,* and some of the children's names. Reverend Singh kept a list of the words and the simple sentences as Kamala spoke them (such as—in Bengali—"Mama come" when Mrs. Singh approached). By 1926 she could carry on a very limited conversation with a vocabulary of about three dozen words. However, her understanding was better than her speaking, and she had no trouble following instructions. By 1929, at the end of her short life, she had a speaking vocabulary of about fifty words and she was able to talk easily with the others who lived at the orphanage and to call them by their names. Her pronunciation was never clear, however.

9   As she took on more human habits, it was observed that her ability to see in the dark, her keen hearing and sense of smell, and her insensitivity to heat and cold left her. She began to like her blanket at night, and insisted on wearing clothes, especially red ones. She would eat and drink only from *her* plate and glass. By 1926 she began to feel affection towards the younger children in the orphanage and would do her best to take care of them, though in very limited ways. By 1927 her relationship with the dogs had changed: they barked at her as though they recognized her as a human, not one of themselves; and she responded[15] with fear and avoided[16] them.

10   Unfortunately, Kamala's health began to fail almost exactly nine years from the date of her capture. On November 14, 1929, she passed away. By this time she must have been around seventeen years old, though in terms of human development she behaved more like a child of about two and a half.

After You Read

COMPREHENSION QUESTIONS

Questions for Part Two:

1. What were the names and ages of the two children?

_____

2. Tell four ways in which they behaved like animals.

    a. _____

    b. _____

    c. _____

    d. _____

3. What was their attitude toward human beings?

_____

Questions for Part Three:
1. What happened to Amala?

_____

2. How did Kamala react to this event?

_____

3. Which human being did Kamala feel closest to?

_____

4. How did this human being win Kamala's trust?

_____

_____

Questions for Part Four:
1. Give four examples of human behavior that Kamala learned.

    a. _____

    b. _____

    c. _____

    d. _____

2. Give two examples of animal behavior that Kamala unlearned.

    a. _____

    b. _____

3. What happened to Kamala at the end of the story? How old was she when this event happened?

_____

_____

REVIEW: COMPLETING THE READING

Now read the whole passage.
Identify the circled reference words.

LEARNING STRATEGY

Forming Concepts: Outlining helps you comprehend information in a simple way.

OUTLINING THE READING PASSAGE

There are ten paragraphs in the story, and each one has one main idea or purpose (as in all good English writing). See if you can identify them. The first has been done for you.

¶1 The children were discovered and were removed from the wolves.

¶2 _____

¶3 _____

¶4 _____

¶5 _____

¶6 _____

¶7 _____

¶8 _____

¶9 _____

¶10 _____

Now read your list from start to finish. It will provide you with a quick summary of the story. Compare it with a partner's list and discuss any differences. Revise your list if you need to.

Vocabulary

KEYWORDS

1. behave ¶2
2. obvious ¶2
3. be unable to* ¶2
4. senses ¶3
5. traumatic ¶4
6. appear ¶4
7. eventually ¶4
8. develop ¶4
9. human nature ¶5
10. eliminate* ¶5
11. indicate* ¶6
12. approach* ¶6
13. gradually ¶7
14. upright ¶7
15. respond ¶9
16. avoid* ¶9

KEYWORD EXERCISE

1. Name some things that (1) you, (2) infants, or (3) wolves are *unable* to do.

   EXAMPLE: Kamala was *unable* to walk upright at first.

2. Name the five *senses.* In your own culture do you have five, or do you have more or fewer? Do you know what a *sixth sense* is?

   EXAMPLE: Kamala's wolflike *senses* enabled her to see in the dark.

3. *Meanings:*
   - To *approach* someone means to come near them.

     EXAMPLE: Kamala *approached* Mrs. Singh when she felt hungry.

   - An *approach* to a problem is one way of thinking about it or trying to solve it.

     EXAMPLE: One *approach* to learning vocabulary is to write the words on little cards and then study them.

   - Explain the similarities between the two meanings.

4. Which of the following objects are *upright?*
   a wall   a road   a rug   a tree   a door

5. Which of the following would you most like to *avoid?*
   a bad meal   a war   an examination   a job   an argument

   EXAMPLE: Kamala *avoided* human company as much as possible.

6. Which of the following words does not mean the same thing as the others?
   obvious   balanced   clear   plain

   EXAMPLE: It was *obvious* that Kamala wanted to rejoin her wolf family.

7. Which of the following experiences would be most *traumatic* for a small child? For an adult?
   getting lost in a shopping center   being in an earthquake
   moving to another country

   EXAMPLE: Amala's death was a *traumatic* experience for Kamala.

8. *Meanings:*
   - *Nature* is all the living beings, things, and processes in the world that were not made or caused by people.

     QUESTION: Name your favorite event or process in nature.

   - *Human nature* is the basic qualities and ways of behavior that most people have.

     QUESTION: Name two characteristics of *human nature.*

   - Explain the similarities between the two meanings.

9. Which of the following words are connected with the idea of *eliminate?*
   realize   misuse   remove   delete   subtract

   EXAMPLE: As the years passed, Kamala *eliminated* her wolf nature and took on a human nature.

10. Which of the following words does not mean the same as the others?
    point out   show   require   *indicate*

    EXAMPLE: Kamala's responses to Mrs. Singh *indicated* that her attitude had begun to change.

REVIEW

Now that you have studied the vocabulary, re-read or re-skim the passage.

Personalizing: Identifying yourself with a person in a story helps you to understand the material better because it becomes more real to you.

Writing: Kamala's Memoirs

Kamala never learned to write, but if she had, she might have written her own story before she died. Imagine that you are Kamala, and write your story. Consider the following questions, but feel free to write this any way that you wish to.

1. What happened to your human parents? How did you come to live with the wolves?
2. Describe what happened when you first came to the orphanage. What did you think of the people? What did they want you to do? How did you feel about this?
3. As the years passed, how did your feelings about your new life change? Why did you decide to learn to walk and talk? Did you like it?
4. Which do you like better, life among humans or life among wolves? Do you miss your wolf family? Do you think you'll ever return to live with them or perhaps to visit them?

READING TWO

As you will see in the following passage, the term "wolf children" is used not just for children brought up by wolves or other animals. In a more general way, it applies to any children who grow up isolated from human society and human models. How was the next child's background different from Kamala's? How were their behavior and development similar?

Reading process: This reading has been divided into six parts. Your teacher will assign you a part in addition to the first part.

THE MYSTERY OF KASPAR HAUSER

Part One

One pleasant May evening in 1828, a very strange-looking young man appeared upon the streets of the German city of Nuremberg. At first it looked as though he were drunk: he was unable to stand upright or to walk well. In his hands he held a letter addressed to a military captain in the city, and he kept repeating a sentence that sounded like, "I want to be a soldier like my father," though the words seemed to mean nothing to him, as though he had merely memorized the sounds. He was given some meat and beer, but he reacted violently to the taste, as though they were poison. Bread and water were all he could take. He was unable to comprehend questions about what his name was and where he came from.

2   He was taken to the captain, who opened the envelope which the young man carried. Inside were two letters. One of (them) was written by an unnamed person who said that when the young man was an infant, (he) had been left with (him) by the mother, who asked him to bring the boy up with his own children. This he had done, but he had been told to bring the boy to Nuremberg when he was seventeen years old so that he could serve in the military. The letter-writer did not identify himself and said that the place where he lived must also be kept secret. In the same envelope was a shorter, much older piece of paper on which someone had written, "You must educate the child. . . . When he is seventeen years old send him to Nuremberg to the sixth [military] regiment, for there his father also was. . . . He was born the 30th April, 1812. I am a poor girl and cannot support him. His father is dead."

3   The young man did indeed appear to be about seventeen years of age, in spite of the fact that he behaved more like a child of two. To everyone's surprise when someone offered him a pen and paper, he took them and wrote in clear letters the name "Kaspar Hauser," though he could not say it.

Kaspar Hauser:
As appearing in Feuerbach's book of 1832

Part Two

4   No one knew what to do with him, so they took him to a local prison, where the kind prison-keeper took him into his family. The man's children began to teach Kaspar how to speak and to sit with them at the dinner table. He could eat only bread and water at first, and only gradually[1] was he able to take other foods. If anyone put even a tiny amount of beer, wine, or coffee in his water, he became sick. He seemed to have had no experience at all with social customs or human ways of thinking. His face at first looked stupid and animal-like, though as the months passed it took on an expression of interest and intelligence and became completely human. When the sun went down he went to bed, but all day long he simply sat on the floor with his legs stretched out straight in front of him. He hardly knew how to use his hands and fingers at all. He was good-natured and sweet-tempered, however, and those who spent time with him became very fond[2] of him.

5   Kaspar's senses seemed much sharper than ordinary people's. He could see so well in the dark that he could even read (later, after he learned to read); in fact, his eyes were oversensitive and sunlight hurt them. His sense of hearing was also as sharp as an animal's. But his sense of smell was so sensitive that it caused him discomfort: some smells that most people consider pleasant, such as the fragrance of flowers, were terrible to him, and the smell of fresh meat made him sick. Years later, after he had learned to eat normal food, he commented that since he had begun to eat meat, his sense of sight had grown much weaker and he was no longer able to see in the dark.

6   He showed great interest in horses, and in particular[3] in toy horses. Noticing this, someone brought him some little wooden horses, and he was overcome with happiness. He would pet (them,) would decorate them with everything shiny and beautiful that he could find, and always put his bread to their mouths before eating and their mouths in his water cup before he took a drink. But as he began to learn more about people and the world around him, he lost interest in these toys.

Threads

The smell of fresh meat was, to him, the most horrible of smells.

Anselm von Feuerbach

Part Three

7   Kaspar was an intelligent, reflective person. When faced with a new object, idea, or behavior, he would withdraw into some inner place in his mind, standing very still and completely lost in thought until he could make sense of (it) by connecting it to something that he already understood. If the new thing were very hard for him to comprehend, his face would begin to twitch and he would become upset. Not surprisingly, after a few weeks of adjusting to so much newness, he actually fell ill. At this point a secondary-school teacher named Daumer offered to give him a home so that he could have a professional tutor and could live a quieter and calmer life. The household consisted of Daumer, his sister, and their mother, and they welcomed the young man into their little family.

8   As Kaspar began his education, one of the most interesting features was his inability to distinguish[4] reality from unreality, living beings from inanimate objects,[5] animal behavior from human behavior. He began to dream at night for the first time in his life, but he was not aware[6] that what he dreamed had not really happened: to him the memory of a dream was like the memory of real events. Someone brought him a mirror, and when he saw his reflection, he looked behind (it) to see who was hiding there. He treated toy animals as though they were alive, and once he became angry because a dirty statue in a garden did not wash itself. If a sheet of paper was blown away by the wind, he thought that it had run away from the table. He became angry at a cat for not sitting up straight and taking its food with its "hands"; he spoke to (it) as he would have to a human, and believed that it was simply unwilling to learn. He felt that animals ought to have to learn the same behaviors as he. At the beginning he used only two words for living creatures: all humans were "bua," and all animals were "ross" (a German dialect word for *horse*). Only their clothing enabled[7] him to distinguish men from women, and he refused to believe that children would one day become adults, or that (this) had happened to him.

9   He had strong feelings about particular colors: he feared anything that was black, disliked green and yellow, cared nothing about white, liked gold very much, and loved anything that was red. The sight of natural beauty did not move him at all; he greatly preferred a view of beautifully painted red houses through his bedroom window to another window's view of a green garden, which appeared to him like so much confusion.

I directed Caspar to look out of the window, pointing to the wide and extensive prospect of a beautiful landscape that presented itself to us in all the glory of summer; and I asked him whether what he saw was not very beautiful. He obeyed; but he instantly drew back, with visible horror, exclaiming, "Ugly! ugly!" and then pointing to the white wall of his chamber, he said, "There are not ugly." To my question, Why was it ugly? no other reply was made, but "Ugly! ugly!"

—*Anselm von Feuerbach*

---

10   Eventually Kaspar Hauser learned to speak very well, but his process of learning language was similar to the process that little children go through with their native language. The first words that he learned were nouns and verbs, then adjectives and adverbs. Words such as prepositions, articles, and conjunctions came much later. He used verbs in the infinitive rather than in tenses. It was a long time before he could understand or use the pronouns "I" or "you"; he would refer to himself as "Kaspar" and would speak to other people always using their names. He would apply a word to anything that it reminded him of, as when he spoke of a fat man as "the man with the great mountain."

Part Four

11   But what was the story of Kaspar's earlier life, that lost period when he could neither understand nor speak? How had he lived, and what accounted for his condition when he first appeared in Nuremberg? Once he had learned to

speak, he was able to tell the story. His only memories were of living in a very small locked room which he sometimes called a "hole" and sometimes a "cage." The only other human whom he knew he called "the man with whom I had always been," (whose) face he never saw but who left bread and water beside him when he was sleeping. In his cage Kaspar sat all day on the floor, barefooted, wearing only a shirt and a pair of trousers. He heard no sounds, saw no one except "the man," and never saw the sunlight. Sometimes his water tasted bitter, and then he fell into a deeper than normal sleep, and when he awoke, he would find himself wearing clean clothing and with freshly cut nails. The only objects in the hole with him were two wooden horses that he played with all day. He knew nothing, saw nothing, thought nothing. Because he had known nothing else, he was content.

> As long as he can recollect, he had always lived in a hole (a small low apartment which he sometimes calls a cage), where he had always sat upon the ground, with bare feet, and clothed only with a shirt and a pair of breeches. In his apartment he never heard a sound, whether produced by a man, by an animal, or by anything else. He never saw the heavens, nor did there ever appear a brightening (daylight) such as at Nuremberg. He never perceived any difference between day and night, and much less did he ever get sight of the beautiful lights in the heavens.
>
> —*Anselm von Feuerbach*

12   One day the man brought a small table into his room, stood behind him, and taught him to write his name with a pencil. Kaspar had no idea what this meant, what writing was, nor even that it was his name; but he enjoyed the activity and copied the letters over and over. Another time the man took hold of him around his waist from behind and tried to teach him to stand upright, but without much success, because Kaspar's legs and feet would not cooperate and it was very painful for him.

13   Then one day the man came and carried him out of his prison and took him on a journey. Even then he never showed his face. He put new clothes on Kaspar, including boots, which hurt his feet very much. He forced the boy to walk, but insisted that he look only at the ground and at his feet, so that he could see neither the man nor the countryside they were walking through. Eventually they stopped and the man put an envelope into his hand and left him. That was how he came to Nuremberg.

Part Five

14   Even so, Kaspar had no hard feelings for "the man with whom he had always been," and he was surprised when other people suggested that he should hate him. For a long time he defended the man. He said, "Man not bad, man me no bad done," and his only complaint was that the man had not returned to take him back "home," where his life had been simple and he had never had to adjust to so much that was unknown to him. He often commented that it seemed unfair that the people he had met since coming to Nuremberg knew so much, even the little children, while there were so very many things which he had yet to learn.

15   This attitude did not change until he had been in human society for about a year and a half. One clear August night, Professor Daumer took Kaspar outside to look at the stars. He had never seen or imagined anything so beautiful. For a long time he stood speechless as his tutor pointed out the different constellations and named the individual stars. Then he said, "That is, indeed, the most beautiful sight that I have ever yet seen in the world. But who has placed all these numerous beautiful candles there? Who lights them? Who puts them out?" When these questions had been answered, he fell silent again and began to cry. He asked bitterly why "the man with whom he had always been" had kept him locked up for so many years so that he could never see such

wonderful sights. He said that the man ought to be locked up himself, so that he could learn what it felt like. This was the first time that he ever said anything against the man.

16   Later he commented to a friend, who asked him why he looked sad,

> "I was just thinking how many beautiful things there are in the world, and how hard it is for me to have lived so long and to have seen nothing of them; and how happy children are who have been able to see all these things from their earliest infancy, and can still look at them. I am already so old, and am still obliged to learn what children knew long ago. I wish I had never come out of my cage; (he) who put me (there) should have left me there. Then I should never have known and felt the want of any thing; and I should not have experienced the misery of never having been a child, and of having come so late into the world."

17   During his stay in Professor Daumer's household he became aware of the deeper meanings of family ties[8], and asked what it meant to have or to be a father, a mother, a brother or sister. Upon thinking of the answers that were given to him, he again shed tears at the thought of how unfair it was that he had no family, and was completely alone as though he were a member of a separate species,[9] the only one of his kind in existence.

Part Six

18   In October of 1829, about a year and a half after he came to Nuremberg, the newspapers announced that the famous Kaspar Hauser was planning to write the story of his life. It was probably this news article that brought on a terrible event and that eventually brought his short life to its tragic end. One day Professor Daumer went out, leaving Kaspar at home. Around midday Daumer's sister noticed spots of blood and bloody footprints on the stairs. She and her mother went looking for Kaspar and found him lying downstairs in a corner of the cellar. He was very weak and was covered with blood, and he kept saying, "Man, man." They called a doctor and carried him to his bed, where he lay in a very bad condition for two days. His forehead had been cut open and he had lost a great deal of blood. But in time he recovered[10] and was able to tell what had happened: He was in the hall of the house when he discovered a stranger whose face was covered with a black handkerchief. The man struck him on the head and he fell to the floor unconscious. When he came to himself, he found that he was bleeding, and became frightened that the man would return to finish him off. He could hardly move, but somehow he managed to pull open the heavy cellar door and found a dark corner to hide in. There he lost consciousness again.

19   No one knew for sure who had tried to kill Kaspar, but people assumed that it was "the man with whom he had always been," and various people reported seeing a stranger come out of Daumer's house, wash his hands in a nearby water-trough, and (several days later) ask someone on the street whether Kaspar were dead or alive.

20   Kaspar recovered fully and continued to learn about the world, surrounded by friends, tutors, and

The gravestone of Kaspar Hauser in Ansbach

others who wished him well. Everyone who knew him was impressed by his honesty, openness, and sweet nature. But this was not the end of the story. In December of 1833, five years after he had discovered the outside world, a stranger approached him in a park and told him that he had news of Kaspar's mother. The man gave him a lady's handbag which had a note in it. When Kaspar opened the purse to look inside, the man stabbed him in the chest with a knife, then ran away. Kaspar, badly hurt, just managed to walk back to his home. He lived for three days, but then he died of his wound.

21   The note in the handbag was written backwards and said, translated into English,

> Hauser can tell you exactly
> How I look and who I am.
> If Hauser will not take this trouble
> Then I will myself say
>
> I come — — — — — —
>
> I come from — — — —
>
> Of the Bavarian border — — —
>
> At the river — — — —
>
> And I will even tell you my name M. L. O.

22   Who was this man, and why did he want to kill Kaspar Hauser? Was he, as most people assume, "the man with whom he had always been"? It remains a mystery, but the most popular answer is that he was killed for political reasons. This theory is extremely complicated, but it concludes that he was killed by someone who did not want Kaspar's real identity to be guessed. It is not clear why the killer, if it was "the man," had not killed him when he was a child, nor why he had brought him to Nuremberg if he feared that Kaspar's identity would become known. Many questions remain unanswered, leaving us with only the puzzling but charming story of a kindhearted young man who came late into life and who left it tragically early.

After You Read

COMPREHENSION QUESTIONS

Questions for Part One:

1. Name two things that Kaspar Hauser couldn't do when he was discovered.

   a. _____

   b. _____

2. Who wrote the two letters?

   a. The newer letter: _____

   b. The older letter: _____

3. What surprising thing could Kaspar do?

   _____

Questions for Part Two:

1. Who were Kaspar's first teachers?

_____

2. Compare Kaspar's senses with ordinary people's.

_____

3. What was something that he liked very much at this point in his life, and what did he do with these objects?

_____

_____

Questions for Part Three:

1. Where was Kaspar's second home after he came to Nuremberg?

_____

2. Give an example of how he confused living beings with nonliving objects.

_____

3. Give an example of how he confused reality with unreality.

_____

Questions for Part Four:

1. Where had Kaspar lived before he came to Nuremberg?

_____

2. Who took care of him?

_____

3. Describe Kaspar's life at that time.

_____

_____

4. What did his keeper teach him to do?

_____

5. Describe his journey to Nuremberg.

_____

Questions for Part Five:

1. At first, what was Kaspar's attitude toward his former keeper?

_____

How and why did this attitude change?

_____

2. What were Kaspar's negative feelings about having come into human society?

_____

Questions for Part Six:

1. Describe Kaspar's first attack.

_____

_____

2. Describe Kaspar's second attack, and tell the result of it.

_____

_____

3. Who was probably responsible for these events?

_____

_____

REVIEW: COMPLETING THE READING

Now read the whole passage.
Identify the circled reference words.

LOCATING INFORMATION

In which paragraph can you find. . . .

1. the point at which Kaspar turned against "the Man"?
2. a description of the final attack on Kaspar?
3. mention of Kaspar's loneliness?
4. a description of Kaspar's trip to Nuremberg?
5. a paragraph in Kaspar's own words?

Distinguishing Between Topic and Main Idea

The *topic* is the general subject of a paragraph; the *main idea* is what the author says about that topic. The topic is usually expressed as a noun or a noun phrase, while the main idea should be expressed in a complete sentence.

Identify both the topic and the main idea of each of the following paragraphs:

Topic	_Main Idea_
¶5 Kaspar's senses	Kaspar's senses were much more sensitive than normal people's.
¶10 _____	_____
¶11 _____	_____

DEVELOPING GOOD HABITS DURING READING

Practice the "Good Habits During Reading" methods that you learned about on page 50. If you need to, review the procedure before you start. Remember the steps:

- Make predictions
- Form mental pictures
- Make connections with your own experience, or with something you already know
- Recognize your reading problems
- Solve these problems

When you finish, fill out the chart on the handout that your teacher gave you earlier.

UNDERSTANDING GRAMMAR

There is one grammar point that may give you a little trouble in this chapter. Here's an example of it:

If the new thing were very hard for him to comprehend, *his face would begin* to twitch and *he would become* upset. Not surprisingly, after a few weeks of having to adjust to so much newness, *he actually fell ill.*

One of the ways that we use *would + verb* is to describe a past habit, an action repeated many times in the past. It is not used in this way to describe present habits. Thus it carries two meanings: one, that the action was habitual in the past; and two, that it is not being done now. Contrast the two examples of this with the final clause *he actually fell ill,* which uses the simple past because it describes one action, not a habit.

Now scan Kaspar's story and mark five examples of *would + verb.* Read them over and note that they inform you of Kaspar's habitual behavior. If you'll take a look at Kamala's story, you'll find similar examples. (You'll notice that Kaspar himself sometimes says *should + verb,* which is an old form that means the same thing. *Should* isn't often used that way today.)

Vocabulary

KEYWORDS

1. gradually ¶4
2. fond ¶4
3. in particular* ¶6
4. distinguish* ¶8
5. object ¶8

6. aware* ¶8
7. enable* ¶8
8. tie ¶17
9. species ¶17
10. recover* ¶18

Forming Concepts: Forming a mental picture of new vocabulary items helps you remember them better.

KEYWORD EXERCISE

1. Which of the following sentences can be said to have happened *gradually?*
   a. She learned Arabic.
   b. The superpowers destroyed their nuclear weapons.
   c. My grandfather grew old.
   d. The boy broke his leg.
   e. We went to Washington D.C. on our vacation.

   EXAMPLE: Kaspar *gradually* learned to speak and even to write.

2. *EXAMPLE:* I like outdoor activities, *in particular* hiking and camping.

   Finish the sentences:
   She's allergic to animals, in particular . . .
   He enjoys movies, . . .

3. *EXAMPLE:* Color-blind people cannot *distinguish* between red and green.

   Finish the sentences:
   When the twins were born, their parents dressed them in different colors until they could distinguish . . .
   Doctors may have trouble distinguishing . . .

4. In ¶8, find and list three inanimate *objects.* _____

   _____

   _____

5. Name some environmental problems that people have gradually become

   aware of over the past several years. _____

   _____

   EXAMPLE: Kaspar was not *aware* of the larger world until he was about seventeen years old.

6. *EXAMPLE:* Their differences in clothing *enabled* Kaspar to distinguish men from women.

   Finish the sentences:
   Winning the lottery would enable me to . . .
   Taking the summer off enabled . . .

7. A *species* is a group of living beings that share the same characteristics and are able to reproduce together. This is the biological classification of human beings:

Kingdom: Animal
Phylum: Chordates
Class: Mammals
Order: Primates
Family: Hominids
Genus: Homo
Species: Sapiens

Human beings are a *species.* National and ethnic categories such as *Japanese, Jews,* and *white people* describe groups within the human species, not separate species.

EXAMPLE: Kaspar felt as though he were the only member of a *species* because there was no one else like him.

8. Which of the following conditions might a person *recover* from?
malaria   good news   bad news   culture shock   a broken bone

EXAMPLE: Kaspar eventually *recovered* from his first attack.

REVIEW

Now that you have studied the vocabulary, re-read or re-skim the passage.

LEARNING STRATEGY

Forming Concepts: Making a chart of related information from different sources helps you learn the material and forms a very helpful study guide.

A Chart Comparing the Wolf Children

The cases of Kamala and Kaspar provide us with interesting similarities and differences that help us to understand human development. A useful study habit is to *synthesize* and reorganize information from two readings in a way that makes it easy to compare them.

Take a piece of paper and turn it sideways (horizontally). You'll use it to make a chart. Down the left side put three categories:

Kamala
Kaspar
Victor   . . . and leave three or four blank lines under each.

Across the top, you're going to write categories of points on which you can compare and contrast the three children. Start with Kamala and Kaspar; later you'll add Victor. Try to come up with at least six categories (for example, "Age at Discovery"). You can work alone or with a partner, but after a time, your teacher will ask you to compare your work in a small group. Use your partners' lists to improve your own.

Writing a Summary of Kaspar's Life

Write a brief article that might have appeared in a newspaper the day after Kaspar's death. Write only three paragraphs: The first will announce his death, the second will describe his background before discovery, and the third will describe his development after discovery. Then count the words. Try to limit your article to 200 words: if it's longer than that, cut it down (without breaking grammar rules).

READING THREE

The third major type of "wolf child" is one who seems to bring himself up with the help of neither humans nor animals. How old do you think such a child would have to be in order to do this? What might cause such a situation to exist? The following story is a classic case of this kind of child. Notice the similarities between his behavior and development, Kamala's, and Kaspar's.

VICTOR, THE WILD CHILD

Part One

1   In the late 1790s several people in a region of south central France reported seeing a "wild boy" in the forest. This youngster wore only a torn shirt, avoided human contact, climbed trees like a monkey, and seemed to survive[1] on such foods as nuts, roots, and raw potatoes that he stole from farms. He appeared to be about twelve years old. Several times he was captured, and several times he escaped; eventually, however, he approached a house and acted as though he wanted to be taken in. The people in the house kept him for a few days and then sent him to a children's hospital in Paris. There he was observed[2], and the following behavior was noted: He showed little interest in his surroundings; his eyes moved restlessly and did not follow anything; his hearing responded neither to loud noises nor to sweet music; he could not speak; he showed no reaction to either bad smells or fine perfume; and he could not use his hands as normal humans do. He was unable to open a door or to climb onto a chair in order to reach objects that he wanted; he seemed to have no memory; and he would not or could not imitate actions or sounds. The doctors at the hospital concluded[3] that he was an idiot, even less intelligent than an animal.

The Wild-boy of Aveyron

2   At this point the doctors wanted to send the wild boy to a special hospital for mentally retarded children, but a Doctor Jean-Marc-Gaspard Itard stepped forward and asked to take over his case. He removed the child to his own house, put him under the care of his housekeeper, Madame Guérin, and attempted to educate him. He gave the boy the name Victor.

Part Two

3   No one ever learned how Victor had come to live in the woods, nor at what age, nor how he had survived with no help from humans or from animals. He had been seen more than five years earlier, so he must have been at least five or six years old when he was abandoned[4] or lost. His body was covered with scars, some apparently the marks of animal bites; but there was one particularly large scar across his throat, and Dr. Itard thought that perhaps someone had tried to kill him and then had left him for dead in the forest. Somehow the boy had survived and had managed[5] to develop the skills for finding food and avoiding humans. Whether he was retarded or not was hard to tell, but he had clearly been isolated[6] from human society long enough that he could not speak or respond to situations in the usual human ways. His interests and thought processes were quite different from those of normal humans.

4   When found, Victor could walk and run easily, though he disliked wearing clothing, especially shoes, and he could run much faster in his bare feet. He seemed insensitive[7] to cold or heat: he would go outside barefooted in the snow, and he could pull burning wood from the fireplace with his bare hands. Although there was no evidence[8] that he had been assisted by animal foster-parents, he did share with animals the habit of smelling everything he came across. His only two emotions were happiness and anger: when happy, he would laugh; when angry, he threw around the room everything that he could lay his hands on. He would spend hours rocking backwards and forwards, his eyes fixed on the window, very much like a caged animal in a zoo. He loved nature and liked nothing more than to be out in the garden or taking walks, and he responded with great joy to thunderstorms and heavy snow. He frequently attempted to escape, but was always found and brought back. Itard remarked, "Indeed, when we consider the little time he has been in society, [Victor] is much less like a simple youth, than an infant of ten or twelve months old. . . ."

5   Gradually he learned some clever ways to make people do what he wanted. For instance, if he tired of visitors, he would bring them their hats and coats and show them to the door. He loved being pushed around the garden in a wheelbarrow, and he would bring it out before guests and put their hands on the handles, then get in it himself. When he wanted to eat, he would put the tablecloth on the table and set out the plates and wait expectantly.

Part Three

6   As time passed, Victor became very fond of Madame Guérin, who was part caretaker, part teacher, and part mother to him. She was extremely patient and understanding. He disliked leaving her side, and rejoining her always filled him with happiness. In his interactions with her, Itard could see evidence of Victor's progress[9] in observing human behavior and in becoming more socialized.[10] A very touching example of this took place when Madame Guérin's husband fell ill and died. That evening at dinnertime, Victor set the usual number of places at the table. When Madame Guérin came into the room and saw her husband's place set out, she burst into tears. Victor, realizing that his actions had upset her, quickly removed the plate and put it away. He never repeated the mistake.

7   He also developed an affection[11] for Itard, in spite of the fact that some of the doctor's methods[12] in educating him might seem cruel to people today. Many times Itard would try to force Victor to perform tasks which he either did not comprehend or simply did not want to do. From time to time Victor would explode in anger and would begin to throw objects around the room. But Itard's will was as strong as his, and the doctor was bigger and was on familiar ground. Once, knowing Victor's fear of heights, he held him upside down out of a fourth-story window until the terrified boy did as he wished.

Part Four

8   Victor never did learn to speak, and Itard finally abandoned attempts to teach him to repeat sounds and even to understand language as others spoke it to him. He did not respond to spoken words in a way that showed that he attached any meaning to them; but he did respond to gesture, expression, tone, and volume of voice. Interestingly enough, Itard's only success with language was in teaching him to make the connection between certain objects and their *written* representation, which seems as though it would have been extremely difficult since Victor had no oral language, and since the very idea of language and of writing was unknown to him.

9   In attempting to teach Victor language, Itard tried to show him the connections between drawings of objects and the objects themselves. If he showed the boy a picture of a comb, for example, Victor was to go and get an actual comb and bring it back. Once Victor understood this, he showed enough intelligence to "overgeneralize": that is, when showed a book, he might bring a newspaper, a letter, or any other example of writing on paper. Itard progressed to showing Victor new ideas in sets of three: a book, a picture of a book, and the written word *book*. Making the connection between the object and the letters was a painfully slow and difficult process for Victor, who of course had no interest in learning to read and write, but eventually he did learn these skills at a very simple level. They did not enable him to tell any interesting details about his past history, but he was able to communicate some of his needs.

Part Five

10   Eventually Victor developed enough responses to heat and cold that he would feel his bath water to make sure it was warm enough; and he would dress himself warmly in cold weather. He learned to perform simple household tasks and to eat "normal" human food at the table with others. But he never really lost his "wild" side, as Itard explains in the following description:

> I would go so far as to say that he has always kept a distinct preference for water. The way he drinks it seems to suggest that it is one of his greatest pleasures. . . . Almost always at the end of dinner, even when he is no longer very thirsty, we see him like a gourmet before a glass of some exquisite liqueur—he fills his glass with pure water, takes a sip and swallows it drop by drop. What adds interest to this scene is its setting. He drinks his water standing at the window, eyes turned towards the countryside as if in this moment of sheer delight this child of nature seeks to unite the only two things which remain from his lost freedom, a drink of clear water and the sight of the sun on the countryside.

11   After several years of working with Victor, Itard moved on to other projects, leaving him in the care of Madame Guérin for the rest of his life. He lived to be about forty years of age.

Threads

Train up a child in the way he should go, and when he is old, he will not depart from it.

Proverbs 12:6, the Bible

After You Read

COMPREHENSION QUESTIONS

Questions for Part One:

1. How old was the "wild boy" when he was found?

   _____

2. Tell two observations that his doctors made.

   a. _____

   b. _____

3. What was the doctors' conclusion about him?

   _____

4. Where did the boy go after he left the hospital, and what name was given to him?

   _____

Questions for Part Two:

1. What might have happened to have caused Victor to live alone in the forest?

   _____

2. How might he have gotten his largest scar? Where was it?

   _____

3. Tell three ways in which Victor was different from a "normal" boy.

   a. _____

   b. _____

   c. _____

4. Tell one way in which Victor showed his intelligence when he wanted something from people.

   _____

Questions for Part Three:

1. How did Victor feel about Madame Guérin?

   _____

   What functions did she fill in his life?

   _____

2. What did he do that upset her?

   _____

   What did he do as a result of having upset her?

   _____

3. How did Dr. Itard force Victor to perform tasks?

   _____

Questions for Part Four:

1. How much success did Victor have in learning to speak?

_____

2. What did Victor respond to when people spoke to him?

_____

3. Tell about Itard's experiments with drawings, objects, and printed words.

_____

_____

4. Eventually, what were people able to learn about Victor's history in the forest?

_____

Questions for Part Five:

1. Name two ways in which Victor became more "normal."

   a. _____

   b. _____

2. In your opinion, did he become very socialized? Why do you think he did or didn't?

_____

3. What happened to Itard and to Victor in the end?

_____

REVIEW: COMPLETING THE READING

Now read the whole passage.

TRUE-FALSE QUESTIONS

				¶ number
1.	Victor was an idiot, even less intelligent than an animal.	T	F	_____
2.	Someone may have tried to kill Victor when he was five or six years old.	T	F	_____
3.	When Victor became angry, he lost control of himself.	T	F	_____
4.	Victor's favorite person was Dr. Itard.	T	F	_____
5.	Victor never learned to speak, but he could understand what other people said to him.	T	F	_____

L E A R N I N G   S T R A T E G Y

Forming Concepts: Thinking about what information *isn't* included in a reading passage makes you a better reader.

CRITICAL THINKING: WHAT ISN'T THERE?

Working alone or with a partner, make a list of three questions about each child that the reading passages do not answer. Your questions should be about information that you would really like to know. Write them on the blackboard. Why do you suppose that information was not included in the passages?

EXAMPLE: Why couldn't Victor learn to talk?

Vocabulary

VOCABULARY IN CONTEXT

1. Look at ¶1 and find the word *idiot.* Read the sentence in which it appears. What do you think an idiot might be?

    What information in the sentence leads you to that guess?

2. Look at ¶3 and find the word *scars.* Read the sentence in which it appears (twice). What do you think a scar is?

    Which part of the sentence is most useful in helping you guess?

3. Look at ¶4 and find the word *bare.* Read both of the sentences in which it appears (three times). What does it probably mean?

    Which parts of the sentence are most useful in helping you guess?

KEYWORDS

1. survive* ¶1
2. observe ¶1
3. conclude* ¶1
4. abandon ¶3
5. manage ¶3
6. isolated ¶3

7. insensitive ¶4
8. evidence* ¶4
9. progress ¶6
10. socialize ¶6
11. affection ¶7
12. method ¶7

KEYWORD EXERCISE

1. *Meanings:*

    • If you *observe* someone or something, you carefully notice what they're doing or what's happening.

    QUESTION: In ¶1, what did the doctors *observe* about Victor?

    • If you *observe* a law or a custom, you obey it or follow it.

    QUESTION: Name a law or custom that is *observed* in your country but not in the United States.

    • Explain the similarities between the two meanings.

2. Which of the following are important elements of the word *conclude?*

    evidence   because   claim   deceive   decide

    EXAMPLE: The doctors *concluded* that Victor was an idiot.

3. Which of the following are important elements of the word *isolated?*
accurate   separate   lonely   distant   useless

   EXAMPLE: Victor grew up *isolated* from human society.

4. Which of the following could be called *sensitive* or *insensitive?*
a movie   a person   your skin   a camera   a drink

   EXAMPLE: At first Victor was *insensitive* to extreme heat and cold.

5. Which of the three wolf children became the most *socialized?* Give evidence for your answer.

   EXAMPLE: Parents *socialize* their children through direct teaching and also through example.

6. If you were lost in the jungle, what would you need in order to *survive?*

   EXAMPLE: Victor *survived* by eating nuts, roots, and raw potatoes.

7. *Meanings:*
   • If you *manage* to do something, you succeed in doing it (even if it is difficult).

   QUESTION: What did Victor *manage* to do before he entered human society? After?

   • If you *manage* a business, you direct its operations.

   QUESTION: Who *manages* the school or institute where you are studying English?

   • Explain the similarities between the two meanings.

8. If a detective were investigating a murder, what *evidence* might she look for?

   EXAMPLE: The large scar across Victor's throat was *evidence* that someone may have tried to murder him.

9. What are some ways that you can measure your *progress* in English?

   EXAMPLE: Victor's *progress* in socialization was very limited.

10. Name two different *methods* of learning a language. Which do you prefer?

    EXAMPLE: Some of Itard's educational *method*s seem cruel to us today.

11. What happens if you *abandon* your exercise program?
If you *abandon* your car on the freeway?
If you *abandon* your attempts to keep in touch with your old friends back home?

REVIEW

Now that you've studied the vocabulary, go back and re-read or re-skim the story.

LEARNING STRATEGY

Overcoming Limitations: Trying to figure out the cause or the pattern of your errors helps you improve your language skills.

Discussion: An Interview with Victor

Victor was the wolf child we know the least about because he never learned to talk at all. But what if he had? Work with a partner and imagine that one of you is Victor, and the other is a reporter who will interview him. Before you begin the interview, together you should write out four or five questions that you want to use, and you should think about (and maybe make notes of) the answers that "Victor" will give. Then practice role-playing the interview. The next time this class meets, your teacher will ask each pair of partners to take turns performing your interviews for the class.

Completing Your Chart

Add information about Victor to the categories on your chart. Then compare your entries with a partner, revising them if you wish to. You will use the information on this chart as the basis for a paper that you will write, so make it clear and easy to follow.

> We must not forget that the human child learns more during the first two years of his life under the influence of his living surroundings than in all the entire period afterwards.
>
> —*Robert M. Zingg, anthropologist*

Writing an Essay: Comparing the Wolf Children

FREEWRITING: THE MOST INTERESTING WOLF CHILD

Which wolf child was most interesting to you, and why?

COMPARING THE WOLF CHILDREN

Write a paper comparing and contrasting the three children. Mention all three, but tell the most detail about your favorite. Consult your chart, but use only the information that you find most interesting: don't use everything. You can organize your paper either this way . . .

    I. Similarities
       A. Kamala
       B. Kaspar
       C. Victor
   II. Differences
       A. Kamala
       B. Kaspar
       C. Victor

. . . or this way:

I. Category (for example, Age at Discovery)
   A. Kamala
   B. Kaspar
   C. Victor
II. Category
   A. Kamala
   B. Kaspar
   C. Victor
     (et cetera)

Don't forget to write an introduction and a conclusion.

LEARNING STRATEGY

Managing Your Learning: Finding out what resources can be useful to you enriches your language. Your teacher and your classmates can suggest some good ones, such as dictionaries, thesauruses, grammar books, encyclopedias, cultural guides, radio and TV programs, and videotapes.

Evaluating Learning Strategies

Look back over the chapter at the learning strategies that were presented. Were there any that weren't especially helpful for you? What wasn't helpful about them? Which ones did you find especially helpful? Think about times and ways that you can keep using them in your future reading.

Evaluating Your Learning

Look at the following list of items that you practiced in this chapter. How did you do on each one? Check your answers (√).

	Very little	*Quite a bit*	*A lot*
You built up your vocabulary.	_____	_____	_____
You can read and understand long passages.	_____	_____	_____
You can explain what you read about.	_____	_____	_____
You can distinguish between topic and main idea.	_____	_____	_____
You can write an essay based on your notes.	_____	_____	_____
You learned about wolf children.	_____	_____	_____

Verbs
abandon
appear (seem)
approach*
avoid*
behave
conclude*
develop
distinguish*
eliminate*
enable*
indicate*
manage
observe
recover*
respond
socialize
survive*

Nouns
affection
approach*
evidence*
function
human nature
method
object
progress
senses
species
tie

Adjectives
aware*
fond
insensitive
isolated
obvious
traumatic
unable*

Adverbs
eventually
gradually
in particular*
upright

Lies and Truth

PLANNING YOUR LEARNING

Review your overall goal statement. How much progress did you make toward it in the last chapter? Do you want to change it? Think about how you can work to meet your goal as you study this new chapter.

- How many words do you want to learn? (minimum 55, the number of keywords in the chapter)
- What grade would you like to make on the vocabulary section of the exam at the end of the chapter?
- What grade would you like to make on the reading comprehension section of the exam?
- What are you going to read outside of class?

PREVIEWING THE CHAPTER

- Think about the title of this chapter. Look in the Table of Contents at the titles of the four readings in it. Look through the chapter at the pictures. What are some things you expect to find out?
- Which reading do you think you'll be most interested in?

PREPARING TO READ: CONTENT (DISCUSSION)

Is Lying Always Wrong?

Imagine yourself in this situation: You are a doctor, and you have just discovered that one of your patients has an illness that cannot be cured. You estimate that he has only about one year to live. He wants to know what his condition is.

- Will you tell him the truth?
- Would most doctors from your culture?
- Will you tell his family the truth?
- If you were the patient, would you want to know the truth?
- If you had only one more year to live, how would you want to spend it?

PREPARING TO READ: CONTENT (FREEWRITING)

A World Where No One Lies

Imagine a world in which everyone always told the truth. What would it be like? Would it be better than this world?

PREPARING TO READ: VOCABULARY

Look at the following vocabulary items. Fill in the blanks with the opposite meaning of the word in the other column. The first one has been done for you.

lie (verb)   tell the truth

_____   honest

_____   true

lie (noun)   _____

_____   truth-teller

_____   trust

fact   _____

LEARNING STRATEGY

Testing Hypotheses: Asking yourself what you expect to find in new material helps to activate your mind and prepare it for the new content.

READING ONE

The following is a general article on lies and lying. Before you look at it, work with a partner and make a list of questions that you might expect such an article to discuss.

Reading process: Now scan the passage for about three minutes, checking off any of your questions that it answers. Then go back and read it carefully.

LIES AND TRUTH

1   What is truth?—and the opposite question that goes with it, What makes a lie? Philosophers, teachers, and religious leaders from all cultures and all periods of history have offered many answers to these questions. Among Euro-North-American writers, there is general agreement on two points. The first is that what we call "a lie" must have been told intentionally[1]—that is, if someone tells an untruth but they believe it to be true, we don't consider them a liar. The second point is that practically everyone lies, and lies frequently. But there the agreement ends.

2   One rather extreme point of view is that lying is always bad and that we should try to find ways to avoid doing it. The reason is that lying hurts not only the listener, but also the liar. Each lie makes the next one easier to tell, and the

Threads

No man is really honest.

Aristophanes

liar comes not only to disrespect herself, but to mistrust others, whom she believes will lie as easily as she. In a society where lying is common, trust[2] becomes impossible, and without trust, cooperation cannot exist. Furthermore, by lying to people, we remove their power to make important choices about (for example) how to spend money, what future career to take, what medical treatment to choose.

3   Toward the opposite extreme is the position that although some lies are evil, many others are not—in fact, they are necessary to hold our society together. We lie in harmless ways to protect each other's feelings and to better our relationships. These are not lies that try to hurt others. We laugh at the boss's joke which we have heard before and which she doesn't tell very well; we pretend interest in a friend's story of something uninteresting that happened to him. If someone asks us a question that is very personal and is none of their business, we may lie in response. Sometimes we lie to protect the reputation or even the life of another person. On a larger scale, government may protect national security by lying.

4   Many people's positions are somewhere between these two extremes. It's common for North American parents to tell their children that lying is bad, that they shouldn't do it and should feel guilty if they do. In Euro-American cultures, a traditional punishment for a child who lies is to wash the child's mouth out with soap. Yet through their actions, parents also teach their children that there are circumstances[3] under which most people do lie. Consequently the children grow up following both teachings—they occasionally lie, but they feel guilty[4] and don't want people to know they've done it.

5   Each person seems to have some point at which they draw the line between an acceptable lie and a bad lie. Obviously, this point varies from individual to individual and from culture to culture. A sometimes painful part of growing up is realizing that not everyone shares your own individual definition of honesty. Your parents and your culture may teach you that liars will suffer,[5] but as you go through life, you find that often they don't: in fact, dishonest people often seem to prosper[6] more than honest ones. What are you to do with this realization? It may make your moral beliefs look weak and silly in comparison, and you may begin to question them. It takes a great deal of strength and courage to continue living an honest life in the face of such a reality.

6   There are many ways to categorize lies, but here is a fairly simple one:

7   *Little white lies:* This is our name for lies that we consider harmless and socially acceptable. (They) are usually told to protect the liar or the feelings of the listener. Most of them would be considered social lies, and they include apologies and excuses: "I tried to call you, but your line was busy." "You're kidding! You don't look like you've gained[7] a pound." Some people, however, would consider it acceptable to lie to save themselves from responsibility in a business transaction: "After I got it home, I noticed that it was broken, so I'm returning it and would like my money back."

8   Occasionally a "little white lie" may have a very profound[8] effect on the lives of the listeners, and may even backfire.[9] Author Stephanie Ericsson tells of the well-meaning U.S. Army sergeant who told a lie about one of his men who had been killed in action. The sergeant reported the man as "missing in action," not killed, so that the military would continue sending money to the dead man's family every month. What he didn't consider was that because of his lie, the family continued to live in that narrow space between hope and loss, always watching for the mail or jumping when the telephone or the doorbell rang. They never were able to go through the normal process of sorrowing for, and then accepting, the death of their father and husband. The wife never remarried. Which was worse, the lie or the truth? Did the sergeant have the right to do what he did to (them)?

9   What we really mean when we call an untruth a "little white lie" is that we think it was justifiable.[10] Into this category fall many of the lies told within the walls of government. A person may lie to government, or a government official may lie to the public, and believe that by doing so, he becomes a hero. Clearly, however, one person's "little white lie" is another person's "dirty lie." Which brings us to the second category:

Listen carefully, because I can only tell this once. I promised not to repeat it.

10   *Dirty lies:* These are lies told with intent to harm[11] the listener or a third party and to benefit the liar. Into this category fall the lies of some dishonest salespersons, mechanics, repairmen; husbands or wives who are having an affair with someone else; teenagers who lie to get out of the house in order to do things that their parents would die if they knew about; drug addicts who beg family members for money to support their habit. Dirty lies may be told to improve one person's reputation by destroying another's, to hurt a colleague's chances of promotion so that the liar will be advanced.

11   *Lies of omission:* Some people believe that lying covers not only what you say, but also what you choose not to say. If you're trying to sell a car that burns a lot of oil, but the buyers don't ask about that particular feature, is it a lie not to tell them? In the United States, a favorite place to withhold the truth is on people's income tax returns. The government considers this an unquestionable lie, and if caught, these people are severely punished. If omission can be lying, history books are great liars. Until recently, most U.S. history textbooks painted Christopher Columbus purely as a hero, the man who "discovered America," and had nothing to say about his darker side. Moreover, most Native American and African-American contributors to science, technology, invention, literature, art, discovery, and other areas of civilization used to be omitted from children's schoolbooks. Many people considered this a lie, and today's history books usually mention at least some of it, though not as much as some people might like.

12   *False promises:* This category is made up of promises that the promiser knows are false, that he has no intention of keeping even as the words leave his lips. While some are fairly harmless and social, others are taken more seriously and can hurt the listener: "I'll never do it again, I promise." Advertisers and politicians suffer from terrible stereotypes because of the false promises of some of their number: "Lose 50 pounds in two weeks." "Read my lips: No new taxes." Probably everyone would agree that if we make a promise but have no intention of keeping it, we lie. But what if we really do plan to keep it, and then something happens to prevent[12] it? Consider the journalist who promises not to identify his sources, but then is pressured by his newspaper or by the law. How far should he go to keep his word? If he breaks his promise, is he dishonest?

13   *Pathological lies:* Pathological liars are persons who lie constantly and for no apparent reason. They will lie about anything. They seem to be unable to control the impulse to lie. Studies of such people find that many of them were badly treated as children, many come from families in which one member was an alcoholic or was mentally ill, many grew up in families in which the truth was simply never valued or practiced. They seem to have an unusually strong

need to be liked and admired by others. But not everyone of whom this is true becomes an uncontrollable liar, and no one knows why some do and some don't. Pathological liars tend to have few if any close or long-lasting personal relationships, because people catch on to (them) and drop (them); (they) are very careful not to introduce their acquaintances to each other for fear that (they) might begin to compare stories.

14   *Lies to oneself:* This is perhaps the saddest and most pathetic kind of lying. These are the lies that prevent us from making needed changes in ourselves: "I know I drank/spent/ate too much yesterday, but I can control it any time I really want to." But there is a fine line between normal dreams and ambitions on the one hand, and deceiving ourselves on the other, and we have to be careful where we draw it. It's common for young people to dream of rising to the top of their company, of winning a Nobel Prize, of becoming famous or rich; but is (that) self-deception,[13] or simply human nature? The term "mid-life crisis" is used to describe the point when some people realize that their life is half over and they are never going to achieve some of those dreams. But were they lying to themselves? More likely, they really believed that such a future was open to them, because they had seen it happen to others. We shouldn't be too hard on ourselves, but if we have turned a blind eye to our faults, we should take an honest look in the mirror.

15   There is no question[14] that the terms "lying" and "honesty" have definitions that vary across cultural boundaries.[15] Members of one culture may stereotype members of another as "great liars," "untrustworthy," or "afraid to face the truth." But what may lie behind these differences is that one culture values factual information even if it hurts, while another places more value on sensitivity to other people's feelings. While the members of each culture believe that of course their values are the right ones, they are unlikely to convince members of other cultures to change over. And that's "the truth."

After You Read

Identify the circled reference words.

DEVELOPING GOOD HABITS DURING READING

Practice the "Good Habits During Reading" methods that you learned about on page 50. If you need to, review the procedure before you start. Remember the steps:

- Make predictions
- Form mental pictures
- Make connections with your own experience, or with something you already know
- Recognize your reading problems
- Solve these problems

When you finish, fill out the chart on the handout that your teacher gave you earlier.

DISCUSSION: COMPREHENSION QUESTIONS

From your own imagination, give an example of each of the categories of lies from the reading.

1. What's a *lie of omission* that a mother might not tell her daughter? Why might she do this?
2. What's a *little white lie* that a daughter might tell her mother? Why?
3. What's a *lie* that you remember having told *to yourself?* Why did you do it?
4. What's a *false promise* that a child might tell a parent? Why?
5. Imagine that you're a *pathological liar,* and tell about something incredible that happened to you the other day.
6. What's the *dirtiest, most hurtful lie* that you can think of?

Now let's review: Try to answer these questions from memory, without looking back at the reading. The answers are the six categories that you just talked about.

1. This kind of lie is like a psychological illness.
2. Some people think that if everything they say is true, they're not lying. But according to the reading, they could still be guilty of what kind of lie?
3. These lies are told by people who don't want to face reality.
4. People tell this kind of lie when they want other people to quit bothering them.
5. Which kind of lie is considered the least serious?
6. Which kind of lie is considered the ugliest and meanest?

Explain this sentence from ¶4: Yet through their actions, parents also teach their children that there are circumstances under which most people do lie.

Paraphrasing and Summarizing

If you really understand something, you ought to be able to explain it to someone else. That's why much academic work in North American colleges and universities requires you to express information from your reading in words of your own. This skill is called *paraphrasing,* and you'll use it every time you write a report, a research paper, a thesis, a dissertation, or any paper that uses other people's writings.

Your ability to paraphrase well depends strongly on your ability (1) to summarize (see pages 86 and 107) and (2) to express the same information in different ways. Let's practice with something fairly simple from the reading above:

> There is no question that the terms "lying" and "honesty" have definitions that vary across cultural boundaries.

A bad method:
Here's what you *don't* want to do: Don't keep the same grammar and just substitute synonyms or similar words. That makes for very bad paraphrasing.
There are two good methods.
Good method one: Read the original sentence several times to make sure you understand it. (Do this now.) Then cover it up with a piece of paper and try to

write down the general idea. (Do this now.) When you finish, compare your sentence with the original. Is the meaning the same? If not, revise it. Are the grammar and vocabulary too similar to the original? If they are, try to change them around without changing the meaning of the sentence.

Now try something else.

Good method two: Highlight the words in the original sentence that can be changed. In this case you can change . . .

There is no question that:_____

terms:_____

definitions:_____

vary:_____

boundaries:_____

Write synonyms or equivalents for these words and phrases. Feel free to use your dictionary or a thesaurus.

There's no reason why you can't change these words and phrases. But you shouldn't change the words *lying, honesty,* and *cultural,* because there aren't any good equivalents. You must change everything you can, but sometimes you're allowed to keep some words.

Now paraphrase the sentence in your own words, changing the grammar around. When you finish, compare your work with a couple of your classmates'. Working together, revise your sentences any way you want to. Then your teacher will ask you to write some of your sentences on the blackboard.

Now practice something on your own. Look at the second and third paragraphs; highlight the topic sentence of each. Then paraphrase each one.

Paragraph two
Topic sentence, paraphrased:

_____

_____

Type of support (reasons? examples? definitions? facts? statistics? comparisons?):

_____

How many supporting details?

_____

Paragraph three
Topic sentence, paraphrased:

_____

_____

Type of support:

_____

How many supporting details?

_____

Identifying Issues

An *issue* is a moral question that different people have very different answers to. There are many issues suggested by the reading above; for instance:

Is lying always wrong?

Where does truth end and a lie begin?

Are some lies worse than others?

Issues are questions of morality, not questions of fact. This is *not* an issue:

What do most Euro-North-American writers agree on?

And finally, issues are questions that apply to everyone, not just to the people in one case. So this also is *not* an issue:

Should the sergeant have lied about his man who was killed in action?

But you could convert this question to an issue by making it apply more generally to everyone:

Is it justifiable to tell a lie in order to benefit people, even though that lie itself might cause them problems?

Look back at Reading One and write another issue-question that it suggests:

_____

FREEWRITING: YOUR OPINIONS ON LYING

Which category of lie is worst? What would you teach your children about lying? What did your parents teach you?

Vocabulary

VOCABULARY IN CONTEXT

1. Find the word *acceptable* in ¶5. Read the sentence it's in. What do you think it means?
2. Find the word *omission* in ¶11. What do you think it means?
   Which sentence explains the meaning?
   Can you find a synonym for *omit* in the third sentence?

KEYWORDS

1. intentionally, intention ¶1
2. trust ¶2
3. circumstances ¶4
4. guilty ¶4
5. suffer ¶5
6. prosper ¶5
7. gain ¶7
8. profound ¶8
9. backfire ¶8
10. justifiable ¶9
11. harm* ¶10
12. prevent* ¶12
13. deception ¶14
14. there is no question that . . . * ¶15
15. boundary ¶15

KEYWORD EXERCISE

1. Which of the following are elements of *intention?*
   accident   planning   affection   function   decision

   EXAMPLE: He has no *intention* of keeping that promise.

2. Find the antonym for *trust* in ¶2.

   _____

   EXAMPLE: In a society where lying is common, *trust* becomes impossible.

3. Look at ¶10. What part of speech is *harm* as used in the first sentence?

   _____

   Find the adjective form of *harm* in the same paragraph.

   _____

   What does this adjective mean?

   HINT: the suffix will tell you.

   _____

   It's not given here, but do you know an adjective that is the antonym of this one, formed of *harm* + a different suffix?

   _____

   EXAMPLE: Dirty lies are told with intent to *harm* the listener.

4. Do you think that animals are capable of feeling *guilty?* If so, what makes you think so?

   _____

   EXAMPLE: Most of us feel *guilty* when we lie.

5. Describe the ideal *circumstances* for learning how to dance.

   _____

   EXAMPLE: There are *circumstance*s under which most people lie.

6. Give an example of how a liar might *suffer.*

   _____

   EXAMPLE: Our parents and our culture may teach us that liars will *suffer.*

7. Give an example of how liars might *prosper.*

   _____

   EXAMPLE: Dishonest people don't always suffer for it; sometimes they *prosper.*

8. The word *gain* has several meanings. Which one applies to this sentence?

   _____

   EXAMPLE: You don't look like you've *gained* a pound.

9. We can use the word *profound* to describe many things: profound ideas, profound hatred, a profound thinker, a profound book, profound silence. The word came into English from the Latin language, where it originally

meant *deep,* as in a deep hole. What's the connection between the idea of depth and the English meaning of *profound?*

_____

EXAMPLE: Sometimes a little white lie may have a *profound* effect on the listener.

10. *EXAMPLE:* Occasionally a "little white lie" may *backfire,* as in the case of the sergeant who lied.

The word *backfire* was originally used in which of the following activities?
fire control   automobile repair   unemployment   shooting a gun

11. If someone lies and says, "You don't look like you've gained an ounce," how would they *justify* this lie?

Do you think it's justifiable? _____

Have you ever said anything like this? _____

12. Note that *prevention* is used before something might happen, not after it has happened. The whole idea is that you don't want it to happen.
What might you do at your house to *prevent* burglars from breaking in?

_____

What do travelers do to *prevent* seasickness or airsickness?

_____

What can people from different cultures do to *prevent* misunderstanding?

_____

13. In North America there lives a very common but peculiar animal called an opossum. Opossums cannot defend themselves very well with teeth or claws, nor can they run very fast. They protect themselves with an unusual kind of *deception* that we call "playing possum." If you don't know what this phrase means, ask a North American. Then write the answer here:

_____

_____

EXAMPLE: Lying to oneself is a form of self-*deception.*

14. *EXAMPLE:* *There is no question that* these words have different meanings in different cultures.

Did you find this phrase in your dictionary? It means that something is so obvious that no one could doubt it. Note that it comes at the beginning of a sentence.
From the following list, choose one statement that you *would* begin with this phrase, and one that you *wouldn't.*
. . . overpopulation is a serious global problem.
. . . everyone learns languages the same way.
. . . a cure for AIDS will eventually be found.

15. What states or provinces share *boundaries* with the one you are now in?

EXAMPLE: These beliefs vary across cultural *boundaries.*

REVIEW

Now that you have studied the vocabulary, re-read or re-skim the passage.

Optional Longer Project: Interviewing Businesspeople in Your Community

Choose a partner. Together, you will survey two businesspeople in the community where you live. You want to find out how important honesty is in their line of work, and whether they trust the people they do business with. Make up a list of three or four questions that you want to ask them.

Now get together as a class and discuss

1. how to select a businessperson to interview.
2. what kinds of things you could say to introduce yourself and your interview to the businessperson.
3. what each partner will do during the interview.

After the interviews, each partner will write up a report. Your teacher will tell you when it is due. You may be asked to summarize your findings orally to the class as well as writing a report.

LEARNING STRATEGY

Managing Your Learning: Review old vocabulary regularly: more frequently at first, then gradually less frequently.

READING TWO

SHOULD DOCTORS LIE TO THEIR PATIENTS WHO ARE TERMINALLY ILL?

Threads

No normal human being wants to hear the truth.

H.L. Mencken

1   If a doctor in your culture discovers that one of her patients has a terminal illness such as cancer, is she likely[1] to tell the patient the truth? Dr. Jimmie Holland, a psychiatrist at a cancer hospital in New York, recently took a survey of cancer specialists in 22 countries. Her findings: "In much of Europe, South America, most of Asia—they consider it unethical to tell. They say, 'America is so brutal, you make it so difficult for the patient, and we are kind and gentle.'"

2   They're right about what Americans would do: nine out of ten U.S. physicians would break the news to the patient in such a case. But the reason is that most U.S. patients demand[2] to know the truth. They believe that knowing the facts will help them to deal with reality. They want to make informed decisions about what kind of treatment to undergo,[3] how to spend their

remaining days, how to put their affairs⁴ in order, and even whether to endure until the end or to commit suicide. Philosopher Sissela Bok writes, "We are also learning that truthful information, humanely conveyed, helps patients cope with illness: helps them tolerate pain better, need less medication, and even recover faster after surgery."⁵

3   Because of the patient's desire to know the truth, most medical schools in the United States train doctors in what to say and how to say it. Obviously breaking the news in a cold and impersonal way could have a negative effect on the patient's welfare.⁶ But what is the best way? Dr. James F. Holland gives one example: "Say a patient asks, 'Do I have a chance?' It serves no useful purpose to say, 'Yes, about one in a hundred,' though that may be statistically so. But it *is* useful to say, 'Yes, but you must work for it, because the treatment won't be easy.' Then they can concentrate on the positive elements of treatment.⁷ People need the possibility of hope."

4   Is his answer honest, and is it as complete as most American patients would want? If not, it may be because many physicians are torn between the belief that they should be honest and the belief that total honesty may drive the patient to despair.⁸ Dr. Stuart E. Lind says, "I saw a woman whose ovarian cancer had come back after three years. The surgeon had never told her it would probably recur. Was it better for her to have those years free of worry? I *think* it's better to know the truth. But I can't be sure. And there may not be a simple answer ever."

5   Realizing this dilemma, some U.S. patients tell their personal physician up front,⁹ "If I ever become terminally ill, I want to know. I want a realistic assessment¹⁰ of how long I have to live, of what the alternative treatments are, and of what experimental treatments are available. I want to know everything."

6   What's behind this desire to possess such painful information? It lies in the U.S. values of independence, making one's own decisions, making informed choices. Many Americans believe that they have a great deal of power over their own lives—they believe less in luck and fate¹¹ than do members of some other cultures. They feel that if they know the truth, they can use that knowledge to control the outcome¹² of their life. They want this control, and if anything is limiting it, they become very upset. Such values run deep, and they persist all the way to the end.

Threads

Take note, take note, O world, To be direct and honest is not safe.

Shakespeare

After You Read

Identify the circled reference words.

TAKING NOTES FROM YOUR READING

In very brief form, write the main idea of each paragraph. Then show how the supporting details are related to it. Try to use your own words. The first one has been done for you.

¶1: *Should doctors tell terminally ill patients the truth?*

       U. S.: Yes   *Europe, S. Amer., Asia: No*

¶2: _____

_____

_____

¶3: _____

_____

_____

¶4: _____

_____

_____

¶5: _____

_____

¶6: _____

_____

_____

TRUE-FALSE QUESTIONS

			¶ number
1. Most patients want to know the truth.	T	F	_____
2. Breaking the news in a cold and impersonal way could have a positive effect on the patient's welfare.	T	F	_____
3. Dr. James F. Holland thinks the doctor should tell the patient the truth.	T	F	_____
4. Many American doctors are not sure that telling the truth is the best thing to do.	T	F	_____
5. Many Americans believe that they have a great deal of power over their lives.	T	F	_____

ANTICIPATING TEST QUESTIONS: MULTIPLE-CHOICE, TRUE-FALSE, FILL-IN-THE-BLANK

One of the best methods of studying for a test is to write your own practice questions. By imagining yourself in your teacher's place, you're better able to anticipate what questions she or he might ask on the actual test. Practice: You write the comprehension questions for this reading. Try three different approaches, each of which is a very common kind of test question in North American education:

1. Write a multiple-choice question.

    EXAMPLE: American patients want to know the truth because . . .

    a. they think it gives them more control over their lives.
    b. they believe in luck and fate.
    c. they believe that knowing the truth will help them to get well.

    Your question: _____

    _____

    _____

    _____

2. Write a true-false question.

    EXAMPLE: Philosopher Sissela Bok believes that doctors should tell the truth to their patients.   T   F

    Your question: _____

    _____   T   F

3. Write a fill-in-the-blank question.

    EXAMPLE: Doctors in many cultures believe that it would be _____ to tell the patient the truth.

    Your question: _____

    _____

    When you finish, find a couple of partners and "test" each other.

TAKING POSITIONS ON ISSUES

The title to this reading is an issue (see page 151). What is your answer to it? Your answer is known as your *position* on the issue. You will give and explain your position in the Discussion/Writing activity that follows.

DISCUSSION/WRITING: SHOULD DOCTORS LIE?

Do you think that doctors should hide the truth from their terminally ill patients? What's the custom in your culture, and what values does it represent? In answering these questions, use some of the concepts and vocabulary from Reading Two.

Vocabulary

VOCABULARY IN CONTEXT

1. Find the word *terminal* in the first paragraph. What do you think it means? What in the context makes you think so?
2. Find the word *endure* in the second paragraph. What do you think it means, and what makes you think so?
3. In ¶4, find the word *recur.* Then find a synonym in a nearby sentence.

KEYWORDS

1. be likely to* ¶1
2. demand ¶2
3. undergo* ¶2
4. affairs ¶2
5. surgery ¶2
6. welfare ¶3
7. treatment ¶3
8. despair ¶4
9. up front ¶5
10. assessment ¶5
11. fate ¶6
12. outcome ¶6

KEYWORD EXERCISE

1. If you told your parents that you were going to stay in North America for the rest of your life, what would they *be likely to* say?

   EXAMPLE: Would they *be likely to* try to stop you?

2. Rank the following verbs in order from weakest to strongest:
   demand   ask   mention   force   request

   EXAMPLE: Most U.S. patients *demand* to know the truth.

3. Note that you *undergo* (¶2) something that is rather difficult and unpleasant, but unavoidable. This word isn't used for things you do for fun.

   Finish these sentences:
   The cancer patient underwent . . .
   In the early 1990s, the Soviet Union underwent . . .

4. *EXAMPLE:* Patients want to put their *affairs* in order.

   NOTE: This meaning is quite different from the meaning in Reading One: Some married people have *affairs* with someone outside their marriage.

Which of the following words might be examples of patient's *affairs* in the sentence from Reading Two?

- writing a will (a legal document that tells who inherits their things when they die)
- paying their bills and taxes
- making arrangements for their young children, if they have any
- cleaning their house

5. You saw the noun *surgery* in ¶2; now look in ¶4 for a word that means the

person who performs *surgery.* What is it? _____

Which of the following is *surgery?*

an operation   diet   exercise   medicine
chemotherapy   radiation therapy

EXAMPLE: Sometimes it takes a long time to recover after *surgery.*

6. Which of the following are elements of a person or group's *welfare?*

physical health   human nature
mental health   comfort   prosperity

EXAMPLE: Breaking the news in a cold and impersonal way could have a negative effect on the patient's *welfare.*

7. Can you recommend a good *treatment* for culture shock?

EXAMPLE: This new *treatment* takes a long time and is expensive, but it works.

8. In ¶3 you can find the antonym for *despair.* What is it?

_____

EXAMPLE: Total honesty may drive the patient to *despair.*

9. When you rent an apartment, do you pay the rent *up front* or at the end of the month?

EXAMPLE: Some U.S. patients ask their doctors *up front* to tell them the truth.

10. *EXAMPLE:* I want a realistic *assessment* of how long I have to live.

Choose one of the following careers—or another of your choice—and explain how *assessment* plays a part in it.

- gymnastics: Judges *assess* the gymnast using a 10-point scale.

_____

- medicine: Doctors *assess* the patient's progress by noticing _____

_____.

- marketing: A company *assesses* the success of its product by _____

_____.

- education: A teacher *assesses* students' performance with _____.

11. *EXAMPLE:* Americans believe less in luck and *fate* than do members of some other cultures.

People who believe in *fate* believe that the end of our life is "written" before we are born, and that we have no power to change it. The ancient Greeks believed that this power was held by three goddesses known as "The Three Fates," each of whom had a specific part to play in the process: One of them spun the thread of a person's life, another measured it and decided where it should end, and the third cut the thread with a pair of scissors. Do you believe in *fate?* Is such a belief common in your culture?

12. *EXAMPLE:* Most Americans would like to control the *outcome* of their lives.

Name three *outcomes* of war—either war in general, or a specific war that you have in mind.

a. _____   b. _____   c. _____

REVIEW

Now that you have studied the vocabulary, re-read or re-skim the passage.

Freewriting: A Personal Experience

Write about a time when someone lied to you. Did you believe the liar? What happened?

LEARNING STRATEGY

Managing Your Learning: Reading aloud for five minutes each day helps you make connections between the printed language and the spoken language.

READING THREE

Reading process: Scanning for information

In which paragraph can you find the following information?

1. The name of the person whose research this essay is based on. _____

2. A list of the four kinds of behavior that can give a lie away. _____

3. Examples of body behaviors that can't be controlled. _____

4. A discussion of different kinds of smiles. _____

5. A list of precautions. _____

HOW CAN YOU TELL[1] WHEN SOMEONE IS LYING?

1   In the children's story, the wooden puppet Pinocchio could never hide a lie because when he told one, his nose grew longer. Wouldn't it be convenient if (that) happened every time anyone told a lie?—or at least everyone except ourselves? But since it doesn't, how can we decide whether someone is lying to us or telling the truth?

2   Psychologist Paul Ekman has made a lifetime study of how people act when they lie. Usually they not only want the hearer to believe the words they are saying; they also want to cover up some strong emotion that they are feeling such as guilt, shame, fear, anger, pain, or even pleasure. In addition to telling the lie, they want

to conceal that emotion, and the easiest way to do this is by trying to substitute the signs of a different emotion. By noticing the contradictions between their words and their behavior, Ekman found that he could often catch them in the act of lying.

3   Ekman concludes that there are four kinds of behavior that can give a lie away[2]: the liar's words, voice, body, and face. He says that liars try hardest to control their words and face, since they assume that that's what the listener will be paying attention to. Consequently "lie catchers" should also pay close attention to the speaker's voice and body signals, which (she) may forget to control. He then points out what the lie catcher should look for in deciding whether he is being deceived.

4   Obviously most lies are untruthful words, and it's these words that we focus on. A common problem for liars is keeping their story straight. As we all know, one lie leads to another, and before the liar knows it, someone will comment, "But that's not what you said a few minutes ago." A less common but more fatal giveaway is what's called a "slip of the tongue," in which the liar accidentally tells the truth instead of the lie she intended to tell. Additionally, frequent pauses may indicate that she is making up the story as she goes along.

5   The liar's voice can also give her away, and the voice is much harder to control than the words. When telling a lie, she may speak unusually loudly or softly, may speed up or slow down her speech for no apparent reason. This can be because of the emotion she's hiding or because she feels self-conscious[3] at telling a lie. The voice-clue that seems to be the most reliable[4] is that when people are upset, their voices tend to become higher. But Ekman points out that vocal changes such as these are not always signs of lying; (they) simply indicate strong emotion which the person may be trying to conceal.

6   Some body behaviors can be controlled, but others can't. When telling a lie, a person may swallow frequently, sweat, or breathe faster. Gestures can give her away: nervous gestures, such as swinging the foot, scratching or rubbing parts of the body, or twisting the hair often increase when a person is self-conscious or under stress.[5] The normal gestures that usually accompany speech are often used less when someone is lying. Or the liar may accidentally use a gesture that contradicts her words, such as nodding "yes" while saying "no."

7   The final thing that can give a lie away is the liar's face. Some facial behavior is impossible to control and can indicate that a person is emotional or self-conscious. Such signs include changes in facial color (reddening or paling), increased blinking, and enlargement of the pupils of the eyes. Some people find it impossible to hold back tears, and almost everyone finds it hard to produce tears in the absence of genuine[6] emotion. But facial expressions fall into both categories: some of (them) are hard to control, while (others) can easily be falsified.[7]

8   Since the liar often wants to mask her true emotion, she is likely to try to substitute a false (one) through her facial expression. The most common and successful mask is a smile. Ekman's research has identified more than fifty different kinds of smiles, to which he has given names like the "felt smile" (this is a genuine smile), the "fear smile," the "miserable smile," the "embarrassed smile." What distinguishes these smiles from each other is the tension and shape of the lips and also the behavior of the muscles around the eyes and in the eyebrows, forehead, and chin. A false smile tends to be a "mouth only" smile, rather than a "full-face" smile that includes the eyes. In addition, the false smile may linger on the person's face longer than a felt smile would. (Think of how uncomfortable you feel holding a smile for the camera, and how unnatural such smiles usually look in pictures.)

9   In addition to smiles, the "lie catcher" should notice the forehead, eyebrows, and eyes. Facial muscles showing anger and surprise are easy to control and are commonly falsified, something we often do during a polite conversation. But forehead muscles that show real sadness and fear are almost impossible to hide, and are equally difficult to falsify.

10   How reliable are these "giveaways"? Taken alone, not very. Ekman provides a list of precautions[8] that can keep the lie catcher from jumping to the wrong conclusion. Here are some of them:

1. Try to identify exactly what the person is doing that makes you suspicious. Doing this will help you to recognize your own mistakes.
2. Keep in mind that you are risking two mistakes: one, that you might believe a lie; the other, that you might disbelieve the truth. Think carefully about both possibilities.
3. Some liars don't give off the signs described above, and some truthful people give them off regularly. In other words, everyone has an individual style of communicating. Looking for changes in a person's usual behavior is more useful than comparing her behavior to other people's.
4. Don't let your own emotions influence your judgment. Are you looking for a lie because you are jealous or angry? If so, you may "see" a lie that isn't there.
5. Bear in mind that a truthful person may "act guilty" if he feels that you believe he is lying.
6. Does the speaker know that you suspect[9] her? If so, what would she gain[10] if you caught her, and what would she lose?
7. Do you know something that only the liar would know? If so, you might catch her with a question about it.
8. Never decide that a person is lying purely on the basis of the behavioral clues described above. Use them as the reason for further investigation.

11   A further precaution concerns cultural differences. Interestingly enough, Ekman's research has convinced[11] him that most facial expressions (of fear, anger, happiness, etc.) are culturally universal, though (their) frequency and the company in which they are shown may vary from culture to culture. For example, Ekman observed Japanese subjects watching emotional films and found that when alone, their facial expressions were identical to North Americans'; but when a person of authority was in the room with them, they masked any expression of negative emotions with a polite smile, as one should in Japanese culture. Euro-Americans are taught to make eye contact when they speak as a sign that they are being truthful; such eye contact may be a sign of disrespect in some other cultures. If you observe a Korean in a conversation with a Brazilian, you'll see great differences in body movements and gestures. As Ekman points out, "When liar and target[12] come from different cultures and do not share a language, detecting deceit is, for a number of reasons, much more difficult." A lie catcher who is not aware of these differences is likely to misinterpret some signals and to miss others completely, leading to serious errors[13] in judgment.[14]

12   As we all know from experience, there are "good" liars and "bad" ones. Some people can "get away with murder," while others somehow fail to make us believe in them no matter how honest they are. But the one group of liars who always succeeds is liars who deceive themselves, who believe their own lies. Ekman says that these people are "undetectable."[15]

After You Read

Identify the circled reference words.

TRUE-FALSE QUESTIONS

			¶*number*
1. At the same time as they are lying, most liars are trying to keep you from seeing their true emotions.	T	F	_____
2. A liar tries hardest to control her voice and body signals, often forgetting to control her face and words.	T	F	_____
3. It's easier to control your words than it is your voice.	T	F	_____
4. People can't control how often they swallow.	T	F	_____
5. There are many different kinds of smiles.	T	F	_____
6. You can always catch a liar by watching for these "giveaways."	T	F	_____
7. Ekman believes that the facial expressions for particular emotions vary from culture to culture.	T	F	_____

ANTICIPATING TEST QUESTIONS: IDENTIFICATION AND DEFINITION

Two other common kinds of test questions are *identification* and *definition*. Each one generally requires a response of a few sentences, maybe a brief paragraph. For instance, these questions might be asked on a test over Reading One:

QUESTION: Define a *pathological liar.*

Example of a good answer:

A pathological liar is a person who lies about everything, and to everyone. He can't control his lying. He generally doesn't introduce his friends to each other because they might compare stories and realize that he's lied to them all. It's unclear what causes this condition, but it's often related to a bad family background or a great need to be liked.

QUESTION: Identify the two extreme moral positions on lying.

Example of a good answer:

The two extreme moral positions on lying are (1) that people should never lie, because lying hurts both the listener and the liar; and (2) that some kinds of lies are justifiable and even helpful to society.

You want your answer to be long enough to convince your teacher that you have a clear understanding of the topic.

Write one definition or identification question about Reading Three. Then get together with a couple of classmates and "test" each other orally.

RECOGNIZING THE STRUCTURE OF THE READING PASSAGE

Reading Three can be divided into four main parts: The introduction, two parts of the body, and the conclusion. Where do these parts begin and end, and what information is contained in the body?

Introduction: ¶s _____

Part I of the body: ¶s _____

   Topic of Part I: _____

   How many main points are there in Part I? _____

Part II of the body: ¶s _____

   Topic of Part II: _____

   How many main points are there in Part II? _____

Conclusion: ¶s _____

DISCUSSION: "BODY LANGUAGE" FOR LYING

In Euro-North-American culture, crossing the first two fingers of one hand is a gesture whose meaning is related to lying (especially if you hold that hand behind your back, where the listener can't see it). Do you know what it means? If not, ask a native. Winking (closing one eye) as one speaks is also related to lying. Find out what it means, too. Are there gestures that carry similar meanings in your culture?

In your culture, what's a traditional punishment for children who lie?

Vocabulary

VOCABULARY IN CONTEXT

1. In ¶4, find the phrase *keeping their story straight*. Read that sentence and the next one.
   What do you think it means?
   What makes you think that this is the meaning?
2. Here's a challenge: Find the phrase *culturally universal* in ¶11. Read the sentence carefully. What do you think it means?
   What makes you think so?

KEYWORDS

1. tell* (distinguish) (title)
2. give something away ¶3
3. self-conscious ¶5
4. reliable ¶5
5. stress ¶6
6. genuine ¶7
7. falsify ¶7
8. precaution ¶10
9. suspect* #6
10. gain #6
11. convince* ¶11
12. target ¶11
13. error ¶11
14. judgment ¶11
15. undetectable ¶12

KEYWORD EXERCISE

1. *EXAMPLE:*   How can you *tell* if someone is lying?

    Did you find this meaning of *tell* in your dictionary? Which of the following sentences uses it?
    • He told everyone my secret.
    • His face told me that he was lying.
    • I can't tell the twins apart.
    This meaning of *tell* is a synonym for a keyword introduced in the story of Kaspar Hauser in the last chapter. Can you find it?

2. *Meanings:*
    • If something *gives something away,* it shows everyone something that someone is trying to hide.

        EXAMPLE: The liar's voice can *give his lie away.*

    • If someone has something but they don't want it, they may *give it away.*

        EXAMPLE: After the children grew up and left home, their mother *gave away* some of their old toys.

    • Explain the similarities between the two meanings.

3. Which of the following are elements of the adjective *self-conscious?*
    uncomfortable   relaxed   natural   nervous   embarrassed

    EXAMPLE: Some people feel very *self-conscious* when telling a lie.

4. Compare the noun *stress,* which means the worry that a person feels when they're under pressure, with the verb *stress* (a keyword from Chapter 4), which means to emphasize something.

    Example of verb: Most parents *stress* the importance of honesty to their children.
    Example of noun: Nervous gestures may increase when a person is under *stress.*

    In this reading we consider the noun. Which of the following situations (or another one that you might name) causes you the most *stress?*
    • taking an examination
    • moving to a new place
    • making a major decision

5. The verb *falsify* is related to the adjective *false.* Note the suffix *-ify,* which makes it a verb. Name three things that a person can *falsify* (you can use examples from this reading if you like).

    EXAMPLE: Some facial expressions can be easily *falsified.*

6. *EXAMPLE:*   Ekman provides a list of *precautions* to keep the lie catcher from jumping to conclusions.

    A *precaution* is something you do if you want to *prevent* (Reading One, ¶12) something unpleasant or dangerous from happening. The expression is to *take a precaution.* As you can see from the sentence above, a *precaution* is also a *warning.*
    What's the connection between the two meanings (preventing and warning)?

7. *EXAMPLE:* What would the liar *gain* if you caught him, and what would he lose?

   In Chapter 2, what did Columbus hope to *gain* when he was planning his first voyage?

8. Note the differences in the grammar that follows *convince:*

   EXAMPLES: His face *convinced* me that he was telling the truth.

   The salesclerk *convinced* me to buy the more expensive item.

   Finish the sentences:
   The weather report . . .
   My teacher . . .

9. *Meanings:*
   • A *target* is a mark that you try to hit when you are practicing shooting a gun or throwing darts.

     EXAMPLE: A good dart thrower can hit the center of the *target* nine times out of ten.

   • A *target* can also be a person whom someone is trying to deceive, usually for the deceiver's gain.

     EXAMPLE: When liar and *target* come from different cultures, detecting deceit is much more difficult.

   • Explain the similarities between the two meanings.

10. Note that *judgment* can also be spelled *judgement.* Both are acceptable.
    In Chapter 1, what was the king's *judgment?*

11. *Matching:*

    _____ **1.** *reliable*   **a.** not noticeable

    _____ **2.** *genuine*   **b.** real

    _____ **3.** *suspect*   **c.** dependable

    _____ **4.** *error*   **d.** a person whom you believe has done something wrong

    _____ **5.** *undetectable*

                                       e. mistake

REVIEW

Now that you have studied the vocabulary, re-read or re-skim the passage.

NOTE: This reading is also on the tape.

Reading process: Scanning for information

In which paragraph would you expect to find the following information?

HINT: Use the *heading*s to help you locate these items.

1. A computer company lied to an advertising agency.
2. You just have to take chances sometimes.
3. Honest businesspeople are proud of their clean names.
4. Most victims don't do anything about it.
5. Most businesspeople trust each other.

HONESTY[1] AND DISHONESTY IN THE BUSINESS WORLD

1   *Are most business people honest?* When they were children, the businesspeople of today were taught by their parents that honesty pays[2] and that the dishonest will suffer. Their parents and teachers told them moral[3] stories about honest people who were rewarded and dishonest people who were punished. Then they grew up and went out into the cold hard world of business. Faced with a choice between honesty and dishonest profit,[4] which road do (these people) take? According to a study conducted by *Harvard Business Review,* most U.S. businesspeople do conduct their affairs honestly. They also are willing to trust other businesspeople, because their experience has taught them that most of (them) are honest too.

2   *Who is dishonest?* But the Harvard team found numerous examples with a different outcome: sometimes dishonesty was greatly profitable. A computer company deceived an advertising agency in order to get good terms, and that single ad helped (them) sell $150,000 worth of software. Expensive department stores in New York City have a reputation[5] for breaking their promises to suppliers and costing the suppliers a great deal. Some investment brokers deceive their clients[6] and lose all (their) money. Yet more clients come along, the suppliers keep working with the department stores, and ad agencies take new chances with unknown firms.

3   *Why does anyone believe them?* Given examples like these, it may seem strange to you that businesses would be so trusting. It's partly due to an assumption[7] in the business world that some dishonest people are going to come your way, and you just have to take it in stride.[8] In other cases the reason is greed[9]: the investor convinces the client that he will make such incredible profits that the client can't resist. The smooth talk of the sales rep may win over[10] the customer. Clients have their lawyer go over the contract with a fine-toothed comb, hoping that they can outfox the deceiver. And another reason that dishonesty pays is because most businesspeople believe that most others are as honest as they themselves are.

4   *How do they get away with it?* You might think that dishonest companies and businesspeople would be sued,[11] but they seldom are. The victim[12] may be afraid of the person's power, they may just not want to spend the time and money and effort, or they might not want to endanger their own reputation.

5   *So why be honest?* It sounds bad, doesn't it? Crime pays, honest people suffer. Yet (these stories) do seem to be in the minority. It's true that you can always find ways to lose your money if you want to take foolish risks with people who have bad track records,[13] but the truth is, most businesspeople told (HBR) that they generally trusted people and that they were very rarely burned. Most of them also said that they themselves were honest in their own business dealings.[14] Why? Not because they believed that it would bring them higher profits, but because of their own self-respect and moral principles. They "took pride in their good names." Said one: "We keep promises because we believe it is right to do so, not because it is good business."

Threads

Honesty is the best policy.

English proverb

After You Read

Identify the circled reference words.

DISCUSSION: COMPREHENSION QUESTIONS

Work with a partner and take turns answering these questions. Try to do it without looking back at the reading.

1. Are most businesspeople honest?
2. Give three examples of dishonest businesses.
3. How are dishonest businesspeople able to find anyone to trust them?
4. How do dishonest businesspeople get away with their deceptions?
5. Why are honest businesspeople honest?

A CULTURAL NOTE

Find the word *outfox* in ¶3. The prefix *out-* means *more than* or *better than;* the second part of the word is the animal *fox.* In English-speaking cultures, the fox is an animal that represents clever deception. In folk stories, smooth-talking foxes deceive stupid chickens and ducks, who end up as dinner on the fox family's table. In the reading, "hoping that they can outfox the deceiver" means "hoping that they can deceive him even more than he is deceiving them."

Vocabulary

SPECIALIZED BUSINESS VOCABULARY

If you're planning to go into business, you may be interested in the specialized business terminology to be found in Reading Four. There are several ways of categorizing these words. See if you can fill them in on this list (some words may be used in more than one place):

• persons (5 words): _____ _____

  _____ _____ _____

• companies (3 words): _____ _____

  _____

- money (1 word): _____

- business relations (2 words): _____ _____

- legal terms often used in business (2 words): _____

_____

- something you want to happen (2 words): _____

_____

- something you don't want to happen (2 words): _____

_____

VOCABULARY IN CONTEXT

1. Close your eyes and make a mental picture of a comb with very fine teeth. Then look in ¶3 and find the sentence that mentions this object. What do you think that sentence means? Is it talking about a real comb?
2. In ¶5, find the word *burned*. What do you think it means to *be burned*? What words in the same sentence help to explain the meaning?

KEYWORDS

1. honesty (title)
2. honesty pays ¶1
3. moral ¶1
4. profit* ¶1
5. reputation* ¶2
6. client ¶2
7. assumption ¶3
8. take it in stride ¶3
9. greed ¶3
10. win over ¶3
11. be sued ¶4
12. victim* ¶4
13. track record ¶5
14. dealings ¶5

KEYWORD EXERCISE

1. Each of these sentences appears in the reading above. Give an example of how each can be true.

   Honesty pays. (¶1)
   Dishonesty pays. (¶3)
   Crime pays. (¶5)

2. A *moral* story is a story with a lesson in it. Here's an example:

   A shepherd boy got bored sitting on the hillside with his sheep, so he shouted, "Wolf! Wolf!" All the villagers came running, but they became very angry when there was no wolf. This was so much fun that the shepherd boy did it again. The villagers were even angrier the second time. Then a wolf really did appear. The boy shouted again, but this time no one came to help him, and the wolf killed one of his sheep.

   What's the *moral* of this story?

3. In Reading One ¶8, there is a word that is the antonym of *profit*. What is it?

   EXAMPLE: Sometimes businesses have to choose between honesty and dishonest *profit*.

4. Your *reputation* falls into which of the following categories?
   a fact   a thing   a belief   an event   an opinion

   EXAMPLE: Some firms have a *reputation* for honesty; some don't.

5. What is the difference between a *client* and a customer? (You can use your dictionary.)

   EXAMPLE: Lawyers have *clients;* stores have customers.

6. *EXAMPLE:* Businesspeople know that some dishonest people are going to come their way, and they just have to *take it in stride*.

   In the literal meaning, your *stride* is the way that you walk when you're relaxed and purposeful. What's the connection between this literal meaning and the meaning of the idiom *take something in stride?*

   When you go to live in a foreign culture, if you let everything bother you greatly, you'd be upset all the time and you'd probably decide to turn around and go back home. What's something that bothered you when you went to a new culture, but which you learned to *take in stride?*

7. What do you think this proverb means?—*Greedy* folks have long arms.

8. *EXAMPLE:* You can always find ways to lose your money if you want to take foolish risks with people who have bad *track records*.

   Were you able to find this phrase in your dictionary? If not, here's a definition: The *track record* of a person or a business is their record of good or bad performance. This term originally came not from business, but from another field of activity. Which of the following do you suppose it was?
   medicine   sports   music   education   science

9. *Matching:*

____   1. *honest*   a. truthful

____   2. *assumption*   b. business relations, trade

____   3. *win over*   c. persuade someone to agree with you

____   4. *be sued*   d. someone who has been wrongfully harmed

____   5. *victim*   e. belief that something is true

____   6. *dealings*   f. a kind of legal action taken against you

REVIEW

Now that you've studied the vocabulary, re-read or re-skim the passage.

Writing an Essay Test

Another common type of test question is the *essay* or *discussion* question. The purpose of this question is to find out how completely you understand a large concept or problem. Your professor may expect an answer that ranges from one well-developed paragraph to a full essay of several paragraphs.

For your essay in this chapter, choose one of the following questions:

1. Compare and contrast U.S. patients' and their doctors' feelings about telling the truth to a terminally ill patient. Then compare and contrast patients' versus doctors' feelings in your own culture.
2. Describe the kinds of behavior that can give a lie away, and explain the risks of believing that you can "catch" a liar in this way.
3. Choose a specific business situation to use as an example for this question: Discuss the risks of trusting an unknown business that you have to deal with. How would you decide whether to trust them? What could you do to protect yourself?

Before you start writing your answer, find the paragraphs in the reading that give you information for each part of the question, and study them carefully for five minutes. You can highlight information and take notes if you like.

Now, without looking back at the reading or your notes, take out a piece of paper and write an answer. Your teacher will tell you how much time you can have. Use this format: Instead of repeating the question, your *very short* introduction should identify the topic (e.g. "Trusting an unknown firm can be risky business, but sometimes you have to do it"). Then continue, keeping one eye on the clock. Make sure that you can cover the entire topic in the time allowed. You'll lose points if your answer is incomplete. If possible, save yourself three to five minutes at the end to re-read what you've written, making revisions and corrections.

LEARNING STRATEGY

Overcoming Limitations: Thinking in English helps you break the habit of translating.

Evaluating Learning Strategies

Look back over the learning strategies in this chapter. Were there any that weren't especially helpful for you? What wasn't helpful about them? Which ones did you find helpful? Think about times and ways that you can keep using them in your future reading.

Evaluating Your Learning

	Very little	Quite a bit	A lot
You learned to use some new vocabulary in your writing.	_____	_____	_____
Your comprehension has improved.	_____	_____	_____
You're getting better at paraphrasing in your own words.	_____	_____	_____
You can identify issues in a reading passage.	_____	_____	_____
You can answer several different types of test questions.	_____	_____	_____
You learned about lies and honesty.	_____	_____	_____

KEYWORDS FOR CHAPTER 6: LIES AND TRUTH

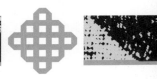

Verbs
backfire
convince*
demand
falsify
gain (2 meanings)
give someone away
harm*
likely to, be*
prevent*
profit*
prosper
sued, be
suffer
suspect*
tell (distinguish)*
trust
undergo*
win over

Adjectives
genuine
guilty
justifiable
moral
profound
reliable
self-conscious
undetectable

Nouns
affairs
assessment
assumption
boundary
circumstances
client
dealings
deception
despair
error
fate
greed
honesty
intention
judgment
mask
outcome
precaution
profit*
reputation*
stress
surgery
suspect*
track record
treatment
trust
victim*
welfare

Adverb
intentionally
up front

Introductory phrase
There is no question that

The Owl and the Logger

7

CHAPTER

PLANNING YOUR LEARNING

Review your overall goal statement. How much progress did you make toward it in the last chapter? Do you want to change it? Think about how you can work to meet your goal as you study this new chapter.

- How many words do you want to learn? (minimum 72, the number of keywords in the chapter)
- What grade would you like to make on the vocabulary section of the exam at the end of the chapter?
- What grade would you like to make on the reading comprehension section of the exam?
- What are you going to read outside of class?

PREVIEWING THE CHAPTER

- Look at the title of this chapter. You'll find out what an owl and a logger are in Reading Two.
- Look in the Table of Contents at the titles of the six readings. Look through the chapter at the pictures, the map, and the drawings. What are some things that you are curious about? What do you expect to find out?
- Which reading do you think you'll be most interested in?

PREPARING TO READ: CONTENT

An endangered species is a kind of plant or animal that is dying out. Working with a couple of partners, make a list of all the endangered species that you can think of. Try to come up with as long a list as possible. When you finish, compare your lists. Which was longest?

Now write all the species on the blackboard. Can you identify a country where each one lives? What has endangered each species? Compared with other problems in the world today, do you think this one is very important?

PREPARING TO READ: VOCABULARY

1. The world of nature, including all life-forms, the land, the sea, and the air, is

   called the e_____.

2. When a species of animal or plant dies out completely, we say that it has

   become e_____.

3. P_____ is the process of dirtying the air, the land, or the water, especially with chemicals that are dangerous to life-forms.

4. Each country contains certain things that it can use for its own people or for sale to other countries. For instance, many countries have petroleum, or good fishing areas, or productive agriculture, or minerals such as gold and diamonds. These are called the country's n_____

   r_____.

5. An area where trees grow closely together is called a f_____.

6. A person who has a job is e_____. A person who loses a job is u_____. These two words are adjectives. What are their noun forms?

7. If people want to get together to discuss a topic or a problem, they may hold a c_____.

8. Many people are working together to try to find s_____ to the world's major problems.

A word about vocabulary: All of the reading passages in this chapter contain some vocabulary items that are specialized for the topic. They'll be marked in the reading by superscript letters (a, b, c, etc.) and defined at the end of each reading passage. You'll need to understand these words in order to follow the readings, but in most cases they aren't terms that you'll need beyond this chapter. (As usual, the most useful items will be listed as Keywords.)

READING ONE

Reading process: Your teacher will give you a minute and a half to skim each of the parts in this reading. After Part One and Part Three, do the exercises in the boxes. After you've skimmed everything, read each part at your own speed, marking vocabulary as usual. When you come to the end of each part, review it and think about its main points.

Endangered Species vs. Human Needs

PART ONE: INTRODUCTION

1 The most famous *endangered species*[a] on earth were the dinosaurs. They died out in one of five "great *extinctions*"[b] that have occurred in the millions of years since life began on this planet—periods in which, for natural causes, a large percentage of the species that existed simply disappeared. We are now in the middle of a sixth great extinction, but this one has been caused by human activity. Consequently, the importance of preserving species is a popular topic today, particularly in the industrialized world.

2 But no discussion of endangered species is complete without an examination of the reasons behind its causes, which are human needs. In Africa, where the world's population is growing the fastest, forests are shrinking as people clear lands for homes and farms and cut wood for fuel. Herds of goats and sheep eat the vegetation, leaving the bare soil to be carried away by wind and water. Humans kill wildlife to protect their crops, and may also kill them for the illegal trade in ivory, rhinoceros horns, furs. In Latin America and Southeast Asia,

rainforests are cleared for farmlands and for fuel and timber. The loss of the forests endangers many species of plants and destroys many animals' *habitats,* or natural homes. And in the oceans, fish supplies have been greatly reduced by overfishing and by *pollution.*[c]

Whom do you favor in this equation—the endangered species, or the human needs? Mark your response on the following scale:

Endangered species   *Both equally*   *Human needs*
1 -------------- 2 -------------- 3 -------------- 4 -------------- 5

Explain your response: Why did you give this weighting to endangered species? To human needs?

PART TWO: _____

3   Humans want to survive just as every other species does. We need food, shelter, and a place to rear our young. So how do our activities endanger other species? Specifically, there are three major ways. We kill off animals directly in some cases. We may want their meat, bones, skins, tusks, horns, or feathers; or we may want to protect our crops and livestock from them. By overhunting, Euro-Americans endangered the buffalo in North America, and in the nineteenth century hunters drove to extinction the passenger pigeon, which was probably the most populous bird species that had ever lived.

4   Another way that we endanger native life-forms is by introducing foreign species into their habitat. A prime[1] example of this was the introduction of European rabbits into Australia, where they multiplied until they endangered the native species of grazing animals by eating all the vegetation. This became a terrible problem that has finally been brought under some control, though not completely solved.

5   The most common way that we endanger other species is by destroying their natural habitats. We do this when we cut down forests, clear land for crops, build towns, dam rivers, drain swamplands of water and then fill them with dirt for construction, and when we pollute the air, the water, the soil. Most species are *habitat-specific;* that is, they depend on the particular[3] offerings of a specific environment,[2] and they cannot simply move to the next province or state and adapt as we can. The greatest diversity of life-forms on our planet are found in the *tropical*[d] rainforests, yet (they) are disappearing faster than any other habitat—at the rate of about 50 million acres (20 million hectares) per year. The loss of the rainforests would mean the loss of most of the species that make their homes in them.

PART THREE: _____

6   But so what? The majority of the animal species on earth are insects and worms anyway, and how important are (they) to us? And tiny populations of tropical plants—the world is covered with vegetation, so what difference does it make how many kinds there are?

7   Many people's answer is that every life-form has a right to exist, and that no other reason is needed for preserving it. A more common reason is the beauty of many species. Certain species also provide[4] humans with economic value. But scientists identify two additional reasons which may not be obvious to most of us.

8   One of these reasons is that each life-form occupies a special place within its *ecosystem*—that is, its community of plant and animal life, in combination with the nonliving components[5] of its environment such as the climate, soil, water, and air. For instance, within a forest the larger trees drop off little twigs and debris, making a layer that holds water in the soil for other plants to use. The roots hold the soil and prevent it from washing away in rainstorms. Whether living or dead, the tree provides shelter for animals and birds and food for insects. As the dead tree rots away, it enriches the soil of the forest floor, enabling other plants to spring up in its place. Such large trees are an example of what we call *keystone species;* if they disappeared from their ecosystem, the consequences would be felt throughout the community of other species living in the forest. "The loss of a keystone species is like a drill accidentally striking a powerline," says biologist Edward Wilson of Harvard University. "It causes lights

An Ecosystem at Work

to go out all over." During the current[6] sixth great extinction, three species of life-forms are dying out every hour, or 74 per day, which equals 27,000 each year. Some of these—and we don't even know which ones—are undoubtedly keystone species.

9   Natural ecosystems are characterized by their *biodiversity,* which means that a good variety of plant and animal life are present there. In many parts of today's world, humans have replaced naturally diverse environments with *monocultures,* in which only one species lives—one that we humans value. A prime example in forested regions of the world is the monocultural "tree farms" that have been planted after the original forests have been cut down. The character of these tree farms is very different from (that) of the original forests.

10   In the case of forests, another extremely important reason for preserving species is illustrated by the Pacific yew tree, which people used to cut down and never replant because they thought it had no particular value. But recently medical researchers discovered that a substance[7] called taxol, produced naturally in the bark of this tree, is an effective[8] medication for treating certain kinds of cancer. Suddenly harvesters began flocking to the forests of the North American Pacific Northwest in search of this tree. If it had become extinct before its value had been discovered, many cancer patients would have died needlessly.

11   Now, consider for a moment that there are around 1.6 million species that we have identified on earth (plus uncounted others that we haven't identified), and most of them have never been studied to see whether they might be able to provide us with food or medicine. About 15 percent of all our medicines are derived[9] from tropical plants, but we have been able to test only about 10 percent of the plants that we know about, and have intensively studied less than 1 percent. Of the 74 species dying out each day, many of them are tropical plants from the rainforests. In most cases, we don't even know the value of what we are losing.

12   If we turn from medicines to food sources, we find that over 50 percent of today's global[10] food supply consists of[11] just three grains—wheat, rice, and corn. If climatic changes or a plant disease suddenly threatened one of these grains, many people would starve unless we could find another species to strengthen or replace it. It is dangerous to be so dependent on such a small number of species. We need to preserve a wider variety of food species.

13   Finally, a very important reason for preserving forestland is that plants produce[12] the oxygen that animals (like us) breathe, and forests produce more of the world's oxygen than any other environment. Forests also make the air more humid, producing rain; and the loss of forests leads to the process of desertification—the creation of deserts where little will grow.

Suppose that you wanted to do something to protect endangered species. How many ways can you think of to do this? Work with your partners to generate a list. When you finish, write your lists on the blackboard and compare them. Copy down any items that you had not thought of. Then look at this larger list. Which of these methods have you heard of before? Which ones do you think are best? Write a + beside them. What drawbacks can you think of for some of the items? Write a − beside them.

PART FOUR: _____

14   Many methods of protecting endangered species are being practiced in different parts of the globe. *Legislation*[e] is a common method: passing laws against killing endangered species or destroying their habitat. Worldwide, over 1200 parks and preserves have been set aside in which wildlife are protected. And certain endangered species are being raised in captivity for later release into their wild habitats.

15   An organization called the World Wildlife Fund recommends nine different methods that can be effective in protecting endangered species. They are:

Protect habitat
Protect individual species
Promote ecologically sound development
Support scientific investigation
Educate the public
Train local wildlife professionals
Encourage countries to design, fund, and carry out effective *conservation*[f]
    activities
Monitor the international wildlife trade
Influence public opinion and the policies of governments and private
    institutions.

16   Only time will tell how effective these attempts will be in slowing the speed of the current great extinction. And the most important factor in this controversy is the demands of a growing human population for natural resources and living space to serve its own needs.

SPECIALIZED VOCABULARY ITEMS FROM THE READING

[a] *Endangered species:* A species of plant or animal that is likely to die out within 20 years unless special steps are taken to protect it.
[b] *Extinct:* We say that a species is *extinct* when all its members have died.
[c] *Pollution:* The act of making the air, water, or soil dirty with harmful or poisonous substances; also refers to the condition of such dirty air, water, or soil.
[d] *Tropical:* The *tropical* area of the earth is the hottest part, which makes a wide band north and south of the equator.
[e] *Legislation:* A law, or the act of making laws.
[f] *Conservation:* The careful management, protection, and use of natural resources.

IDENTIFYING ISSUES AND TAKING POSITIONS

Working in a small group, identify three issues from the reading. Formulate them as questions.

1. _____
_____

2. _____
_____

3. _____
_____

After You Read

Identify the circled reference words.

COMPREHENSION: NAMING THE PARTS OF THE READING

Look at Parts Two through Four. Choose a title for each one that gives a good idea of its content.

COMPREHENSION QUESTIONS

1. What are seven human activities that are causing the current great extinction?

   a. _____   e. _____

   b. _____   f. _____

   c. _____   g. _____

   d. _____

2. What are five reasons why this should worry us?

    a. _____   d. _____

    b. _____   e _____

    c. _____

3. What are two advantages that biodiversity has over monocultures?

    a. _____

    b. _____

4. Look in ¶15 at the World Wildlife Fund's nine methods of protecting endangered species.
   • Which one or ones can be accomplished by legislation?
   • Which one or ones use parks and preserves?
   • Which one or ones use zoos?

TAKING NOTES FROM YOUR READING

On a separate sheet of paper, take notes for each part of the reading. The comprehension questions that you've just answered will provide you with good information to include.

First look at each part and determine how it is organized:

• a list of examples or reasons?
• comparison/contrast?
• cause and effect?
• problem and solution? etc.

Look for the markers that will give you clues to the organization. Then take your notes in a graphic form that makes it easy for you to see the information and how it's organized. Work on one section at a time. (You may want to refer to page 98 in Chapter 4 for some examples of graphic forms for notes. These are only possibilities; use your own creativity to find ways to display your own notes clearly.)

To get you started, here's an example. Finish it.

> Human activities causing 6th great extinction → pollution
> → habitat destruction (most common cause)

Try your best. Taking notes in this way is exactly what college and university students in North America have to be able to do. At the end of this chapter, you'll be using information from your notes in a paper that you'll write, so the better your notes are, the better your paper will be.

Managing Your Learning: Find and use the best conditions and time for you to learn vocabulary.

Vocabulary

VOCABULARY IN CONTEXT

1. Find the phrase *habitat-specific* in ¶5. What do you think it means?
    What phrase does the author use to introduce the definition?
    (Always notice this phrase if you're looking for meaning in context. It's a common signal that the author is about to explain or define something new.)
2. Find another example of a definition signaled the same way in ¶8. What word is being defined?
    What does it mean?

KEYWORDS

1. prime ¶4
2. environment ¶5
3. particular* ¶5
4. provide ¶7
5. component ¶8
6. current* ¶8

7. substance ¶10
8. effective ¶10
9. derived ¶11
10. global ¶12
11. consist of* ¶12
12. produce ¶13

KEYWORD EXERCISE

1. What's a *prime* example of a very dangerous occupation? _____

    EXAMPLE: The passenger pigeon was a *prime* example of a species that was made extinct by overhunting.

2. What's the meaning of *environment* in this sentence: Some people study better in a quiet *environment*, such as a library, while others prefer a noisy *environment* like a café.

    _____

    What's the connection between this meaning of *environment* and the natural *environment*?

    _____

3. Which of these words could be substituted for *particular* in the following phrases from the reading?

   acceptable   specific   uncertain   special   individual

   . . . the *particular* offerings of a specific environment . . .

   _____

   . . . had no *particular* value . . .

   _____

4. Name at least three *components* of a camera.

   _____   _____   _____

   EXAMPLE: Climate, soil, water, and air are nonliving *components* of an ecosystem.

5. *EXAMPLE:* The tree *provides* shelter for animals and birds.

   Finish the sentences:
   My family provides . . .
   Doctors . . .

6. Look at ¶8 and find the word *current*. What part of speech is it?

   _____

   You'll note that there are several definitions of it in your dictionary. Which

   one is correct for the sentence in the reading? _____

   EXAMPLE: The *current* great extinction is the sixth.

7. What *substance* makes leaves green? _____

   EXAMPLE: Taxol is a *substance* produced in the bark of the Pacific yew tree.

8. In your opinion, which of the following would be the most *effective* way to reduce violent crime in the United States?

   gun control   construction of more prisons
   greater employment opportunities

   EXAMPLE: Taxol is an *effective* treatment for certain kinds of cancer.

9. What is a good-smelling substance that can be *derived* from flowers?

   _____

   EXAMPLE: Fifteen percent of all of our medicines are *derived* from tropical plants.

10. What shape is a *globe* map? _____

    Some people call the earth today a "*global* village." What do you think they mean?

    _____

    EXAMPLE: The *global* weather patterns are driven mainly by the oceans.

11. **EXAMPLE:** Over 50 percent of the global food supply *consists of* just three grains.

   Finish the sentences:
   Water consists of . . .
   This class . . .

12. **EXAMPLE:** Forests *produce* more of the world's oxygen than any other environment.

   Finish the sentences:
   Iran produces . . .
   Automobiles . . .

Remembering New Material: Making up paragraphs that contain several new words helps you remember them more easily.

REVIEW

Now that you've studied the vocabulary, re-read or re-skim the passage.

READING TWO

Reading process: Developing good habits during reading

Practice the method that you learned about on page 50. If you need to, review the procedure before you start. Remember the steps:

- Make predictions
- Form mental pictures
- Make connections with your own experience, or with something you already know
- Recognize problems that you are having
- Solve these problems

When you finish, fill out the chart on the handout that your teacher gave you earlier.

The Owl and the Timber Industry

PART ONE: INTRODUCTION

1   One of the hot spots in the war between endangered species and human needs is the Pacific Northwest of the United States. Here the mountains and valleys of Washington, Oregon, and northern California are blanketed with some of the most beautiful forests in the world. They are also a profitable source of wood. When the white settlers moved into the region around 150 years ago, the timber industry became an important part of the *economic base,*[a] and it seemed as though this ocean of giant trees would last[1] forever. Yet by now most of the diverse ancient forest (called *old-growth*) has been cut and replaced by *second-growth* monoculture tree farms of Douglas fir, a tall, large, straight tree whose wood is very valuable for construction. *Environmentalists*[b] of the 1970s began to worry that before long, the few old-growth forests that were left would fall to the saws of the *logging companies.*[c] But there didn't seem to be much (they) could do to stop (it.)

PART TWO: _____

2   Onto the battlefield flew a small bird, the northern spotted owl. Environmentalists discovered that this bird makes its home almost exclusively in old-growth forest. Each pair of owls needs an area of about four square miles (264 hectares) for its survival. And with the disappearance of the old-growth, the owls' numbers were also shrinking as their habitat was being eaten away.

3   The environmentalists used the owl as the basis for action to stop the cutting of the ancient forests. They turned to a law known as the Endangered Species Act, which requires the *federal*[d] government to identify and to protect life-forms in danger of extinction. In 1991 the northern spotted owl, though not considered "endangered," became listed as "*threatened,*" which means likely to become endangered if nothing is done to protect it. So the United States government reserved 8.2 million acres (3.3 million hectares) of forest in California, Oregon, and Washington as "critical[2] habitat" for the owl. Some of the areas consisted of "owl circles," areas of 6600 acres (264 hectares) whose center was the nest of a pair of owls. These areas were declared "off limits" to activities (particularly tree cutting) that might damage the owls' habitat. In fact, in 1990–91 the federal government and the three states spent a total of $9.7 million in efforts to protect the spotted owl. Such efforts included locating owls, mapping their circles, communicating with timber companies to declare the areas off limits, enforcing these efforts, and prosecuting violators.

4   The heart of the controversy is this: at one extreme stand some environmentalists who believe that no more ancient forest should be cut. Some of them are willing to go to any means to stop the cutting: they will secretly drive metal spikes into the trunks of giant trees, then inform logging companies that in a particular area, certain trees have been "spiked." The *loggers*[e] know that if their saws hit a spike, (they) can be injured or even killed, so they won't cut in that area. At the other extreme stand members of the timber industry who depend for their livelihood[3] on the availability of wood to be cut. By 1993 many *sawmills*[f] in the Northwest had closed down because of the unavailability of giant old-growth logs, and the workers lost their jobs. Whole[4] families with little children lost their homes and had nowhere to go. Some took to the woods and lived there in their cars or in tents. These people are desperate[5] for their employment. They know that there is great demand for wood products in the United States today, and they can see the remaining[6] ancient forests waiting to be cut. It seems to them that as human beings, their needs should outweigh those of birds.

Based on your own opinion and what you have learned so far, whom do you favor in this particular situation—the owl, or the humans? Mark your response on the following scale:

Northern spotted owl　　　　　　*Both equally*　　　　　*Timber workers*
1 -------------- 2 -------------- 3 -------------- 4 -------------- 5

Explain your response.

PART THREE: _____

5   But it's not that simple. Few really important controversies are. Suppose we took the most extreme timber-industry position and went ahead and cut all of the old-growth forests. Some jobs would be saved temporarily,[7] but eventually all of the giant trees would be gone, and then what? There really isn't an endless supply of (them.) And with them would go all of the plant and animal species that are part of the old-growth ecosystem. For the environmentalists, the most important thing is not the owl: the bird is simply an indicator of the health of the ecosystem, which is the larger issue.

6   Furthermore, the drop in timber-industry jobs is due in part to other factors.[8] (One) is increased automation in the mills. (Another) is that industry owners find it profitable to export "raw" logs and wood chips overseas instead of processing them in the United States. Critics[9] point out that if those logs were sawn into lumber and converted into finished products at home, if those wood chips were converted into paper in the Northwest, jobs would be saved there.

7   But suppose we took the other extreme point of view. If we closed off all of the remaining ancient forests from any cutting, what would happen to the unemployed timber workers? There are larger issues involved here, too: the timber industry provides money for public schools and other local and statewide social programs. Particular areas of Washington, Oregon, and northern California are totally dependent on this industry and have no other economic base to fall back on. Many unemployed workers do not have a college education or specialized training for other employment; they never thought they would need it. They have worked their whole lives in the woods and the mills, and there is nothing else that they are trained to do or want to do. For some entire communities, working in and around the forests is more than a job: it is a way of life, and has been for generations.[10] What are these people to do, especially since they can see that there is still wood that has not been cut, wood that is being preserved for the use of a bird? It's no wonder that you can find pickup trucks in the Northwest with bumper stickers that read "Have an owlburger for lunch" and "Save people, not trees." Human needs have to be addressed.

PART FOUR: _____

8   However, these human problems cannot all be blamed on[11] the environmentalists. Another larger issue is the question of how forests should be managed. The whole concept behind the career of forestry is that forest resources should be managed for human benefit. Part of this, of course, involves keeping the forests healthy, since an unhealthy forest cannot benefit humans. In the United States, forests on federal, state, and local-government-owned lands equal about 140 million acres (56 million hectares), about twice as much as is owned by the forest products industry. The public forests are managed in order to provide for multiple uses: timber for the manufacture of lumber, plywood, paper, and other wood products; water supply; recreation for the public; and wildlife habitat.

9   Until the mid-1990s, the most common method of tree harvesting in the Pacific Northwest was *clearcutting*. This method involves just what the name suggests: clearing a particular area of all the vegetation on it. The valuable logs are trucked off to the sawmill; the remaining stumps and debris are bulldozed into a pile, which is burned. Then people are supposed to come in and replant the area, usually with a monoculture of trees such as Douglas firs. Obviously, clearcutting completely destroys the original forest ecosystem. A closely planted monoculture tree farm does not provide for the variety of species that make their homes in a natural forest, including many kinds, sizes, and ages of trees, smaller undergrowth plants, and not only living trees but also fallen logs in various stages of decay.

10   Until (it) can be replanted or until the new trees become well established, a clearcut area's soil is open to the elements. Wind and rain carry the fragile[12] topsoil away, uncovering the poorer soil below, eroding it with deep scars, especially on steep hillsides. Rains carry the exposed[13] soil into the nearby streams and rivers, filling them with mud; this pollutes the water and harms the fish and other life-forms that make their homes (there.) So the practice of clearcutting also affects the fishing industry.

11   In the Pacific Northwest, fishing is a billion-dollar industry involving over 60,000 persons per year. The best-known fish is the salmon, which used to be plentiful in the streams and rivers of the

A Clearcut

area. An interesting feature of salmon behavior is that they hatch from eggs in freshwater streams and rivers, then swim out into the ocean for most of their lives. Not long before they die, they swim back inland up the very same river in which they were born to lay their eggs. If they cannot get to that exact place, they will not reproduce. Human activities such as the damming of rivers for lakes and hydroelectric power have made it very hard for them to do this. Clearcutting of forests has also taken its toll: it has removed14 riverside trees that provided shade and whose roots in the water provided protection for the salmon, and eroded topsoil has polluted the streams. In fact, the American Fisheries Society claims that the endangerment of at least 90 salmon runs in the Pacific Northwest is due to the practice of clearcutting on federally managed public land.

12   But clearcutting is the most economical method of cutting trees. "*Selective cutting,*" in which loggers carefully take out only particular trees, leaving the rest of the forest intact, is much more difficult to do and is therefore expensive. Some members of the industry insist that they should not be forced to give up clearcutting, should just be encouraged to give it up voluntarily, or should be given a period of several years to make the transition from clearcutting to selective cutting. They say that in this way, jobs will be saved and more wood will be produced for the increasing global population, whose number is expected to double every 39 years at present rates.[15] More people means growing demands for *natural resources*[g]—land, water, fuel, construction materials for housing—and jobs. Protecting industry profits means protecting jobs.

CONCLUSION: ─────────────────────────────

13   So should we protect the environment, or should we protect the economy? Most people in (the area) have come to believe that we must do both. If we don't protect the environment, there will soon be no more timber industry. And if we don't protect the industry, human beings will continue to suffer because of unemployment. But the industry is clearly going to have to make changes in how it operates. Each side of the controversy must protect the other. In April, 1993, the Society of American Foresters (the world's largest association of professional foresters) recommended an approach to forestry that was twofold: to harvest trees at a rate equal to replanting, but also to manage the forest in such a way as to protect wildlife, water quality, and overall ecosystem health.

14   When he was running for President of the United States in 1992, Bill Clinton visited the Northwest and promised that if elected, he would return to the region and listen to all sides of the controversy. (This) he did in April, 1993, at a gathering known as the White House Forest Conference in Portland, Oregon. All day President Clinton, Vice President Al Gore, and members of the Cabinet listened as 53 people gave them a wide variety of information and points of view that ranged from extreme-environmentalist to middle-of-the-road to extreme-timber-industry. Their purpose, as President Clinton stated in his introductory remarks, was to help answer the following difficult questions: "How can we achieve a balanced and comprehensive policy that recognizes the importance of the forests and timber to the economy and jobs of this region, and how can we preserve our precious old-growth forests, which are part of our national heritage and that once destroyed, can never be replaced?" At the end of the day, Clinton appointed a team of specialists to study the problem and asked them to recommend a solution within 60 days.

SPECIALIZED VOCABULARY ITEMS FROM THE READING

[a] *Economic base:* The primary money-making activity or activities of a region are called its *economic base.*

[b] *Environmentalist:* A person who takes action to try to protect the health of the natural environment from human activities that threaten it.

[c] *Logging company:* A *logging* company cuts down trees.

[d] *Federal:* The *federal* government of the United States is the national government.

[e] *Logger:* A *logger* is a person who cuts down trees for a living.

[f] *Sawmill:* A *sawmill* is a place where logs are cut up into flat boards.

[g] *Natural resources:* Substances that can be found in nature and can be used by humans. Besides timber, examples include petroleum, natural gas, iron, some wildlife.

After You Read

Identify the circled reference words.

COMPREHENSION: NAMING THE PARTS OF THE READING

Look at Parts Two through the Conclusion. Write a title for each one that gives a good idea of its content.

COMPREHENSION QUESTIONS

1. What legal action did the environmentalists take in order to protect the old-growth forests?

_____

_____

_____

What did the government do as a result of their action?

_____

_____

_____

2. What is the most extreme environmentalist position?

_____

What problems would result if we acted on this position?

a. _____

b. _____

c. _____

3. What is the most extreme timber-industry position?

_____

What would happen if we acted on this position?

_____

4. The basic principles of forest management are keeping forests

_____ and keeping them _____ for humans.

What are four uses we have for forests?

a. _____   c. _____

b. _____   d _____

5. What does clearcutting result in?

a. _____   c. _____

b. _____

What does selective cutting result in?

a. _____   c. _____

b. _____

6. What two things does the Society of American Foresters want to do?

a. _____

b. _____

7. What did President Clinton do in an effort to find a solution to the forest controversy?

_____

_____

IDENTIFYING ISSUES

The two central issues of this controversy are stated somewhere in the last part of the reading. Can you identify them?

TAKING NOTES FROM YOUR READING

On a separate sheet of paper, take notes for each part of the reading. As before, you should use the information in your comprehension questions to help you. Consider the organization of each part as you decide how to present your notes in a graphic form that makes it easy for you to see and understand the information.

Vocabulary

VOCABULARY IN CONTEXT

1. Find the phrase *old-growth* in ¶1. What do you think it means?
   How does the author use punctuation marks to show you the meaning?
   (Remember this technique! It's a very common signal of a definition in a
   textbook.)
2. Find the word *inland* in ¶11. What do you think it means?
   Which words and phrases give you clues to its meaning?
   (Remember, if you are looking for meaning from context, check for word
   clues in the same sentence.)
3. Find the word *reproduce* in ¶11. What do you think it means?
   Which sentence in the paragraph gives you the clues to its meaning?
   (Remember, if you are looking for meaning from context, check the sentence
   before and the sentence after.)

KEYWORDS

1. last (verb)* ¶1
2. critical ¶3
3. livelihood ¶4
4. whole* ¶4
5. desperate ¶4
6. remaining ¶4
7. temporarily ¶5
8. factor ¶6
9. critic ¶6
10. generation ¶7
11. be blamed on* ¶8
12. fragile ¶10
13. exposed ¶10
14. remove ¶11
15. rate ¶12

KEYWORD EXERCISE

1. *EXAMPLE:*   It seemed as though this ocean of giant trees would *last* forever.

   The word *last* has several meanings. Which part of speech and meaning are
   used in the sentence above?

   _____

2. *EXAMPLE:*   The government reserved 3.3 million hectares of forest as
   "*critical* habitat" for the owl.

   You'll notice in your dictionary that *critical* has two meanings. Which of the
   sentences below contains the same meaning as the sentence in the reading?
   • He looked at his son with a critical eye.
   • Her doctor reported that she was in critical condition and might not live.
3. Look at the parts of the word *livelihood.* What's the connection between the

   meanings of the parts and the meaning of the word? _____

   _____

   EXAMPLE: Loggers depend for their *livelihood* on the availability of trees to
   be cut.

4. *EXAMPLE:* *Whole* families with little children lost their homes and had nowhere to go.

   Finish the sentences:
   The power blackout affected the whole . . .
   I feel really sick because I ate a . . .

5. Rank the following words from weakest to strongest.
   desperate   worried   concerned
   a.   b.   c.

   EXAMPLE: These people are *desperate* for their employment.

6. Which of the following is an example of a *temporary* condition?
   a. "Children, your father and I are going on a little trip this weekend, and your grandmother is in charge."
   b. When I was ten, my family emigrated to Canada.
   c. At the moment the Democrats are enjoying a majority over the Republicans in Congress.

7. *EXAMPLE:* The drop in timber-industry jobs is due in part to other *factors.*

   Name two other *factors* that have contributed to the loss of these jobs.

   a. _____   b. _____

8. *Critics* (¶6) are persons who are *critical.* Review Item #2 in this exercise.

   Which meaning of *critical* is *critic* related to? _____

   EXAMPLE: *Critics* review books, films, and plays for newspapers and magazines.

9. Which of the following words are elements of *remain*?
   defend   still   stay   eliminate   exist

   EXAMPLE: Only about 10 percent of the old-growth forests *remain.*

10. How many *generations* are there between you and your great-great-grandparents? _____

    EXAMPLE: Three *generations* of my family have attended this university.

11. Which of the following are elements of the word *blame?*
    essential   good   bad   genuine   responsible

    EXAMPLE: These problems cannot all be *blamed* on environmentalists.

12. A crystal flower vase is very *fragile.* If you wanted to ship one to someone in another country, how would you pack it?

    _____

    EXAMPLE: Wind and rain carry the *fragile* topsoil away.

13. *EXAMPLE:* Clearcutting *exposes* the soil to the wind and rain.

    Finish the sentences:
    That plant will die if you expose . . .
    X-rays . . .

14. *EXAMPLE:* Clearcutting *removes* all the trees in an area.

    Finish the sentences:
    The doctors wanted to remove . . .
    In a Japanese house, people should . . .

15. You have two minutes to catch a train that is three kilometers away. You travel the first two kilometers at a *rate* of 60 kilometers per hour. At what *rate* will you have to travel the remaining kilometer in order to catch the train?

    _____

    EXAMPLE: The global population is expected to double every 39 years at present *rates*.

REVIEW

Now that you have studied the vocabulary, re-read or re-skim the passage.

ANTICIPATING TEST QUESTIONS

Choose either Reading One or Reading Two, and write one of each of the following kinds of test questions:

True-false	Identification
Multiple-choice	Essay
Fill-in-the-blank	

When you finish, get together with your classmates. Put all the "tests" for Reading One in one stack, and the ones for Reading Two in another. Then find a partner and "test" each other orally with these questions.

An Important Note About the Following Reading Passages in This Chapter

All of the rest of the readings in this chapter are unsimplified transcriptions of speeches that participants gave during the White House Forest Conference. Some of them are easier to read and some of them are more difficult. For each one, you will have the same comprehension activities: (1) to take notes of the most important points, and (2) to briefly summarize the main idea(s) in your own words. So when you run into difficult English, don't panic! You aren't responsible for understanding every word or every sentence.

You'll note that some of the speakers will address President Clinton directly. Remember that they were all sitting around a table together, discussing these issues.

The White House Forest
Conference

READING THREE

NOTE: This reading is also on the tape.

PHYLLIS SHRAUGER, MAYOR OF HOQUIAM, WASHINGTON

1   Mr. President, if I might add, this conference is too late for my city. My city got hit on November the twelfth with the closure of a three-unit mill, and our unemployment is now 19.5 percent and climbing; we expect it to go over 20 percent. My *budget*,[a] which buys my policemen, my firemen, my parks, my keeping my city hall open, got a direct hit of 15 percent. That's an immediate hit. When all of the extrapolated *taxes*[b] do not come in, we fully expect to have a $25 million hit and cutback[1] because this company spent $40 million in our city. We expect a $600,000 shortfall,[2] which by the time we pay self-insured unemployment, could affect[3] 22 employees, and we're doing everything we can not to make it that bad. But I cannot describe to you the feeling that I have in the pit of my stomach when I know that I have to add to this unemployment. I've never had to lay people off[4] before in my whole life. And unlike the federal government, it's against the law for me to operate in the *deficit*,[c] so I have to balance.

2   I have a community where 92, you heard me right, 92 percent of our kindergarten children are on free and reduced lunches. That, Mr. President, you are paying for. It goes down to 50 percent by the time they get into high school because the high school kids don't like to sign up for it.

3   I've often heard you say that you are a child of the sixties. Mr. President, I'm a child of *the Depression*.[d] The stock market crashed, creating the Depression, the year after I was born, and I never knew anything else growing up except the poverty of the Depression. . . . And when I hear people start to talk about putting these good workers back to work building picnic tables and cutting trails, it's unacceptable to me. Because we are a proud[5] people, a proud community, and they deserve[6] full-time, family-*wage*[e] jobs. They've got to have some timber freed up, and I just admire[7] you more than you can believe for putting together this kind of a table, seeking solutions. They've got to have some sufficiency,[8] they've got to know where they stand, so that . . . they are not constantly being jerked back and forth from one rope to the other.

4   I think probably the instances that hurt me the most are the time that a millworker came into my office not too long ago and he told me what it was like to stand in his first *food line*ᶠ. . . . He said, "Mrs. Shrauger, I made it back to the car," and then he said, "I sat there and I cried." Another man came and told me, he's 50 years old, how he was going to lose his house, and he said, "I'm just desperate, Ms. Shrauger. I don't know why I've come to talk to you, but," he said, "I'm going to lose my house." . . .

5   A friend of mine went up the Wynoochee River and found two families camping in a tent with little children. . . . in order to keep their kids in school, they had gone to the nearest community and had bought a post office box, because that gave them an address. But they didn't want those kids to tell anybody where they were, and (they) were cautioned not to do that at school, because (they) were afraid that somebody would take the children away from them when (they) found them living like that.

6   The last and worst case, that affects me the deepest, is there was a young couple up in the Quinault area, he was a logger, they got laid off. They were down to the point where the only food they had was out of the *food bank*ᵍ and that was it. She became pregnant and had her baby, and the baby died. . . . Afterwards they learned that for three days before that baby was born, that mother had not had anything to eat. Anything she had had, she had given to the two little kids they already had. . . . This afternoon when I leave this conference, Mr. President, I'm going to drive out to southwest Portland, and I'm going to sit and rock my little eight-month-old grandson. . . . I know that I'm not going to be able to help but think of this woman who doesn't have her child. . . . It just seems to me that surely, surely, this planet⁹ is big enough to support the wildlife species and the human species. And I just want to wish you all of the cooperation and all of the help from all of the people at this table to bring about a solution to what has become a regular *logjam*.ʰ Thank you for asking me to participate.

[Shrauger is asked what her town is doing to try to diversify their economic base]

7   Tourism is something we had been working on even before this hit. . . . We are working on tourism, and we're doing everything we can to diversify,¹⁰ but our biggest problem with diversification¹⁰ is that we have no industrial park, we have no warehouses, I don't know how many times we get inquiries¹¹ for *warehouse*ⁱ space. All we have to market is an empty log truck and a rusty *spar pole*.ʲ Our county has been 85 percent timber, and it just has never been necessary to have the kinds of things you need to diversify. We are working very hard toward that. We are seeking all of the help from the federal and state government that we can get. . . . we know we have to diversify, we know that. . . . I hope that I never ever see a 650-employee mill again in my city, because every time they sneeze, we all get cold. I would much, much rather have a series of smaller mills and smaller businesses, and a variety of businesses. But this is not going to be an easy *turnaround*ᵏ for our area, because we are not equipped¹² for it.

A Jobless Timber Family
Living in the Woods

SPECIALIZED VOCABULARY ITEMS IN THE READING

ᵃ *budget:* a plan or a record of money spent and money received, whether by a business, a family, or an individual person.

ᵇ *taxes:* money that individuals and businesses have to pay to the government.

ᶜ *deficit:* If a country or organization spends more money than it receives, that negative amount of money is called a *deficit.*

ᵈ *the Depression* (with "the" and a capital "D"): the period of time beginning late in the 1920s and lasting through the 1930s when the economy was very bad in many parts of the world.

^e *wage:* the money that a person earns for work done, especially when they are paid by the hour.

^f *food line:* a place similar to a restaurant where poor people can go to receive free meals, maybe from the government or maybe from a private organization.

^g *food bank:* a central place where poor people can go to receive free groceries from the government.

^h *logjam:* When logs are floated down a river, sometimes they pile up together and can't move. Shrauger is comparing the owl-timber controversy with this inability to move.

ⁱ *warehouse:* a large building used to store materials or products for a business.

^j *spar pole:* a piece of logging equipment.

^k *turnaround:* a sudden improvement in the success of a business or in the economy of a city, area, or country.

After You Read

Identify the circled reference words.

COMPREHENSION QUESTIONS

1. In Hoquiam, Washington, the main employer was a lumber mill that employed 650 people. When it closed, what were the results?

_____

_____

_____

_____

_____

2. Hoquiam needs to diversify its economic base. What are three reasons why it's having a hard time doing this?

_____

_____

_____

TRUE-FALSE QUESTIONS

¶ number

1. Timber formed the economic base of the area   T   F   _____
around Hoquiam, Washington.
2. Hoquiam is making good progress toward   T   F   _____
replacing timber with other economic bases.

TAKING NOTES; SUMMARIZING AND PARAPHRASING

On a separate sheet of paper, take notes for Shrauger's speech.

What did you learn from this speech? Write a one-paragraph summary in your own words, not more than 75 words long. Use your notes as a reference.

Now compare your Shrauger notes with the ones you took for the first two readings in this chapter. What connections can you see? Think of them as three parts of one big picture. When you write your paper later, you can use parts of all of them to support your points.

Vocabulary

KEYWORDS

1. cutback ¶1
2. shortfall ¶1
3. affect* ¶1
4. lay people off ¶1
5. proud ¶3
6. deserve* ¶3
7. admire ¶3
8. sufficiency ¶3
9. planet ¶6
10. diversify, diversification ¶7
11. inquiry ¶7
12. equipped ¶7

KEYWORD EXERCISE

1. *EXAMPLE:* Mayor Shrauger is facing *cutbacks* in her budget because of economic hard times.

   Examine the word *cutback.* What is the connection between the meanings of the parts and the meaning of the whole word? _____

   _____

2. *EXAMPLE:* Mayor Shrauger expects a $600,000 *shortfall.*

   What is the meaning of *short* in this word? _____

   What's the connection between the meanings of the two parts and the

   meaning of the whole word? _____

   _____

3. How do the sun's rays *affect* the skin of white people with blond or red hair?

   _____

   EXAMPLE: The cutbacks could *affect* the jobs of 22 city employees.

4. What's the difference between *laying* workers *off* and firing them? Which would look worse on a worker's record?

   _____

   EXAMPLE: The mayor has never had to *lay* people *off* before.

5. *EXAMPLE:* Mayor Shrauger says, "We are a *proud* people, a *proud* community."

   Proud has several meanings, some positive and one negative. Which one do you think the mayor meant?

   _____

6. *EXAMPLES:* Timber workers *deserve* full-time, family-wage jobs.
             He *deserves* to be rewarded for saving that child's life.

   Finish the sentences:
   A company that doesn't take care of its employees deserves . . .
   Homeless people . . .

7. *EXAMPLE:* Mayor Shrauger *admires* the President.

   <u>*Finish the sentences:*</u>
   I admire a person who . . .
   No one admires . . .
   Young boys . . .

8. Which of the following is a synonym for *sufficient*?
   obvious   enough   luxurious   isolated

   EXAMPLE: A part-time job isn't *sufficient* to feed a family of four.

9. How many *planets* are there? _____

   Can you name them (in either English or your own language), from the

   nearest to the sun to the farthest from it? _____

   _____

   EXAMPLE: Surely this *planet* is big enough to support the wildlife species
   and the human species.

10. *EXAMPLE:* Mayor Shrauger's town needs to *diversify* their economy.

   Suggest some ways they could do that.

   _____

   _____

   _____

11. Which of the following letters represents an *inquiry*?
   a. a letter complaining about poor service
   b. a letter requesting information
   c. a letter of thanks

   EXAMPLE: We get *inquiries* for warehouse space.

12. If people are *equipped* for something, which of the following elements
   might they have?
   training   experience   tools   ideas   intervals

   EXAMPLE: We are not *equipped* to change our economic base overnight.

REVIEW

Now that you have studied the vocabulary, re-read or re-skim the passage.

LEARNING STRATEGY

**Personalizing: Think of a way that you can benefit from each
language-learning task you do, either in class or outside of class.**

NOTE: This reading is also on the tape.

Reading process: Let's work on speed. Your teacher will give you two minutes to read as far as you can in the following passage. Mark where you stop. Then you'll start at the beginning again and be given another two minutes. See how much farther you can go this time. Then do it a third time. Finally, just read straight through without any time limit.

NAT BINGHAM, COMMERCIAL SALMON FISHERMAN

1   Thank you, Mr. President. On behalf of the commercial and recreational fishing industry in California, Oregon, and Washington, I would like to express the gratitude that all of us feel that you have recognized that this problem is more than just spotted owls, but that there is another industry which is dependent on a healthy forest: the salmon fishing industry. For 30 years I've been privileged to participate in that fishery and it was a wonderful way of life. I can't tell you how rewarding[1] it is to go out on the ocean and work all day out there and come back with a catch of fish and sell them and be a provider for your family.

2   That way of life is fast disappearing. We are now faced with almost an identical situation[2] that the timber harvesting families are. Next week the Federal Pacific Fisheries Management Council . . . will decide whether we are going to be allowed to fish at all on the Pacific coast this coming season. Last year, 500 miles of the West Coast was closed to commercial[3] salmon fishing, including my home port in Fort Bragg, California. I didn't even try to travel the several hundred miles I would have had to have traveled by boat and spend the whole summer away from my family. I just left my boat tied to the dock. Only 25 fishermen even left my home port and went south to try to survive in a fishery that has been so severely[4] restricted[5] to protect these stocks of salmon, even though the managers have acknowledged that fishing has not been the cause of the decline[6] of the salmon. The destruction of the salmon's habitat has been the cause of the decline of the salmon. The loss of freshwater habitat in the forest, the siltation of streams, cascades of sediment pouring into the streams, loss of shade from removal of the overstory trees and loss of character of the streams have destroyed the home of the salmon.

3   So what I did was, I tied my boat up and got in my pickup truck and traveled inland, and I went wherever the salmon go, and I tried to understand what the problem was. And what I found out was, there are a lot of folks just like the fishing families back there in the woods that shared[7] all the same concerns[8] about family values that we did. And they wanted to try to help solve the problem.

4   I've been working with the farmers over in the central valley of California, and I've discovered two things. The first thing is, we're about to[9] lose the salmon resource. It's very, very close to extinction with many stocks, particularly coho salmon right along the coast where the old-growth forest is. If we don't do something right now to protect the remaining habitats, we're going to see listings of salmon that will be of an order of magnitude under the Endangered Species Act that will make the spotted owl situation pale by comparison. And I don't think that's something that any of us want to see happen: it'll put me out of business, and it'll put the forestry industry out of business too. That's what's coming.

5   The other thing I found out when I went inland and started talking to folks is, there are a lot of people out there that want to work with us to solve this problem. The fishing industry has been working for years developing model programs, putting our own dollars to work through a program we've innovated in California to try to solve the inland habitat problems. We know how to do the job, but we need your help. We want to get together with the forest people, with the Indian tribes and the farmers and work on a *watershed*[a] base to empower local communities to go to work to solve this problem. I know we can do it with your help. Thank you.

[*Vice President Al Gore questions Bingham*]

6 *AG:* How many jobs are involved in the commercial fishing industry in Oregon, California, and Washington?

NB: We estimate,[10] with support industry, around 65,000 jobs.

AG: Now your presentation makes it sound as if there is a direct link between those jobs and the avoidance of damage[11] to the habitat of the fish on which those jobs depend.

NB: Yes, that is correct. We're down to a place now where we have to protect the remaining existing habitats. We have to identify (them,) we have to be certain what the limiting factors are, and we have to ask folks to get them out of denial that what's going on in the land is impacting those fish. We're in a critical situation here, and we have to act now. So we have to find those critical habitats (most of the fish folks already know where they are), designate them for special protection, and then start the rebuilding process based on those last refuges.

SPECIALIZED VOCABULARY ITEM IN THE READING

[a] *watershed:* A *watershed* is the area of land whose rainfall drains into one particular river, stream, or lake.

After You Read

Identify the circled reference word.

COMPREHENSION QUESTIONS

1. What is causing the decline of the salmon? Explain how this is happening.

_____

_____

_____

2. What are three solutions that Bingham recommends?

_____

_____

_____

TRUE-FALSE QUESTIONS

¶ *number*

1. Fishing families are facing the same problems   T   F   _____
   that the timber families are facing.
2. Clearcutting has caused the decline of the   T   F   _____
   salmon.

TAKING NOTES; SUMMARIZING AND PARAPHRASING

On a separate sheet of paper, take notes for Bingham's speech.

What did you learn from Bingham's speech? Write a one-paragraph summary in your own words, not more than 75 words long.

Now compare your Bingham notes with the ones you took for the earlier readings in this chapter. What connections can you see?

Vocabulary

KEYWORDS

1. rewarding ¶1
2. situation ¶2
3. commercial ¶2
4. severely ¶2
5. restricted ¶2
6. decline ¶2
7. share* ¶3
8. concern ¶3
9. are about to* ¶4
10. estimate* ¶6
11. damage ¶6

KEYWORD EXERCISE

1. If *commercial* means "involving or relating to commerce and business," what is Nat Bingham's purpose in catching fish? _____

   What is a noncommercial fisherman's purpose? _____

   EXAMPLE: Last year, 500 miles of the West Coast was closed to *commercial* salmon fishing.

2. *Meanings:*
   • A *reward* is something nice that you receive because you have done something useful or good.

     EXAMPLE: She received a *reward* for returning the ring that she found.

   • A *rewarding* activity is one that you find it very satisfying to do.

     EXAMPLE: Bingham finds fishing a very *rewarding* occupation.

   • Explain the similarities between the two meanings.

3. Which of the following words is a synonym for *situation*?
resource   circumstance   technique   version

   EXAMPLE: Fishermen are faced with the same *situation* as timber workers.

4. Rank the following words from weakest to strongest.

   The driver was _____ injured in the accident.

   severely   fairly badly   critically   somewhat

   EXAMPLE: Salmon fishing has been *severely* restricted.

5. *EXAMPLE:*   The government has *restricted* fishing in order to protect the remaining salmon.

   Name a cause and an effect of this *restriction.*

   Cause: _____   *Effect:* _____

6. As you'll notice in your dictionary, the word *decline* has several meanings. Choose the sentence below with the same meaning as the sentence in ¶2.
   • Fishing has not been the cause of the *decline* of the salmon.
   a. Membership in our organization has *declined* steadily since 1992.
   b. There was a sharp *decline* in unemployment during the war.
   c. We had to *decline* their invitation.

7. *EXAMPLES:*   Timber families and fishing families *share* some of the same concerns.

   I *shared* my lunch with my roommate.

   <u>*Finish the sentences:*</u>
   Children have to be taught to share . . .
   Rich nations should . . .

8. What part of speech is *concerns* in this sentence: We all share the same *concerns.*
   Which of the following sentences contains the same use and meaning?
   a. There's great *concern* in the United States about the high cost of health care.
   b. The public is also *concerned* about the problem of homelessness.

9. *EXAMPLE:*   Bingham says we'*re about to* lose the salmon resource.

   <u>*Finish the sentences:*</u>
   After years of rule by the military or by dictators, several African countries . . .
   Let me call you back in about an hour. My favorite TV program . . .

10. Which of the following words are related to *estimate?*
    guess   involve   approximate   about   opinion

    EXAMPLE: Bingham *estimates* that around 65,000 jobs related to the fishing industry are in danger.

11. Which of the following words are unrelated to the others?
    damage   hurt   linger   observe   harm

    EXAMPLE: Clearcutting has *damaged* the salmon's habitat.

REVIEW

Now that you have studied the vocabulary, re-read or re-skim the passage.

NOTE: This reading is also on the tape.

The following reading is fairly difficult. When you read it, highlight or underline everything that you *do* understand. Then re-read the highlighted or underlined parts.

LOUISE FORTMANN, PROFESSOR OF NATURAL RESOURCE SOCIOLOGY AT THE UNIVERSITY OF CALIFORNIA AT BERKELEY

1   I shall address community well-being in northern California focusing on poverty, the problem of outside influence, and the need for locally[1] based management and planning in forest-dependent communities. Let me stress that forest dependence is *not* synonymous with timber dependence. There are diverse forest-based livelihoods. Poverty is a long-standing and persistent feature of these communities. In 1989, nearly a fifth of California forest-dependent counties had poverty rates that were equal to or greater than inner-city rates. In the decade between 1979 and 1989, forest counties in northern California that experienced increases in the timber cuts did not experience decreases in their poverty rates. The lesson is that at least in California, large timber harvests will not automatically resolve the poverty problem, particularly when profits are not reinvested in the communities or counties to any significant extent.

2   Local[1] people are angered by outside influences on their communities. The decisions that affect the well-being of these communities are often taken or influenced by timber *corporations*[a] with out-of-county or out-of-state *headquarters,*[b] by the staff of state and national natural resource agencies, and by the urban-based[2] *staffs*[c] of national environmental organizations. These are people who are not personally affected by the adverse consequences of their decisions. They often lack the detailed knowledge of the local ecosystem that local people have. They do not have family ties or a personal stake in the well-being of those communities. And they often tend to see their jobs in terms of uniform policy and uniform[3] regulations.

3   Is there a remedy[4]? There is. . . . We need healthy forest communities, communities that can take responsibility for successfully solving their own problems. For this we need locally based planning processes that enable local people to develop and implement diverse policy options[5] that take into account[6] the social and ecological diversity of their communities. And we need state and federal policies that will facilitate[7] these local processes. We need community-initiated[8] and locality-based planning and management units[9] that make ecological sense and social sense. Locally based management will involve local people and others of their choosing in gathering scientific evidence about local social and economic conditions and about local ecosystems. It will involve community members and others meeting to establish community goals and planning and implementing actions to achieve them.

4   Now this takes a lot of time. People need a lot of time to learn to trust each other, for starters. . . . While this process is going to be painful and time consuming,[10] I know of no effective alternative to end the rancor and to return people's attention and creative abilities to strengthening their communities.

Threads

A culture, a way of life, prized and reverenced in our timber communities, is dying.

Thomas Murphy
Catholic Archbishop
of Seattle, Washington

And it does work. We have successful examples of local loggers, ranchers, businesspeople, environmentalists sitting down and solving their problems. . . . I think that the success of these and many other community-based experiments in change tell us that facilitating local process is going to be the most important product of this conference. Thank you very much.

SPECIALIZED VOCABULARY ITEMS IN THE READING

[a] *corporation:* a company.
[b] *headquarters:* the central offices of a company, agency, or organization.
[c] *staff:* employees. This is an uncountable noun, so it's grammatically singular.

After You Read

Identify the circled reference words.

COMPREHENSION QUESTIONS

1. What problem for timber communities does Fortmann describe in ¶1?

_____

_____

_____

What problem does she describe in ¶2?

_____

_____

_____

2. What solutions does she recommend in ¶3?

_____

_____

_____

3. Is she optimistic that these problems can be solved?

_____

_____

_____

TRUE-FALSE QUESTIONS

¶ number

1. If more trees could be cut, poverty would   T   F   _____
decline in Northern California timber
communities.
2. Local people want experts and specialists from   T   F   _____
outside their area to come in and solve their
problems for them.

TAKING NOTES; SUMMARIZING AND PARAPHRASING

On a separate sheet of paper, take notes for Fortmann's speech.

What did you learn from Fortmann's speech? Write a one-paragraph summary in your own words, not more than 75 words long.

Now compare your Fortmann notes with the ones you took for the earlier readings in this chapter. What connections can you see?

Vocabulary

KEYWORDS

1. local(ly) ¶s 1, 2
2. urban ¶2
3. uniform ¶2
4. remedy ¶3
5. option* ¶3

6. take into account ¶3
7. facilitate ¶3
8. initiate ¶3
9. unit ¶3
10. time consuming* ¶4

KEYWORD EXERCISE

1. If you are living in another country now, what are some *local* foods that you can't find in your home country?

   _____

   _____

   EXAMPLE: Local people are angered by outside influences on their communities.

2. Name two elements of *urban* life that you like, and two that you don't like.

   Like

   a. _____

   b. _____

   Don't like

   a. _____

   b. _____

   EXAMPLE: Urban life is very different from life in small timber-dependent communities.

3. Which of the following sentences contains the same meaning as this sentence: These jobs offer *uniform* retirement and health benefits.
   a. Many schools require their pupils to wear *uniforms.*
   b. All the branches of our company follow a *uniform* policy toward overtime work.

4. What is a good *remedy* for homesickness?

   EXAMPLE: It's hard to find a *remedy* for the problem that everyone will agree with.

5. If you want to travel this coming summer, what are your *options*?

   EXAMPLE: We need to find an *option* that will save both the timber workers and the environment.

6. When planning your summer trip, what do you have to *take into account*?

   EXAMPLE: A teacher has to *take into account* the different abilities of all the students in the class.

7. *EXAMPLE:* We need state and federal policies that will *facilitate* these local processes.

   Finish the sentences:
   Living in a foreign country facilitates . . .
   Earning a university degree . . .

8. Which of the following words are not synonyms for the verb *initiate*?
   conclude   begin   start   open   eliminate

   EXAMPLE: Solutions that the timber workers have *initiated* are different from those that the environmentalists have *initiated*.

9. Name a *unit* of measurement for length. _____

   . . . for weight. _____

   . . . for volume. _____

   . . . for electricity. _____

   . . . for sound. _____

   . . . for radiation. _____

10. Rank the following items from least to most *time consuming*.

    _____   **a.** Mastering the art of Chinese cooking.

    _____   **b.** Learning enough English to enter a university in Canada or the United States.

    _____   **c.** Crossing the North American continent by bicycle.

    _____   **d.** Writing a book.

    EXAMPLE: This process is going to be painful and *time consuming*.

REVIEW

Now that you've studied the vocabulary, re-read or re-skim the passage.

LEARNING STRATEGY

Personalizing: Try to find out how language learning works, and apply what you learn to your own situation.

NOTE: This reading is also on the tape.

RICHARD NAFZIGER, FORMERLY THE WASHINGTON STATE GOVERNOR'S SPECIAL ASSISTANT FOR TIMBER POLICY

1   Mr. President, this summit confronts two issues: how we care for the earth, and how much we care about each other. We need to preserve both our forests and our communities, because both are essential to a sustainable American democracy. All of us are going to have to be going to take some risks and make some changes if we're going to do that. . . . I want to talk about five fundamental[1] changes that I think need to be made.

2   The first one . . . is, we must begin to manage our forests differently. We heard that [timber] stands managed in a new way not only contain a diversity of wildlife, but also can produce higher quality wood products. We can strive to develop an entire landscape of natural forests. . . . What we need to reach for is a sustainable ecological system that includes old growth, wildlife, and people who live in rural[2] communities. But we can't achieve this goal by ramming new regulations down private landowners. Everybody's got to be at the table, everybody's got to contribute[3] to this forest landscape. But we need to create[4] *market incentives,[a]* like generous[5] *capital-gains tax treatment[b]* for environmentally sensitive forest investments, so that protecting the earth can become a question of economic self-interest.

3   Number two, we must extract more value out of each tree harvested, and there was a little bit of discussion about that earlier, and if we want to protect both jobs and ecosystems, we have to scale the value-added pyramid in an attempt to get more jobs out of each *board-foot[c]* harvested. We can't afford anymore to export one quarter of our logs overseas. We have to develop a bigger remanufacturing and secondary manufacturing industry, . . . building more cabinets, more modular houses right here. *Investment tax credits[d]* can help create an incentive for value-added investments.

4   Thirdly, we must adjust our *trade[e]* policies. Landowners cannot be expected to stop exporting logs when our trading partners put up barriers[6] to finished products but not to raw logs. The wood products industry in the U.S. cannot be expected to compete[7] with foreign nations in finished product markets when we have higher environmental standards[8] than our competitors.[7] Trade policies must create a *level playing field.[f]*

5   Fourthly, . . . we must attract *capital[g]* to rural timber communities through the creation of community development banks. The *redlining[h]* and uncertainty created by the timber crisis have cut off the lifeline of capital to (these towns). . . . [C]apital is essential if there's going to be any diversification or any value added. And a government/private partnership through community development banks could *leverage private capital.[i]*

6   Fifth, we must develop a coherent national retraining policy to help workers who've lost their jobs. Regardless of what level of timber supply we decide on, there are going to be thousands of job losses. Workers who have lost their jobs must be able to *see the light at the end of the tunnel.[j]* This conference must not evade or minimize[9] the shared responsibility to those whose way of life we are affecting.

7   I want to conclude by saying that we can solve this problem, and the problems of people who depend on forests, but first, environmentalists, the industry, and the public must take risks and make investments. Environmentalists must allow innovation and recognize new ways of doing business, rather than trying to stop the industry from doing any business at all. Secondly, the forest industry must think in the long term and act in their own long-term[10] economic interests rather

than in the interest of quarterly profits. And the public must recognize that if we want both forest products and ecological protection, the price must be paid by all of us, not by timber communities alone. Mr. President, we need your help. We need you to help us come together and build a new paradigm for sustainable communities and a sustainable environment. Thank you.

> There are no simple or easy answers. This is not about choosing between jobs and the environment, but about recognizing the importance of both. . . . A healthy economy and a healthy environment are not at odds with each other; they are essential to each other.
>
> —*President Clinton*

SPECIALIZED VOCABULARY ITEMS IN THE READING

[a] *market incentives:* reasons that make people want to do something that you want them to do because it will be profitable for them.

[b] *capital-gains tax treatment:* one kind of tax "break" for businesses that have profited from selling their assets.

[c] *board-foot:* a unit for measuring lumber, equal to 1 foot × 1 foot × 1 inch.

[d] *investment tax credit:* one kind of tax "break" for people who invest money in businesses.

[e] *trade:* the buying and selling of goods, or the exchange of goods.

[f] *a level playing field:* a situation that's fair to everyone who's involved in a competition.

[g] *capital:* the money that is invested in a business.

[h] *redlining:* illegally discriminating against investments in certain communities because they are believed to be a poor risk.

[i] *leverage private capital:* set up one system for borrowing money that makes private lenders want to invest in a business because it will be profitable for them.

[j] *see the light at the end of the tunnel:* see the end of the problem.

After You Read

Identify the circled reference words.

COMPREHENSION QUESTIONS

1. What five changes does Nafziger recommend?

   a. _____ d. _____

   b. _____ e _____

   c. _____

2. What must environmentalists do to enable this problem to be solved?

   _____

   _____

   What must the timber industry do?

   _____

   _____

   What must the general public do?

   _____

TRUE-FALSE QUESTION

¶ number

1. Everyone must give up some of what   T   F   _____
   they want if this problem is going to be
   solved.

TAKING NOTES; SUMMARIZING AND PARAPHRASING

On a separate sheet of paper, take notes for Nafziger's speech.

What did you learn from Nafziger's speech? Write a one-paragraph summary in your own words, not more than 75 words long.

Now compare your Nafziger notes with the ones you took for the earlier readings in this chapter. What connections can you see?

Vocabulary

KEYWORDS

1. fundamental ¶1
2. rural ¶2
3. contribute* ¶2
4. create* ¶2
5. generous ¶2
6. barrier ¶4
7. compete, competitor ¶4
8. standard ¶4
9. minimize ¶6
10. long term ¶7

KEYWORD EXERCISE

1. Nafziger recommends five *fundamental* changes. The word *fundamental* comes from a Latin word that means *bottom*.
   Which of the following words are synonyms for *fundamental*?
   basic   essential   central   successful
2. Timber workers live in *rural* communities. Look on page 204 at Reading Five, ¶2, and find a keyword that is an antonym for *rural*. What is it?

   _____

   Name two things that you like and two things that you dislike about *rural* life.

Like	*Dislike*
a. _____	a. _____
b. _____	b. _____

3. *EXAMPLES:*   Everybody's got to *contribute* to this forest landscape.
   Christians are supposed to *contribute* at least 10 percent of their income to the church.

   Finish the sentences:

   Everyone helped to build the village's new school. A rich family contributed . . .
   Two builders contributed . . .
   Even the children . . .

4. Which of the following is an antonym for the verb *create*?
   make   develop   destroy   produce

   EXAMPLE: The President's Forest Conference *created* a climate where everyone's point of view could be heard, and could be taken seriously.

5. Which of the following are elements of the adjective *generous*?
   give   too much   a large amount   helpful   friendly

   EXAMPLES: Our company has a *generous* pension plan.
   She's a kind and *generous* old lady.

6. Should nations create trade *barriers* to give an advantage to their own companies?
   Name one way this is commonly done.

   _____

7. Find the words *compete* and *competitors* in ¶4. Think of a situation in which *competition* is better than cooperation.
   Now think of a situation in which cooperation is better than *competition.*

8. Name a university in Canada or the United States that has very high entrance *standards.*

   EXAMPLE: Different nations have different environmental *standards.*

9. *EXAMPLE:*   This conference must not evade or *minimize* its responsibilities.

   What part of speech is this word? _____

   What is the noun form? _____

   The adjective form? _____

10. *EXAMPLE:*   The forest industry must think *in the long term* and act in their own *long-term* economic interests rather than in the interest of quarterly profits.

    The antonym of this phrase is *in the short term.* In Nafziger's sentence above, what represents the short term?

    How long is *the long term*, in Nafziger's opinion? _____

REVIEW

Now that you've studied the vocabulary, re-read or re-skim the passage.

Writing a Longer Paper: Advice to the President

Imagine that the President has asked you for your ideas on how this controversy should be solved, since you, as an international student, have a point of view that's fresh and that's different from a North American point of view. You have read all of the reading passages in this chapter, have taken notes, and have summarized most of the passages in your own words. You are well informed. Your voice should be heard.

Begin by freewriting for about 15 minutes. In your heart, where do your sympathies lie? Why? In the best of all possible worlds, what would you like to see happen?

Now review your notes and summaries (not the reading passages). Highlight the information that supports your point of view or that you think should be included. Remember, you don't have to explain everything—the President was there at the conference. But you can use certain people's ideas to support your own.

How shall you organize your paper? Make a list of what you want to say first, then second, and so on—these are your main points. Then add the details (reasons, examples, statistics, etc.) that support each point. You can plan your paper any way you like: in a formal outline or an informal graphic presentation (similar to the format of your notes).

Now you're ready to write your first draft. Concentrate on clear content and organization. Don't worry about grammar and vocabulary at this point. Just try to get your ideas across and to support them well. When you finish, exchange papers with a classmate and tell each other if your ideas are clear and well developed.

In your second draft, focus on grammar and vocabulary. What are your common problems in these areas? Try to find them and correct them. Use your dictionary. When you finish, work with a partner again—preferably not someone who speaks your native language, because you might miss each other's mistakes.

Finally, look for places where you have copied the exact words of the passages in this chapter. Change them as much as possible. If you cannot change them, you are permitted to use them if you put "quotation marks" around them—but don't put more than five *brief* quotations in your paper, and when you do, you must identify the original writer.

When you're satisfied that your letter is as good as you can make it, give it to your teacher.

LEARNING STRATEGY

Personalizing: Find reading material in English that fits your personal interests to make reading in English easier and more enjoyable.

Evaluating Learning Strategies

Look back over the learning strategies in this chapter. Were there any that weren't especially helpful for you? What wasn't helpful about them? Which ones did you find helpful? Think about times and ways that you can keep using them in your future reading.

Evaluating Your Learning

	Very little	Quite a bit	A lot
Your vocabulary is larger.	_____	_____	_____
You can comprehend unsimplified readings.	_____	_____	_____
You can take good notes from your reading.	_____	_____	_____
You write better than you used to.	_____	_____	_____
You understand something about endangered species versus human needs.	_____	_____	_____

KEYWORDS FOR CHAPTER 7: THE OWL AND THE LOGGER

Verbs
about to, be*
admire
affect
blamed on, be*
compete
consist of*
contribute*
create*
deserve*
diversify
facilitate
initiate
last*
lay people off
minimize
produce
provide
reduce
remove
share*
take into accout

Adverbs
severely
temporarily

Nouns
barriers
competitor
component
concern
critic
cutback
damage
decline
diversification
environment
estimate*
factor
generation
inquiry
livelihood
option*
planet
rate
remedy
shortfall
situation
standard
substance
sufficiency
unit

Adjectives
commercial
critical
current*
derived
desperate
effective
equipped
exposed
fragile
fundamental
generous
global
local
particular*
prime
proud
remaining
restricted
rewarding
rural
time consuming*
uniform
urban
whole*

Prepositional Phrase
long term, in the

Bigfoot and
Company

PLANNING YOUR LEARNING

Review your overall goal statement. How much progress did you make toward it in the last chapter? Do you want to change it? Think about how you can work to meet your goal as you study this new chapter.

- How many words do you want to learn? (minimum 61, the number of keywords in the chapter)
- What grade would you like to make on the vocabulary section of the exam at the end of the chapter?
- What grade would you like to make on the reading comprehension section of the exam?
- What are you going to read outside of class?

LEARNING STRATEGY

Understanding and Using Emotions: Regular exercise, a healthy diet, and good rest periods improve your language-learning ability.

PREVIEWING THE CHAPTER

- Think about the title of this chapter. What do you think "Bigfoot" refers to?
- Look through the chapter at the pictures and the map. What are some things you're curious about?
- What do you expect to find out?

PREVIEW ACTIVITY

For this activity you'll need a tape measure in feet and inches and a scale that measures in pounds. Take the following measurements of yourself:

- Your weight in pounds: _____
- Your height in feet and inches: _____
- Your foot length in inches: _____
- Your stride (the distance of one normal footstep): _____

PREPARING TO READ: CONTENT

From around the world come reports of peculiar animals that most people don't believe in because they have never seen them and because no one has ever captured one to show to the public. One of the most famous examples is the Loch Ness Monster of Scotland. Can you name any others? If so, where do they live? Are there any in your home country?

Can you name such an animal that is reported to live in North America? Where does it live—if it really exists?

Cultural Survey: What Is "Bigfoot"?

Over the next week, interview several North Americans and ask them what they can tell you about "Bigfoot," or "Sasquatch." Find three people who can tell you something they've heard about it. Do they believe in it? Why or why not? Do they know any stories about it?

In about a week, you'll be asked to tell your classmates what you've learned from your survey and to write a brief summary of your findings.

PREPARING TO READ: VOCABULARY

Working alone or with a partner, write all the English words you know that are related to the following concepts. Feel free to use your dictionary and to ask your teacher questions. Try to think of three words for each.

animal _____ _____ _____

find _____ _____ _____

dangerous _____ _____ _____

proof _____ _____ _____

surprise _____ _____ _____

fear _____ _____ _____

not believe _____ _____ _____

false _____ _____ _____

READING ONE

Reading process: Scan the passage for the following information. Your teacher will give you a time limit.

1. How was Big Al captured?

_____

2. What size is his vocabulary?

_____

3. Can he make sentences?

_____

4. Name something he likes.

_____

After you finish scanning and comparing your answers, read the passage carefully.

CAPTURED BIGFOOT CAN TALK!

560-lb. creature bagged in Montana is communicating with scientists!

Half-man half-beast speaks four words and has intelligence of a 5-year-old child!

Scientists face their toughest decision: Keep him, or let him go!

CATEGORY: _____

By Rick Tracy, Special Correspondent

1   A towering, 560-pound Bigfoot captured in Montana last month can talk and scientists say they may even be able to teach him the alphabet and how to count. Though still dangerous and unpredictable,[1] the giant creature can communicate with his captors when he's hungry, thirsty, or frightened.

2   During an extraordinary[2] demonstration for a select group of scientists at a private research facility near Helena, primate expert Professor Eric Belvit was shown teaching words to the furry, seven-foot-tall creature. "Prof. Belvit has made unbelievable progress with the beast we've since named 'Big Al,' in just a few short days," said zoologist Dr. Leonard Owens, who headed up the team that captured the beast, as *The NEWS* exclusively reported last month.

3   Putting his hand to his mouth several times as if eating, Prof. Belvit asked Big Al if he was hungry. "Hungee! Hungee!" Bigfoot replied and mimicked[3] Belvit by putting his hand to his mouth. Prof. Belvit held an apple in his hand and asked the giant beast if he liked apples. Much like a baby learning to talk, the half-man, half-creature grunted and said "a . . . a . . . peel" as he grabbed the apple out of Belvit's hand. "Drink, drink," said Bigfoot when the professor held a glass of water in front of him. And when the professor put his hands in front of his face and cowered behind them trembling,[4] Bigfoot copied his actions and screamed, "Fraid . . . fraid."

4   "We are both pleased and amazed at what we've been able to teach him," said Dr. Owens, who with three assistants captured Bigfoot with a tranquilizer dart on March 27. "It's already apparent[5] that this creature is considerably more intelligent than apes and functions at the level of a 5-year-old child," said Dr. Owens.

5   A team of scientists has spent hour after hour watching and recording Bigfoot's every move. From this constant observation, they have learned that Big Al prefers to stay by himself unless he's hungry or thirsty. "He growls when he's angry and grunts when he's happy and content," said Prof. Belvit. "We haven't been able to teach him to use the toilet, but he likes to shower."

6   The huge beast is being treated for parasites, but otherwise[6] is in reasonably good health. Big Al appears to be between 30 and 35 years old with 20-inch feet and hands the size of a baseball catcher's mitt. Bigfoot has super human eyesight and sense of smell. He eats mostly nuts and berries and other fruit, but got angry when Dr. Owens fed him a peanut butter sandwich. Strangely, the giant creature likes soft dreamy music, especially the late Glenn Miller's *Moonlight Serenade.* "When he gets ornery, we play that song and he's as gentle as a baby," Dr. Owens said.

7   "We want to learn as much as we can about Bigfoot before we're forced to make that inevitable[7] decision—keep the creature indefinitely[8] for research—or let him go," said Dr. Owens.

After You Read

COMPREHENSION QUESTIONS

1. What kind of passage is this?
   - encyclopedia entry
   - tabloid article
   - newspaper article
   - transcription of a personal taped account
   - written report about someone else's experience

   Write the category under the title.
2. What do you think a Bigfoot is? Talk it over with a partner. Write down a one- or two-sentence explanation.
3. What choice do the scientists face?

TRUE-FALSE QUESTIONS

				¶ number
1.	Big Al has learned the alphabet and how to count.	T	F	_____
2.	He is as intelligent as a human being.	T	F	_____
3.	He likes to be alone.	T	F	_____
4.	His senses are sharper than those of most humans.	T	F	_____
5.	The scientists are going to keep Big Al indefinitely for research.	T	F	_____

Beginning a Chart of Information

Begin a chart of information about Bigfoot. Turn a piece of paper sideways, horizontally. Down the left side, from top to bottom, list the readings in this chapter: Readings One through Eight. Across the top from left to right, write categories of information about Bigfoot: Size, Color, Features, Footprints, Method of Movement, Voice, Personality, Food, Habitat, Behavior, Evidence, Human Reactions to, Life Span.

Fill in the information that is contained in this article. Summarize it as briefly as you can. If there is no information for a particular category, just leave it blank. When you finish, compare your chart with a classmate's. (At the end of this chapter you may use the collected information on your chart to write a "profile" of Bigfoot.)

Freewriting: Can This Be True?

Do you believe this story? Do you think the author believes it? How could you find out if it is true?

Vocabulary

VOCABULARY IN CONTEXT

Do you think that *parasites* (¶6) are something that you would like to have? What clues in the sentence make you think this?

KEYWORDS

1. unpredictable ¶1
2. extraordinary ¶2
3. mimic ¶3
4. tremble ¶3

5. apparent* ¶4
6. otherwise* ¶6
7. inevitable ¶7
8. indefinitely* ¶7

KEYWORD EXERCISE

1. ***EXAMPLE:*** Big Al is still dangerous and *unpredictable*.

   Break the word *unpredictable* down into parts and define them.

   _____

   _____

   _____

   _____

   What part of speech is it? _____

   What's the connection between the meanings of the parts and the meaning

   of the whole word? _____

   _____

2. ***EXAMPLE:*** Big Al's captors gave an *extraordinary* demonstration of what he had learned.

   What part of speech is *extraordinary*? _____

   If you break this word down into its two parts, you might think that it means "very ordinary," but in this case the prefix *extra-* means "beyond," so its real meaning is "unusual, not at all ordinary."

Name and describe an *extraordinary* person that you know personally or know about. _____

What makes her or him *extraordinary*? _____

_____

3. Which of the following words are synonyms of the verb *mimic?*
   admire   copy   imitate   repeat   consist of

   EXAMPLE: Bigfoot *mimicked* Professor Belvit's gestures.

4. Name three different things that can cause people to *tremble*.

   a. _____   b. _____   c. _____

   EXAMPLE: The professor covered his face with his hands and cowered behind them, *trembling*.

5. The word *apparent* is the adjective form of the verb *appear* (a keyword from Chapter 3). From the list below, circle the (synonyms) and underline the antonyms.

   hidden   secret   clear   covered   obvious

   EXAMPLE: It's already *apparent* that this creature is more intelligent than apes.

6. *EXAMPLE:*   The huge beast is being treated for parasites, but *otherwise* is in reasonably good health.

   Finish the sentences:
   I wish I didn't have to study for this exam; *otherwise* . . .
   Listening comprehension in English is still a little hard for me; . . .

   Otherwise is a marker for what kind of relationship?
   similarity   contrast   cause and effect   chronology

7. According to an English proverb, the only two things that are *inevitable* are death and taxes. Do you agree that they're *inevitable?* Can you think of some other *inevitabilities?*

   _____

8. If you are studying in a foreign country now, are you planning to stay there *indefinitely*? _____

   To study English *indefinitely*? _____

   EXAMPLE: The scientists may keep Big Al *indefinitely* for research.

REVIEW

Now that you have studied the vocabulary, re-read or re-skim the passage.

As you read the two passages below, try to decide whether the authors want you to believe in or to doubt the existence of Bigfoot. At the end of each reading you'll be asked how the author's use of language makes you believe or doubt.

BIGFOOT

CATEGORY: _____

1   Bigfoot is a humanlike creature said to live in the Pacific Northwest. Bigfoot has been reported most often in the mountains of California, Oregon, and Washington, and of British Columbia in Canada. Canadians call it *Sasquatch*. Bigfoot stories resemble those about the Abominable Snowman, a hairy beast said to live in the Himalaya and other mountainous areas of central and northeastern Asia. . . .

2   Hundreds of people have reported seeing the bigfoot or its footprints. They describe the creature as standing from 7 to 10 feet (2 to 3 meters) tall and weighing more than 500 pounds (230 kilograms). Like an ape, it has thick fur, long arms, powerful shoulders, and a short neck. It supposedly[1] walks like a human being and leaves footprints that measure about 16 inches (41 centimeters) long and about 6 inches (15 centimeters) wide.

3   The evidence for the bigfoot's existence has so far not been sufficient[2] to convince most scientists. Many believe that some evidence, which includes footprints and photographs, has been faked.

BIGFOOT

CATEGORY: _____

1   Bigfoot is an apelike creature believed by some persons to exist in certain areas of the United States and Canada. It has been called *Sasquatch* by Canadian Indian tribes. Stories about it resemble those of the abominable snowman, or *yeti,* of Asia.

2   Hundreds of persons since 1840 have reported sighting such a creature in wooded areas of the Pacific Northwest, California, New Jersey, Pennsylvania, Ohio, Illinois, and British Columbia, and one photographer took a brief movie sequence supposedly showing a bigfoot in northern California in 1967. Tracks measuring up to more than 17 inches (43 cm) long and 7 inches (18 cm) wide, and attributed to[3] bigfoot, have also been found. However, no specimen[4] has ever been captured or photographed clearly.

3   Bigfoot is generally described as a primate resembling a man or ape, 6 to 8 feet (1.8–2.4 meters) tall, standing erect[5] on two feet, with massive shoulders and a body covered with gray, black, or brown hair. It flees when approached, and generally makes no sound. Although most scientists do not recognize its existence, a few believe that it may be the descendant[6] of an extinct apelike creature, Gigantopithecus, that may have crossed the Bering land bridge from Asia to North America in prehistoric times. Indians of the Pacific Northwest and western Canada for generations have perpetuated legends[7] about *Sasquatch* and similar creatures with other names.

After You Read

COMPREHENSION QUESTIONS

1. Under the title, write the category of these passages (they're both the same):
   - encyclopedia entry
   - tabloid article
   - newspaper article
   - transcription of a personal taped account
   - written report about someone else's experience
2. The author of Reading Two says that Bigfoot is a *humanlike* creature, but the author of Reading Three says that it is *apelike.* Look at Reading One, ¶3: What did that author say? Which author is correct?
3. Did the authors present this information in a way that makes you believe in the existence of Bigfoot, or doubt it?
   How did their choice of words and grammar tell you their position on this issue?

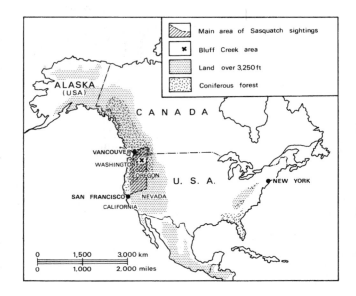

IN WHICH PARAGRAPH CAN YOU FIND . . .

Question	Reading Two	Reading Three
1. Names for this animal	_____	_____
2. Comparison with the "abominable snowman"	_____	_____
3. Habits	_____	_____
4. Size	_____	_____
5. Habitat (location)	_____	_____
6. Evidence	_____	_____

TRUE-FALSE QUESTIONS

			Reading and ¶ number
1. Bigfoot supposedly lives in South America.	T	F	_____
2. The "abominable snowman" is also known as the "yeti."	T	F	_____
3. Most scientists doubt that Bigfoot really exists.	T	F	_____
4. Bigfoot looks similar to an ape.	T	F	_____
5. "Sasquatch" is another name for "Bigfoot."	T	F	_____

Threads

From southwestern Mongolia come reports of humanoid creatures who are called *Almas.* They are supposedly about the same height as the local humans and are often seen in family groups.

CONTINUING YOUR CHART

Continue your Bigfoot chart by adding the information contained in these two readings. When you finish, compare your work with a classmate's.

Vocabulary

KEYWORDS

1. supposedly 2¶2
2. sufficient* 2¶3
3. attributed to 3¶2
4. specimen 3¶2
5. erect 3¶3
6. descendant 3¶3
7. legend 3¶3

KEYWORD EXERCISE

1. Compare the following two sentences:
   • The movie sequence *supposedly* shows a bigfoot in northern California.
   • The movie sequence shows a bigfoot in northern California.

   What's the difference in meaning? _____

   What does the word *supposedly* contribute to the meaning of a sentence?

   _____

2. Think of the number of levels in the English program where you're now studying. In your opinion, what level of English is *sufficient* to prepare you

   for success in a college or university program? _____

   Do your classmates and your teacher agree with you? _____

   EXAMPLE: The evidence has not been *sufficient* to convince most scientists that Bigfoot exists.

3. **EXAMPLE:** Those large tracks were *attributed* to Bigfoot.

   Finish the sentences:
   The great amount of damage was *attributed* to . . .
   Her success in the business world . . .

4. Which of the following words is not a synonym for *specimen*?
   example   factor   case   illustration   instance   sample

   EXAMPLE: No *specimen* has ever been captured or photographed clearly.

5. **EXAMPLE:** Bigfoot stands *erect* on two feet.

   What part of speech is this word? _____

   You'll find more than one meaning for *erect* in your dictionary. Which of the following sentences contains the same meaning as the sentence in the reading?
   • We decided to erect a greenhouse in the garden behind our home.
   • The soldiers stood erect as the general reviewed them.

6. Which of the following family terms are used to identify direct *descendants*?
grandmother   granddaughter   nephew   son   cousin

   EXAMPLE: Bigfoot may be the *descendant* of Gigantopithecus, an extinct apelike creature.

7. Who is the original author of a *legend*? How old are *legends*?

   _____

   How did people originally learn about them—by reading them, or by hearing

   them? _____

   Do you know many *legends* from your own culture? _____

   EXAMPLE: There are many Native American *legends* about Sasquatch.

REVIEW

Now that you have studied the vocabulary, re-read or re-skim the passage.

LEARNING STRATEGY

Managing Your Learning: Before an exam, make a schedule to review the material every day for a week.

READING FOUR

[TITLE] _____

CATEGORY: _____

Reading process: Before you read the passage, scan it for information to add to your chart. Your teacher will give you a time limit. Then when you read carefully, you can make any necessary corrections.

1   Man or beast, or both? Whatever it was that sent John Bringsli of Nelson fleeing[1] in blind panic[2] from the head of Lemmon Creek, hurling his huckleberry pail into the bush and racing for home in his early-model car, it had pulled a speedy disappearing act by the time he and a group of hunters returned to the scene.[3] Mr. Bringsli, woodsman, hunter and fisherman in the Kootenay district for more than 35 years, swore on his reputation as an outdoorsman that it was "definitely[4] not a bear."

2   In an interview, Mr. Bringsli related[5] his experience with an "unknown creature" seen while on a huckleberry picking expedition alone near Six-Mile, and unashamedly told of his frantic race over 100 yards of stunted bush and dwarfed underbrush to his car. "I had just stopped my 1931 coupe on a deserted logging road a couple of weekends ago and walked about 100 yards into the bush. I was picking huckleberries. I had just started to pick berries and was moving slowly through the bush. I had only been there about 15 minutes.

Threads

More than 1,000 Sasquatch sightings have been reported in the Pacific Northwest of North America.

Sasquatch footprint

For no particular reason, I glanced up and that's when I saw this great beast. It was standing about 50 feet away on a slight[6] rise in the ground, staring[7] at me. The sight of this animal paralysed[8] me. It was seven to nine feet tall with long legs and short, powerful arms, with hair covering its body. The first thing I thought was, 'What a strange-looking bear.' It had very wide shoulders, and a flat face with ears flat against the side of its head. It looked more like a big hairy ape. It just stood there staring at me. Arms of the animal were bent slightly[6] and most astounding was that it had hands, not claws. It was about 8 A.M. and I could see it clearly," Mr. Bringsli said. "The most peculiar[9] thing about it was the strange bluish-grey tinge of color of its long hair. It had no neck. Its apelike head appeared to be fastened[10] directly to its wide shoulders."

3 Mr. Bringsli stood with mouth agape staring at the thing for about two minutes. Then it began to slowly walk, or rather shuffle, towards the paralysed huckleberry hunter. It was then that Mr. Bringsli decided it was time for him to find another berry-picking location. He sprinted the 100 yards to the car and drove recklessly[11] down the old logging road and home.

4 Mr. Bringsli returned to the scene next day with a group of friends armed with high-powered rifles and cameras but the strange beast did not reappear. They did find one track nearby. It was from 16 to 17 inches long. There were no claw marks but rather a "sharp toe" print as described by Mr. Bringsli.

Threads

No report has ever described Sasquatch as walking on all fours, as gorillas and chimps often do.

"They were beautiful," says Bond. "I remember them that way even though I had only a short glimpse of them before I started running away. No one should harm them; try to shoot them, or anything like that," he continued. "They made no move as if to harm me. I was simply startled and frightened."

—*from a Bigfoot report*

After You Read

Identify the circled reference word.

COMPREHENSION QUESTIONS

1. Write a good title for the passage.
2. Categorize the passage:
   - encyclopedia entry
   - tabloid article
   - newspaper article
   - transcription of a personal taped account
   - written report about someone else's experience
3. What animal did Mr. Bringsli think the creature was at first?

   _____

4. What did the creature do? _____

5. What evidence was Mr. Bringsli able to show to his friends?

   _____

6. In your own words, summarize Mr. Bringsli's reaction to the creature.

   _____

TRUE-FALSE QUESTIONS

				¶ number
1. It was evening when this event happened, so the light was poor.	T	F	_____
2. The Sasquatch had blue-gray fur.	T	F	_____
3. It had a long apelike neck.	T	F	_____
4. It approached Mr. Bringsli.	T	F	_____
5. The only evidence the next day was a single footprint.	T	F	_____

CONTINUE YOUR CHART

Vocabulary

VOCABULARY IN CONTEXT

1. Find the phrase *1931 coupe* in ¶2. What do you think this means? What clues in nearby sentences make you think so?
2. Find the verb *sprinted* in ¶3. What do you think it means? What clues make you think so?

KEYWORDS

1. flee ¶1
2. panic ¶1
3. scene ¶1
4. definitely* ¶1
5. relate (tell) ¶2
6. slightly* ¶2

7. stare ¶2
8. paralyse/paralyze ¶2
9. peculiar ¶2
10. fasten ¶2
11. recklessly ¶3

KEYWORD EXERCISE

1. Which of the following animals are most likely to *flee* from danger?
   a rabbit   an elephant   a cat   a rhinoceros   a leopard
   Grammar note: This verb is irregular: *flee, fled, fled*

   EXAMPLE: The Sasquatch sent Mr. Bringsli *fleeing* back to his car.

2. Which of the following are elements of *panic*?
   sudden anger   a very strong feeling   fear
   acting without thinking carefully

   EXAMPLE: Mr. Bringsli fled from the creature in blind *panic*.

3. ***EXAMPLE:***   Bringsli returned to the *scene* the next day with some of his friends.

   What part of speech is this word? _____

   Which two of the following words are synonyms for it?
   victim   resource   attitude   place   location

4. Which of the following words is the weakest, and which is the strongest?
   definitely   possibly   probably   maybe   surely

   EXAMPLE: Bringsli said the creature was "*definitely* not a bear."

   NOTE: *Definitely* is not the antonym for *indefinitely* (Reading One ¶7). Review the definitions of the two words, and explain the difference to a classmate.

5. ***EXAMPLE:***   Mr. Bringsli *related* his experience to a newspaper reporter.

   You'll find more than one meaning for this verb in your dictionary. Which of the following sentences contains the same meaning as the sentence in the reading?
   • The sailor *related* his adventure to everyone in the bar.
   • Children need to learn to *relate* properly to other family members.   ·

6. Rank the following words and phrases from least to most.
   somewhat   a great deal   quite a bit   totally   *slightly*

   EXAMPLE: The animal's arms were bent *slightly*.

7. In your culture, is it considered rude to *stare* at a person who looks different from other people—for example a foreigner, a very old person, a very overweight person, a person in a wheelchair? _____

   EXAMPLE: It just stood there *staring* at me.

8. What can't a *paralyzed* person do? _____

Name three causes that can *paralyze* a person.

   a. _____

   b. _____

   c. _____

   EXAMPLE: At first Bringsli was *paralyzed* by the sight of the creature; then he turned and fled.

9. Why did Mr. Bringsli think the beast's color was *peculiar?*

_____

What would have been a less *peculiar* color? _____

10. What is used to *fasten* the front of a shirt? _____

What is used to *fasten* a shoe? _____

What is used to *fasten* a door? _____

   EXAMPLE: Its apelike head appeared to be *fastened* directly to its shoulders.

11. Mr. Bringsli drove *recklessly* down the old logging road and home. How would he have driven if he had driven in the opposite manner?

_____

REVIEW

Now that you've studied the vocabulary, re-read or re-skim the passage.

Discussion and Freewriting: Report on Cultural Survey

Tell a small group of your classmates what you learned from three North Americans in the cultural survey that you took (from page 217). Then freewrite a brief summary of your findings.

LEARNING STRATEGY

Managing Your Learning: Control your time wisely by working on your most important tasks first.

Reading process: You may find the following reading rather difficult. Focus on what you can comprehend, not on what you can't. First skim the passage; then go back through and highlight everything you can understand; then re-read the highlighted parts from start to finish. How well do you understand the general idea? Use your dictionary only for the parts where you are totally lost, and then only if you think those words are really important to a comprehension of the whole.

[TITLE] _____

On the night of 21 October 1972, Alan Berry, a journalist living in Sacramento, California, recorded the voice of Bigfoot, at an altitude of about 8,500 ft. in the high Sierras of northern California, some 2,000 ft. above the nearest road and eight miles from the nearest trail. Members of his group made previous and subsequent recordings at the same location, but (this one) is of exceptionally high quality. (It) has a wide range of sounds, some of which seem quite humanlike, and even some whistles. Subsequent[1] work on the tapes involved techniques of signal processing, and the range of the recorded pitch and vocal length indicated a creature whose vocal tract was much larger than man's. The tape was not pre-recorded, nor had it been tampered with[2] in any way, obviating the possibility of a hoax. Data from an "average" man (5 ft. 11 in. high, 7-in. long vocal tract and average pitch of 115 Hz) suggested that the creature on the recording had a proportional[3] height of up to 8 ft. 4 in., but slightly different results were obtained[4] depending on which sound was analyzed.[5] (The "grr" growl sound, for example, yielded a height for the creature of between 7 ft. 4 in. and 8 ft. 2 in.) Serious analysis[5] of the sounds having precluded hoaxing, (one) is left with the conclusion that the tape was genuine, and moreover, that more than one Bigfoot seems to have been heard.

Threads

There are tales in Siberia of the *Chuchunaa,* humanoids who are the height of tall humans, who wear clothing made from skins, and who use fire.

After You Read

Identify the circled reference words.

COMPREHENSION QUESTIONS

1. Write a good title for the passage.
2. Look at the first sentence, which is rather long. What is the main point?

   HINT: Look for the independent clause. _____

3. What's the main point of the third sentence? _____

4. How was Berry's recording different from other recordings? _____

_____

5. Which are the two most important sentences in the paragraph? _____

_____

_____

6. Do you think this author believed that the tape was genuine? _____

_____

What makes you think she did or didn't? _____

TRUE-FALSE QUESTIONS

				¶ number
1.	Berry's recording was made in a very isolated location.	T	F	_____
2.	This is the only known recording of a Bigfoot's voice.	T	F	_____
3.	The author believes that the tape is probably a hoax.	T	F	_____
4.	More than one Bigfoot has listened to the tape.	T	F	_____

CONTINUE YOUR CHART

Continue your Bigfoot chart by adding the information contained in this reading.

Vocabulary

KEYWORDS

1. subsequent
2. tamper with
3. proportional
4. obtain
5. analyse/analyze, analysis

KEYWORD EXERCISE

1. Find the word *subsequent* in the reading. Near it you'll find an antonym.

What is the antonym? _____

EXAMPLE: Members of his group made previous and *subsequent* recordings at the same location.

2. How might people *tamper* with a tape like Berry's? _____

How might they *tamper* with a passport?_____

EXAMPLE: The tape had not been *tampered* with in any way.

3. *EXAMPLE:* Data from an "average" man suggested that the creature on the recording had a *proportional* height of up to 8 feet 4 inches.

- Proportional is a word used in comparing things that are similar in the relationship between (for instance) height and width, or between weight and height, or in other statistics. Thus we might say that Bigfoot and human beings are different in size but similar in proportion because the bodies of both have the same general shape.
- Name two other pairs of animals that are different in size but similar in proportion. _____ _____

4. How could you *obtain* information about colleges and universities in Canada or the United States? _____

What's a very short, general synonym for *obtain*? _____

EXAMPLE: Slightly different results were *obtained* depending on which sound was analyzed.

5. What parts of speech are the words *analyzed* and *analysis?*

_____ _____

NOTE: In the United States the spelling is *analyze,* but in Canada it's *analyse.*

If you did a research experiment and wanted to *analyze* the data you obtained, what would be a useful tool? _____

EXAMPLES: Different sounds were *analyzed.*
An *analysis* was made of the tape.

REVIEW

Now that you have studied the vocabulary, re-read or re-skim the passage.

READING SIX

Reading process: Begin by skimming the reading from start to finish for two minutes, then skimming again for five minutes. Then read carefully.

As you read, use the "Good Habits During Reading" methods that you learned about on page 50. If you need to, review the procedure before you start. Remember, these are the steps:

- Make predictions
- Form mental pictures
- Make connections with your own experience, or with something you already know
- Recognize your reading problems
- Solve these problems

When you finish, fill out the chart on the handout that your teacher gave you earlier.

[TITLE] _____

1   The most controversial and at the same time potentially convincing evidence for the Sasquatch so far is the film shot on 20 October 1967 by Roger Patterson when trekking on horseback high up in the Bluff Creek Valley of northern California, an area where many footprints had already been found. Patterson himself had followed the Sasquatch saga for several years and even published a flamboyant journalistic paperback called *Do Abominable Snowmen of America Really Exist?* For this reason alone critics dismissed his film as a hoax, or at least a fraud designed to cash in on the subject.

René Dahinden and Roger Patterson with casts of Sasquatch footprints.

2   Patterson and his partner Bob Gimlin were crossing rough country along the base of a bluff when they rounded a sharp bend in a creek and the horses reared, throwing both men. The cause of the alarm was a large animal which they could see across the creek about 90 ft. away, conforming closely to known descriptions of the Sasquatch. Patterson grabbed his movie camera (fortunately already loaded) and started running towards the creature, filming as he went. Since he was running, the resulting film is jerky and the image rather blurred, and in his haste[1] he forgot to note the film speed, two facts which inflamed the subsequent controversy. The result, however, is a continuous sequence[2] of 20 ft. of color film which seems to show a female Sasquatch, about 7 ft. high and weighing an estimated 350 pounds. Her pendulous breasts are clearly visible,[3] and she is covered with short shiny black hair, with the exception of the area just around her eyes. On the back of her head there is a kind of ridge (a bony crest observed on other Sasquatch, which also occurs, incidentally, on large female gorillas), and she has a very short neck, heavy back and shoulder muscles. The creature walked upright, swinging its arms, in a humanlike manner. Patterson, running as fast as he could after the creature and trying to focus the camera at the same time, was surprised when she turned to face him and did not seem at all frightened by his proximity. Of course, she was much the larger animal. However, this enabled him to get a head-and-shoulders shot before she ambled off into the forest.

> Patterson's Bigfoot's tracks were 14–15 inches long (35.6–38 centimeters).
> The largest Sasquatch footprint ever reported measured 30 inches in length (76.2 centimeters) and 10 inches in width (25.4 centimeters). But the average length is 14–18 inches (35.6–45.7 centimeters) and the average width is 7 inches (17.8 centimeters). How long is your foot?

3   Gimlin, meanwhile, had been trying to control the horses, which seemed to have been frightened either by the appearance of the creature or by its foul smell—the latter* being a feature remarked by both men at the time, and one which has been noted in association with other sightings (and of the Yeti). The two men followed the creature's tracks (she had moved with a pace of 40–42 in.) until they were cut off by a tributary stream. They then headed[4] back for the nearest town to get the film processed and to summon[5] some scientific help. René Dahinden, an acknowledged Sasquatch expert, arrived at Bluff Creek the day after filming, but it had rained heavily in the night and the creek had risen quickly. Although they managed to make a cast of one of the prints the danger of flooding forced them to leave the area. Further corroborative evidence being denied[6] them, the burden of proof rested on the film alone,** which generated a vast[7] amount of

public interest when news of (its) existence was released.[8] It has since been shown on many occasions in the USA, in Russia, Britain, Europe, on television, at conferences, and to interested scientists. There is still no firm consensus.[9] Everything hangs on one question—would it be possible for the figure to be that of a hoaxer, an actor in a fur suit, and could such a deception be carried out sufficiently well to fool the scientific establishment[10]?

---

* *The latter* is a reference to the second of two items that have just been mentioned. It's a very common expression. A reference to the first of the two items would be *the former.*

** This clause means "Because they were not able to obtain any other evidence, their only proof was the film."

After You Read

Identify the circled reference words.

COMPREHENSION QUESTIONS

1. Write a good title for the passage.

2. What was the quality of the film? _____

3. Give a reason why people might doubt the film. _____

_____

4. What was Patterson's reaction to the Bigfoot? What was its reaction to him?

_____

_____

5. ". . . this enabled him to get a head-and-shoulders shot. . . . "
   What does this sentence mean—what did Patterson do to the Bigfoot?

_____

_____

6. What was the distance between the Bigfoot's steps? _____

   Convert it from inches into centimeters. (1 inch = 2.54 cm)

_____

TRUE-FALSE QUESTIONS

			¶ number
1. Patterson had no idea that there might be any Sasquatches in that area.	T	F	_____
2. Patterson did not have a reputation as a serious scientific researcher.	T	F	_____
3. The Sasquatch was not afraid of Patterson.	T	F	_____
4. Many Sasquatches have been reported to smell bad.	T	F	_____
5. Patterson and Gimlin had to leave the area because of bad weather.	T	F	_____

IN WHICH PARAGRAPH CAN YOU FIND . . .

1. The reaction of the public to Patterson's film _____

2. The reaction of the horses to the Sasquatch _____

3. The location of the sighting _____

4. A description of the Sasquatch _____

CONTINUE YOUR CHART

LEARNING STRATEGY

Remembering New Material: Putting new words into meaningful sentences helps you remember them.

Vocabulary

VOCABULARY IN CONTEXT

1. Find the phrase *cash in on the subject* in ¶1. What do you think it means? What clues make you think so?
2. Find the word *reared* in ¶2. What do you think it means? What clues make you think so?

KEYWORDS

1. haste ¶2
2. sequence ¶2
3. visible ¶2
4. head (verb) ¶3
5. summon ¶3
6. deny* ¶3
7. vast ¶3
8. release* ¶3
9. consensus ¶3
10. the establishment ¶3

KEYWORD EXERCISE

1. An English proverb says, "*Haste* makes waste." What do you think this means?

_____

_____

Do you agree? _____

Do you have a proverb in your culture that means the same thing?

_____

EXAMPLE: In his *haste* Patterson forgot to note the film speed.

2. Put the following events into a normal *sequence*.
   death   job   birth   marriage   education

   > *EXAMPLE:*   The result is a continuous *sequence* of 20 feet of color film.

3. *EXAMPLE:*   Many stars are not *visible* without binoculars or a telescope.

   What part of speech is *visible?* _____

   From the context in ¶2 and from the parts, what do you think this

   word means? _____

4. *EXAMPLE:*   After the Sasquatch disappeared, the two men *headed* back for
   the nearest town.

   What part of speech is *head* in this sentence? _____

   What's the connection between this word and the noun *head,* the part of

   the human body? _____

5. *EXAMPLE:*   Patterson and Gimlin *summoned* scientific help.

   This very formal verb means to call for or order. In which of the following
   situations might you use it?
   • A child wakes in the night and calls for his mother to bring him a drink of
     water.
   • A judge orders a person to come and speak at a trial.
   • The CEO of a company calls for an employee to give a report at a
     meeting.

6. Find the verb *denied* in ¶3. Be sure to read the footnote explaining the
   sentence. Then choose the sentence below that contains the same meaning
   as the reading.
   • The judge *denied* the prisoner's request.
   • Many scientists *deny* the existence of Sasquatch.

7. Which of the following are *vast?*
   • St. Peter's Cathedral in Rome
   • The Great Plains of the United States
   • The Amazon River in South America
   • Mount Everest in Asia
   • The Sahara Desert in Africa
   • The city you are living in now

   > *EXAMPLE:*   The film generated a *vast* amount of public interest.

8. *EXAMPLES:*   Patterson *released* the news of the film's existence.
   The police *released* the wrong person.

   Finish the sentences:
   The kidnaper. . .
   The laboratory assistant. . .
   In an accident, the nuclear power plant. . .

9. Find the word *consensus* in ¶3. If a group of people with different points of view have to come to a *consensus*, what's the best way for them to do it?

_____

_____

Are people in your culture good at reaching *consensus*? _____

Do you think that most North Americans are good at it? _____

10. *EXAMPLE:* Could such a deception be carried out sufficiently well to fool *the* scientific *establishment?*

This particular meaning of *establishment* may not be in your dictionary. *The establishment* refers to any group of people who have great power and influence, especially if they have had it for a long time and are unwilling to give it up or share it. The sentence in the reading refers to *the scientific establishment.* Name three other areas of society that have *establishments.*

_____   _____   _____

REVIEW

Now that you have studied the vocabulary, re-read or re-skim the passage.

Discussion: Arguing Both Sides of an Issue

In the following activity, each of you will argue your own position on the existence of Sasquatch. You will also receive a brief reading that will give you some additional information. Read it ahead of time and paraphrase it in the discussion.

READING SEVEN

NOTE: This reading is also on the tape.

The following reading is written in conversational English. It contains some language that is a little different from "classroom" grammar and vocabulary. If you find any examples of this and want to ask your teacher about it, do so. You may also notice that the English is very informal.

Reading process: Read as far as you can in three minutes. Mark where you stop. Then start over and see if you can get farther in the next three minutes. Finally, read the whole passage.

The following story is told by a young man who was traveling with a friend when night fell. Rather than pay for a motel, they decided to camp out along a lonely forest road in their sleeping bags. Here's what happened to them after they settled down for the night:

[TITLE] _____

CATEGORY: _____

1 My friend started talking about different calls, you know. He said he was from Missouri, said he could make a black panther sound, like a woman's scream. So he did that, and I did a wolf call. About that time, after we completed our calls, we first noticed a big form on top of the hill. . . . To me it looked a good nine feet tall,[1] very very broad. I didn't get a good look at it. . . .

2 We thought we got a glimpse[2] of it coming down to the left of us and that was the last time we seen it for a while. About half an hour later it was coming down the road. N—— shone the light on it. He started screaming "Look! Look! There it is!" and it was coming down the road and I turned around and saw it.

3 He said he was going to stop it by blinding it in the eyes and it stopped cold and jumped behind the embankment, behind some bushes, and it looked like it was going to stalk us. We could see its hair and the outline[3] of it and the eyes. You know, like you'll shine another animal in the eyes, in the light they'll glow.[4]

4 I jumped in the car and accidentally locked the door on N—— and the thing got up and rushed us[5] and poor N—— couldn't get in because the door was locked. (He) started screaming and everything else so I got the door unlocked and he jumped in the car and all of a sudden (that thing) just hit the car and really made a ruckus.

5 It seemed to want to get in for some reason, or maybe it was trying to be friendly or curious. Whatever it was, we didn't like it. So then it went away and we decided, well, we're going to split, take off, but he couldn't find his keys. He figured he left them in the trunk. So we got out and sneak[6] around there and no keys.

6 Then we . . . saw the thing so we think we better get back in the car, it would be safer'n out there, so we kept hearing this thing, kept seeing it and we decided well we've got to get out of here. We decided the keys have got to be around there, so we both got out and I took a pop bottle and I busted it as a weapon, but I busted it all to pieces so we stood there and here (the thing) came and we never got nothing . . . had no chance of leaving 'cause we didn't have the keys and couldn't find them.

7 So the thing started rushing around . . . just walking around us out of curiosity. . . . Well it didn't do any more damage after that, didn't attack the car and we just stayed there all night.

8 Next morning, it was about eight o'clock, we got out of the car and walked around to make sure the thing wasn't there. Actually we looked around first, we figured it wouldn't show in the daytime. We found the track, down in the cut we noticed these big tracks of this here particular thing, and (they) was good sized, they looked like a human's footprints.

> The most impressive thing about the big footprints is neither their size nor their shape, but the depth to which they are impressed in the ground. . . . False feet worn by a person would show the opposite effect, tending to sink in less than the normal amount, as with snowshoes.
>
> —*John Green, Sasquatch researcher*

9   We followed the tracks down the road for quite a ways and we lost them going into the brush. They went down towards a ravine. We could see some of the tracks and then we lost them. We searched around again for more tracks but they just all seemed to lead down that way.

10   The face was sort of a human-type face. It was pointed like on the top, it had a large pointed forehead on the top. A human's is sort of rounded off, his wasn't. It was dome[7] shaped. It wasn't really that it had a lot of hair on its face, except the side features, it had hair on that. And he had a nose. It resembled a human's nose except it was flatter and wider than a human's nose would be.

11   His mouth was somewhat like a human's except it was bare, but a larger mouth. And he had something like carnivorous teeth, like a dog's teeth, and his eyes were good sized, and like I said, (they) shone in the dark. Real bright, like whitish-yellow, very very glowing. He had a bull neck, didn't have an extremely long neck, in fact there wasn't hardly a neck there, it was a bull's.

12   His skin had a yellow tinge to it like it had been bleached in the sun, like leather would be, buckskin would be, sort of tanned like you get in a taxidermist's and stuff, that's what it looked like. His torso was very muscular.[8] I didn't get a good look at his hands because we didn't have the light actually on his body that much, you know, when we were trying to blind him in the eyes is when we actually shone the light on him outside. And he was bent over, stooped over. He had a pretty long stride[9] to him. His legs were long and muscular and his waist tapered. He did have actually a large waist. I didn't really get a good view of his back. He had brown hair, real good shape, wasn't ragged or nothing.

13   He was about nine feet. I'm six-two, and he stood a good three feet taller than I was. Weight I'd say a thousand two hundred, something like that.

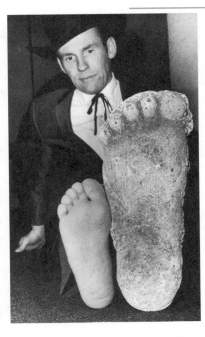

Roger Patterson comparing his foot with a plaster cast of a Bigfoot track.

For the first time I had a chance to appreciate the tremendous pressure with which the prints are made. Where they sank an inch deep in the sand my boots made only a heel print and a slightly flattened area in the center of the soles. To make a hole an inch deep I had to jump off a log about two feet high and land on one heel.

—*John Green*

Threads

The average human stride is less than one meter long.

After You Read

Identify the circled reference words.

COMPREHENSION QUESTIONS

1. Write a good title for this passage.
2. Categorize the passage:
   • encyclopedia entry
   • tabloid article
   • newspaper article
   • transcription of a personal taped account
   • written report about someone else's experience

3. What were the two people doing in ¶1? _____

4. In your own words, tell what happened in ¶4. _____

_____

5. In your own words, tell what happened concerning a bottle in ¶6.

_____

_____

6. What was the creature's height in centimeters? (1 ft. = 12 in.; 1 in. = 2.54 cm)

_____

What was its weight in kilograms? (1 lb =.4536 kg) _____

7. Have you ever slept out in the open as the two friends were planning to do?

After reading this account, would you want to? _____

CONTINUE YOUR CHART

Vocabulary

KEYWORDS

1. a good nine feet tall ¶1
2. glimpse ¶
3. outline ¶3
4. glow ¶3
5. rush (someone) ¶4

6. sneak ¶5
7. dome ¶10
8. muscular ¶12
9. stride ¶12

The following words from the passage are very informal: *ruckus, split, busted, . . . and stuff*

KEYWORD EXERCISE

1. *EXAMPLE:* To me it looked *a good* nine feet tall.

   Finish the sentences:
   They stayed in Hawaii for a good . . .
   I suppose my suitcase must weigh . . .

2. Which of the following are elements of the word *glimpse*?
   hear   see   brief   careful   study

   EXAMPLE: We thought we got a *glimpse* of it as it came down the hill.

3. Draw an *outline* of a classmate's profile (side view).

   EXAMPLE: We could see its hair and the *outline* of it and the eyes.

4. Name three things that can *glow.*

   EXAMPLE: You know, like you'll shine another animal in the eyes, in the light they'll *glow.*

5. *EXAMPLES:* The thing got up and *rushed* us.
              The thing started *rushing* around.

   What's the main element of the verb *rush?*

6. *EXAMPLE:* We got out and *sneak* around there and no keys.

   (This verb is regular; most speakers would have said "sneaked.") Under what circumstances might a person *sneak*?

   What are some elements of the word *sneak*?
   quiet   loud   open   secret

7. Name a world-famous *dome,* and tell where it is.

   EXAMPLE: His head was *dome* shaped.

8. *EXAMPLE:* His torso was very *muscular.*

   What part of speech is *muscular*?
   What's the noun form?
   Who's the most *muscular* person in your class?

9. Look at your measurements in the Preview Activity on page 216. Who has the longest *stride* in your class?
   How does it compare with a Bigfoot's *stride*? (Refer to your chart.)

REVIEW

Now that you've studied the vocabulary, re-read or re-skim the passage.

READING EIGHT

Reading process: Read the following passage as many times as you can in five minutes. Then try to answer the questions.

[TITLE] _____

On October 23 [1975], at 7:30 P.M., the police sergeant answered a call to a house where something had been heard pounding[1] on the back wall. The woman who lived there had gone next door to her son's house and there was no prowler to be found, but something had apparently torn some plastic that covered a back doorway, and there was a window broken. At 2:20 A.M. the same night something was again reported behind the house, and when the sergeant arrived, along with several other people, his spotlight quickly picked up what looked like a very large ape standing in the back yard. While someone else held the light on it the sergeant walked to within 35 feet of the animal, which made no attempt to run but crouched down[2] as he got near. There they stayed for "many minutes," while the sergeant wondered what to do next. He had a shotgun loaded[3] with buckshot but he was not sure if the thing was some kind of human, and if it wasn't, he didn't know how much buckshot it could take. He noted afterwards in his report that it was black in color, would stand seven to eight feet tall and appeared to have no neck. It was covered with short hair, except on the face. He could see no ears. The eyes were small. It appeared to have four teeth larger than the others, two upper and two lower. Its nose was flat. He could see the nostrils. At the end there were seven people watching it, although only two others approached close to it. Then there were noises heard off in the dark at both sides, and the man with the spotlight swung it off to the right and called that there was "another one over there." At that point the sergeant decided to return to his patrol car.

Threads

Sasquatches are very rarely seen together. Most reports are of a single animal only.

After You Read

Identify the circled reference word.

COMPREHENSION QUESTIONS

1. Write a good title for the passage.

2. How many animals were seen? _____

3. Why didn't the policeman shoot? _____

4. Where was the owner of the house? _____

5. How helpful was the policeman to the homeowner? _____

6. Work with a partner. One of you play the part of the policeman, the other of the Bigfoot. Role-play their behavior as they confronted each other.

COMPLETING YOUR CHART

Add the information from this reading to your chart. Now it's complete. Compare it with two or three classmates' work, adding anything that you left out.

Vocabulary

KEYWORDS

1. pound   2. crouch down   3. load (a gun)

KEYWORD EXERCISE

1. *EXAMPLE:*   The Bigfoot had been *pounding* on the back wall of a woman's house.

   To show that you understand this word, *pound* the wall or your desk. Which part of your body do you use if you *pound* something?

   _____

2. *EXAMPLE:*   The animal *crouched down* as the policeman approached it.

   What is the antonym for *crouched down*? _____

   Give two reasons why someone might *crouch down*.

   _____   _____

3. *EXAMPLE:*   The policeman had *loaded* the shotgun with buckshot.

   Finish the sentences:
   We had forgotten to load . . . with film.
   The movers . . .

REVIEW

Now that you have studied the vocabulary, re-read or re-skim the passage.

ANTICIPATING TEST QUESTIONS

Write one of each for any of the readings in this chapter: multiple-choice, true-false, fill-in-the-blank, definition/identification, essay/discussion. Then work with a small group to "test" each other orally.

Writing an Essay About Sasquatch

Threads

Which counts for more: The fact that no one can prove that Bigfoot exists, or the fact that no one can prove it doesn't?

Choose one of the following alternatives:

1. A Profile of Sasquatch
   Using your chart for information, write a paper that is a *profile* of Sasquatch— that is, a composite of information about several of the categories you took notes on. You may use the name Sasquatch or Bigfoot, whichever you prefer.
2. Argue For or Against the Existence of Sasquatch
   Using the list that you helped put together of arguments for and against Bigfoot's existence, write a paper that explains your own position on this issue. Support your position with reasons and examples.

Writing process: First, freewrite about each category or argument. Then decide where to divide the information into paragraphs in the body of your paper. Next, write a first draft of the introduction, body paragraphs, and conclusion. At this point you should concentrate only on content and organization: try to develop your points well and clearly.

Trade papers with a partner (preferably someone who doesn't speak your native language). Encourage each other about the clear and interesting parts, and advise each other about points where the content and organization seem incomplete or confusing. Think carefully about what your partner says, and make your decisions about which advice to take. Then revise.

Now read your second draft carefully, paying attention to vocabulary, grammar, and punctuation. Think about your usual weaknesses when you write in English. Work with a partner again. Make decisions about which advice to take, and revise for a third draft. This is the one that you will hand in to your teacher.

If you ever see a Bigfoot or its tracks, take a photograph if you can. Write down everything you can about what happened, where, and when. Then contact the International Society of Cryptozoology, P.O. Box 43070, Tucson, Arizona 85733, U.S.A.

LEARNING STRATEGY

Personalizing: Using English outside the classroom improves your language skills.

Evaluating Learning Strategies

In this chapter you have been presented with several new learning strategies. Look back over them. Were there any that weren't especially helpful for you? What wasn't helpful about them? Which ones did you find especially helpful? Think about times and ways that you can keep using them in your future reading.

Evaluating Your Learning

	Very little	Quite a bit	A lot
You increased your vocabulary.	___	___	___
Your comprehension has improved. You can identify different categories of writing.	___	___	___
You can argue both sides of an issue. You can use a chart to compare information from different readings.	___	___	___
You learned what Bigfoot is (or is it?).	___	___	___

KEYWORDS FOR CHAPTER 8: BIGFOOT AND COMPANY

Verbs
analyze
crouch
deny*
fasten
flee
glow
head
load
mimic
obtain
paralyze
pound
relate
release*
rush
sneak
stare
summon
tamper with
tremble

Nouns
consensus
descendant
dome
establishment
glimpse
haste
legend
outline
panic
scene
sequence
specimen
stride

Adverbs
definitely*
indefinitely
otherwise*
recklessly
slightly*
supposedly

Adjectives
apparent*
attributed to
erect
extraordinary
fake
good + quantity
inevitable
muscular
peculiar
proportional
subsequent
sufficient*
unpredictable
vast
visible

Appendix

Chronological

Chronological is an adjective that means "by time." Chronological organization (also called "time order") means giving information in the order in which it happened. We use this organization when we are telling a story, giving historical facts, or describing a process. Here are some common *markers* or *signals* that will help you recognize chronological organization:

EVENTS IN A NARRATIVE, STEPS IN A PROCESS

to begin with	first	the first step is to	
second	next	then	
after that	after	afterward	later
finally	at last	the final step is to	
when			

in 1848	by 1830
already	yet
gradually	
eventually	

SIMULTANEOUS EVENTS

as
at the same time
during
simultaneously
while

OTHER TIME EXPRESSIONS

after	following
as long as	
as soon as	
before	prior to
by the time	
in	for
once	
until	
whenever	

ADDITIONAL INFORMATION

and	additionally	also	as well	furthermore	moreover

Comparison, Contrast

COMPARISON

both
either/neither
in like manner
like
likewise
parallels
similarly

CONTRAST

although	though	even though	while
but	yet		

in spite of the fact that   despite the fact that   regardless of the fact that
instead
in contrast
on the contrary
on the other hand
otherwise

still	however	nevertheless

Cause and Effect, Problem and Solution

as a result   consequently   therefore because of this   thus so
because   since   as because of
be responsible for   contribute to result in   lead to
result from   be a consequence of be due to   be a result of
so much/many . . . that   such . . . that

Listing Reasons, Examples, Characteristics, or Features

e.g.   for example   for instance   such as
The reason is
The answer is
furthermore
additionally

Restatement or Equivalence

i.e.
to put it another way
in other words